Eating Culture

Eating Culture

Ron Scapp and
Brian Seitz, Editors

State University of New York Press

Grateful acknowledgment is made to Susan Bordo and the University of California Press for permission to reprint "Hunger as Ideology," which originally appeared in *Unbearable Weight: Feminism, Western Culture, and the Body.* Copyright © 1993 The Regents of the University of California.

Published by
State University of New York Press, Albany

For information, address State University of New York Press,
State University Plaza, Albany, N.Y. 12246

Production by E. Moore
Marketing by Dana E. Yanulavich

Library of Congress Cataloging-in-Publication Data

Scapp, Ron, 1955–
    Eating culture / Ron Scapp and Brian Seitz, editors.
        p.   cm.
    Includes bibliographical references.
    ISBN 0-7914-3859-7 (hardcover : alk. paper). — ISBN 0-7914-3860-0
(pbk. : alk. paper)
    1. Food habits.   2. Dinners and dining.   I. Seitz, Brian, 1954–
II. Title.
GT2850.S27   1998
394.1—dc21   97-37147
                                                              CIP

10 9 8 7 6 5 4 3 2 1

In memory of
Erika Jacobson
and her desire for sushi to the end

Contents

Introduction

Ron Scapp and Brian Seitz

Eating practices embody some of the most dramatic philosophical conundrums, including the puzzling divisions and linkages between culture and nature as well as those between appearance and reality. Obsessed with the connections between image and substance—the meat of the matter—an idle philosopher finds food for thought in the relationship between plastic sushi and "the real thing." The remarkably literal plastic representations somehow take the place of the food itself. They deliver sushi to the viewer, the potential diner on the street, who is outside, not eating, just looking.

However, the models are not merely a visual substitution. They indicate the significance of both presentation and representation for eating in general. The plastic sushi may not be edible, but it is a feature of the discourse of sushi, part of a specific aesthetics of eating. And since it is not just food for thought but eating itself that seems to be the pertinent measure of aesthetics and reality here, the diner might well derive something more satisfying from substitutions other than the fake variety represented by plastic *tekka maki*. They trigger the appetite through the imagination, but deliver no real pleasure to the palate.

Consider, for example, the gastronomic possibilities and likely epistemological confusion that the following "international" substitutions present to the diner in the form of cooking tips: not only can a whole wheat tortilla (not a Mexican staple) stand in as a mock chapati, but a chapati can also function as a whole wheat tortilla, and the tortilla can devolve into a "wrap." This contextually oblivious reversibility does not hold, however, for the prepackaged egg roll wrapper used in lieu of chile relleno batter. The material properties require a concoction that coats rather than wraps, an irreducible culinary reality. Or perhaps for the diner or cook caught up in the play of substitution, such considerations don't really matter.

Can ingredients used in Mexican, Indian, and Chinese cuisines really stand in for each other? Can culturally diverse cuisines—for instance, French and Thai, cream and fish sauce—be gracefully fused? It seems so now, and not only according to the leveling logic offered by the adage, "it all goes to the same place." Eating is seldom merely about destination or purpose. Eating is largely about creation and self-creation, and about the production and reproduction of human life.

While humans have basic nutritional needs, they are born into widely divergent fields of material and cultural availability (which includes lack). So much that pertains to eating goes well beyond purely practical issues, particularly nowadays, when, in some parts of the world, agricultural and transportation technologies seem to make everything available, regardless of season or location, time or space. Here and now we truly move from the possibilities of an aesthetics of eating to a hyperaesthetics—that is, to an aesthetics unbound by natural constraints. A simple desire, a whim, an idea can surpass the practical limitations—season and region—traditionally imposed by nature. Destination often immaterial, everything moves now, everything crosses the old borders (usually in one direction), all food circulates.

One form of evidence for this is phenomena such as durable rather than tasty tomatoes, which seem to be available practically anywhere, anytime, thanks to applied agricultural science, semitrucks, trains, and planes. Of course in the United States, a significant proportion of produce comes from elsewhere, including from Mexico and farther south, where environmental regulations do not forbid the use of agricultural chemicals banned in the U.S. and where also people on the whole do not eat as well as they do in America.

As another form of evidence for this transition to a hyperaesthetics, note the familiarity of Japanese, Mexican, Chinese, Indian, Italian, and other widely divergent cuisines to Americans from a range of lost or conflated ethnic backgrounds. Indigenous figures such as Betty Crocker, Aunt Jemimah, Tony the Tiger, and the Pillsbury Doughboy once dominated store shelves. Now, large supermarkets across America—in small towns as well as large cities—routinely stock pita bread, frozen bagels, "oriental" condiments, fresh pasta, kiwi, tofu, "French" roast coffee, specialty vegetables, and on and on. The foreign has become the familiar, the different has been domesticated by Albertsons, Safeway, Pathmark, Winn Dixie, Grand Union, Kroger's, King's Sooper, and the other chains that provide a source of food for the masses, and link so much of "this eating culture" together. Part of the same domestication of difference is Euroamerica's expectation that chopsticks are the appropriate utensils in an Asian restaurant (even a Thai restaurant), although the Western eater tends to use them like a fork—that is, to carry the food all the way from the tabled plate to the palate, rather than engaging the chopsticks with the bowl held to the mouth.

This is one side of the new internationalism. Then there are the other sides of the globe, such as the new universal-specific eating and drinking decisions that "we" face in common (e.g., Classic Coke or Diet Coke or Caffeine-free Coke or Caffeine-free Diet Coke or Cherry Coke, etc.)—that is, the consumer decisions that constitute a collective appetite.

Not reducible to an imagined melting pot, mixed ethnicity goes back to the beginnings of eating in colonized America. Early European settlers survived by adopting native farming, hunting, and gathering techniques, not to mention the food itself. The Pilgrims of Plymouth Colony—the most iconized beneficiaries of the fruits of native America—celebrated a plentiful harvest and their very survival in the autumn of 1621, which was formalized by Governor William Bradford's proclamation declaring a three-day festival. This was the original Thanksgiving in America. Pilgrim hunters were sent out for meat, and bagged a fine string of turkeys (which Benjamin Franklin would later propose as the national bird). Massasoit and some of his Wampanoag were invited to the feast, and they contributed five deer. Complete with "friendly Indians," this mythologized image is still absorbed by American schoolchildren when they are very young, with the meal at its center.

Thanksgiving is a wholesome eating ritual, unique because it is the only meal shared and celebrated by America as a nation, ostensibly able to efface ethnic and religious differences, if only for a day. But to avoid sacrificing the specificity of America's past

to the apparent universality of the holiday, we might remind ourselves that just two years before that original Thanksgiving, the
first black slaves had arrived in Virginia. One wonders what those
slaves were fed on the ship, and one wonders what the ritual meal
meant for the still-enslaved descendants of these first slaves,
when—168 years after the "original" Thanksgiving—President
George Washington proclaimed November 26, 1789, a national
day of giving thanks to God—of, that is, Thanksgiving. Did slaves
share this official Thanksgiving in a capacity other than their
servitude? Or did it remain something foreign, a ritual owned by
the culture of the masters? Later, in 1863, President Abraham
Lincoln institutionalized the event by declaring the last Thursday
of November a national holiday. The Civil War was of course
tearing the country apart that particular autumn. Whether or not
the turkey dinner actually helped to reinforce national identity,
the effort was made in its name, and it has been made annually
ever since then. Finally, and in order to encourage holiday shopping by lengthening the gap between Thanksgiving and Christ-
mas, President Franklin Roosevelt changed the official date from
the last Thursday of November to the fourth Thursday, which is
where it has remained.

It seems appropriate that this latest adjustment to the national meal was a blatantly commercial one, since the machinery
of food production and distribution in America—think of those
millions of November and December totem turkeys—is in one of
its fundamental profiles the machinery of big business. Consider
the phrases, "Nature's Best," and "Healthy Choice," which are
now registered brand names. As such they have ceased to reach out
as descriptive signifiers, and are no longer secured in life as simple
use-values.

Nature itself has acquired a curious status in connection with
eating practices lately too, having become something not just to
use or exploit but to actively manipulate and transform. Tech-
nologized science intervenes in nature and reconfigures what nature provides through genetic engineering applied to plants and
animals: hybrid grains developed to specification, designer meats
and dairy products generated or enhanced by hormone stimulation,
cloning, etc. Advanced irrigation techniques tap ancient aquifers
deep beneath the planet's surface. Enthusiasts claim that hydro-
ponically grown vegetables are the food of the future (a scenario
different from the one projected in the film *Soylent Green*).

Further, the food industry now harnesses and thus appropriates the idiosyncrasies of natural processes. In salmon "ranching," for example, the anadromous salmon return from the sea to their freshwater birth site, just as they have always done, but the human-made hatchery they were born in has now been converted to a butcher block, which the salmon swim right up onto. Out at sea, new methods of old-fashioned exploitation invade the water, such as the "squid" boats which have combed the planet's oceans, *mining* fish with nylon-monofilament gill nets up to forty miles long; little escapes the haul. In the supermarket, cans labeled "dolphin-free" tuna do not provide the reassurance that we might desire for guilt-free consumption.

Meanwhile, back on the farm, time-tested and apparently efficient but also clumsy, modern methods are deployed to combat nature. These include chemical pesticides, herbicides, and—to compensate for nature's inadequacies—fertilizers. Clearly, the traditional practice and significance of *the harvest*, the one associated with the original Thanksgiving, has been radically transformed, a mutation brought about by technology and by the fundamental value ascribed to efficiency and quantitatively maximized production, which can be linked not only to the profit motive, but also to the continual growth of the planet's perpetually and increasingly hungry population.

All of these elaborate apparatuses exist in a conflicted universe. Along with the alternate gauge provided by growing levels of pollution, depletion, and desertification, the perfection of the food machine may also be measured by a universe of hunger and malnutrition. In the long run this universe will be determined by the natural limitations of the planet's capacity to provide for its inhabitants, whose numbers grow exponentially. For the time being, this universe is a problem largely caused by the distribution of wealth. For some people, the range of eating possibilities has never been better. But for hundreds of millions of others, it remains as empty and bleak as it ever was.

While convenience stores are packed with microwave burritos and twelve-packs of beer, and while McDonald's is establishing new forms of globalism by reaching its next billion-served in Moscow, hunger remains a widespread problem throughout the world, not only in "developing" countries, but on the streets of postindustrial nations too. Technology may have helped create one world, but it is still a divided world, a world bifurcated by the difference between empty bellies and full. According to some, water supply problems projected for the future may have a certain equalizing effect on all such disparities. For the time being, we can only speculate about these matters.

All of these global references may suggest an end to the regional dimensions of eating, which would be too facile. One need only note recent American food trends, with their fetishistic desire for everything from blackened red snapper to tandoori chicken, from the new Northern California style to Pacific Rim cuisine, from Perugina chocolates to Perrier, from Corona to Coors, and a continued craving for sushi, which persists despite warnings about parasites and the trade deficit. Some sophisticated restaurants go so far as to identify oysters as being not just from, for instance, Washington state, but from individually named bays and estuaries in Puget Sound, catering to the endless desire for particularity.

Led not by Pepsi's "freshness dating" but by Chez Panisse in Berkeley, the nouvelle cuisine from California has over the years transformed fresh into another fetish, another form of particularity. This desire for the fresh and natural that drives many postmodern eaters is part of an obsession with inspiring food, food that will take the diner somewhere special. A serving of *gado-gado* might send us, if not to Indonesia, at least somewhere fleetingly different, transported by the peanut sauce as it crosses the tongue. Eating food from other regions of the world, however, is no substitute for travel, and the distinction between place and taste remains critical. The difference marks not only distances measured by air travel, but also distances between neighborhoods.

For instance, Manhattan's East Sixth Street is widely known for its Indian restaurants among diners in search of "the exotic." Yet, by and large, these sophisticated diners do not venture out to the Queens neighborhoods where so many Indians live and eat. Wherever East Sixth vindaloo takes the adventurous gourmand, it is not necessarily somewhere Indian. In this case, the place remains familiar Manhattan. That is to say, the obsession with the special and the different remains attached to and perhaps even part of an apparently competing desire for the comfort of the known. McDonald's success in flirting with the unusual—fajitas—is only possible within its supremely generic universe.

If eating serves as a safe form of travel, then it seems increasingly important to travel light. That is, part of the new obsession with food is linked to a passionate concern about health, or about being slim, two related but not identical values connected to eating (some say that Californians care about their bodies, while New Yorkers care instead about the way they look). Organically grown food is highly valued, although its exorbitant price represents the elitist reality of its production and its market niche; this is a cultural contradiction in North America, where the vast growth of the organic food industry grew out of the ideologically egalitarian counterculture of the sixties. But health concerns have come to permeate all food types, not just the elite variety. Cholesterol-free cooking oils are in, Crisco is out. Oat bran is still good, salt is not. Liver continues to provide a lot of iron, bacon contains fats and sodium nitrates. Eat a lot of roughage, peel your fruits, and avoid too much barbecue. Salad is especially slenderizing if you leave out the dressing, red meat is bad for you, and fish is good from a diet standpoint, although some fish may also contain significant traces of carcinogenic chemicals.

The endless goal is to slim down, be healthy, look good. This goal—this desire—fuels many new products (lean cuisine, lite beer, lite potato chips, lite ice cream, "fat-free" muffins, and the whole universe of Nutrasweet products, etc.). While exercise may remain the key to losing weight and staying fit, the new tactic for many seems to be solely dietary—it would be so nice if we could just eat ourselves thin (although the opposite holds true for many living with AIDS). Of course, men can get away with extra pounds a little easier than women, which reminds us that the disequilibriums of sexist culture permeate eating practices as much as any others.

Sexism continues to inform the preparation as well as consumption of food. Things change, so men cook at home more than they used to (often "gourmet"), but women still tend to be associated with the domestic cooking scene. Although women have begun to claim some territory as chefs in the most elegant dining establishments and even as cooks in greasy spoons, heterosexual white men remain the dominant force in professional kitchens; the often caricatured truckstop cafe survives as the basic model of sexist and racist hierarchy. Traditional roles and power relations continue to limit and constrain workers throughout the eating industry. For some diners, however, the possibilities appear to grow without end.

New prospects for diners derive from a range of sources. One source is a by-product of immigration patterns; the number of Vietnamese restaurants that have opened throughout the U.S. since the war is a good example. Emphasizing a different side of eating out, though, this also has to do with shifts in widely dispersed cultural habits and values. Americans are filing out of the family dining room and lining up to be served. Sometimes this is an elegant, formal, and expensive affair. More often, though, it has to do with efficiency, apparent thrift, and even laziness, or at least a change of routine ("You deserve a break today . . ."). The change of routine pertains not only to where people eat, but also to what they eat and the way they eat it. For many, this does not always coincide with health concerns. Nor does it coincide with aesthetic concerns, not in a traditional sense. Here, again, the values put into play are those of a hyperaesthetics, which is largely a value associated with speed, with motion, with a fast modern lifestyle.

The dominant value here is often that of convenience, which has brought us frozen food, microwave meals, instant noodles, instant coffee, Instant Breakfast, Wendy's, Pizza Hut, and Taco Bell. Fast food in particular has become a way of life, even far from the fast-paced lifestyle associated with big cities. Perhaps the dissemination of fast food is one of the agents that has undermined the once clearer difference between the urban and the rural. The pick-and-run salad bar has become a central fixture in all sorts of eating establishments, from chicken and hamburger franchises to supermarkets to Korean delis. The salad bar in particular is a real advance in the history of fast food in that it enables the fit-but-fast segment of the population healthier possibilities than existed in earlier days, which were dominated by traditional deep-fried and other greasy delights.

Another alternative to heavy food is the lightest food of all, food online—check out www.epicurious.com—and televised eating possibilities, which the Food TV Network has pushed to the next level ("kick it up a notch," says Emeril). Electronic food is the fastest food of all.

The immediate availability of fast food has an apparently democratic character; we all have equal access to the same food lines. Of course mass food does not have to mean fast food. One of the more obvious examples of this is the ubiquitous, nationally advertised Red Lobster, where, we are told, you don't have to stand in line if you call in advance (make a reservation?). There are also other varieties of food lines, including the line in the all-you-can-eat, smorgasbord restaurant, the line in the cafeteria chains so popular in certain parts of the country, and, quite different, the line at the soup kitchens that have proliferated throughout this country in recent years. But there are also the lines associated with the kinds of places where people are seated by a maitre 'd. These are the lines of exclusivity that divide mass eaters from the privileged diner, who can afford not only to eat ("to fill the hole"), but to eat very well, with wine to match. This is the line that keeps most eaters out of certain restaurants, the bottom line.

But the differences between kinds of eating experiences are clearly not determined by socioeconomic factors alone, and demand a broader cultural analysis. For example, eating practices were transformed by the dating-dancing-dining phenomenon of the '70s, when restaurants shifted from being primarily places to eat to, explicitly, places to meet. Eating and sex combined in novel ways, fusing desires into a new atmosphere, as well as a new market, a new kind of "meat market." Restaurants continue to evolve into more subtle and often wild formations, even into artworks. In downtown New York, for example, a once flashy steak house called "Teddy's," which featured dated photos of celebrities and other chic diners, reopened in the '80s as "El International," an ultratrendy, outrageously decorated hangout that served Spanish food to a sexy, fast-paced clientele. Since then, it has metamorphosed into an equally trendy Mexican restaurant, "El Teddy's," now a point of intersection for a variety of diners, all of whom are willing to pay the price for this exotic, if contrived atmosphere.

What is noteworthy about Teddy's/El International/El Teddy's, is that each of its new incarnations retains strong and eclectic traces of its previous identities, including the original photos of famous diners. The current restaurant's aesthetic proudly incorporates abundant archaeological evidence of its past, which determines its particular atmosphere. A postmodern restaurant such as this may strike some as too clever for its own good, particularly since it does not preserve so much as appropriate the past for its own purposes. Interestingly enough, however, it does not efface its past by succumbing to a modernist obsession with uncorrupted originality, an originality equally threatened by the other end of postmodernism, the infinite repetition represented by franchises such as Howard Johnson's.

Eating has never been simple, and contemporary eating practices seem more complicated than ever, demanding a multidimensional analysis that strives not for a reductive overview but for a complex understanding. The purpose of this collection of essays is to offer a number of diverse outlooks on some of the prominent practices and issues associated with the domain of eating in contemporary culture.

We think that the range of topics, perspectives, and possibilities presented here makes for an unusual and interesting menu. It is our hope that *Eating Culture* stimulates your appetite.

Chapter 1

Hunger as Ideology

Susan Bordo

The Woman Who Doesn't Eat Much

In a television commercial, two little French girls are shown dressing up in the feathery finery of their mothers' clothes. They are exquisite little girls, flawless and innocent, and the scene emphasizes both their youth and the natural sense of style often associated with French women. (The ad is done in French, with subtitles.) One of the girls, spying a picture of the other girl's mother, exclaims breathlessly, "Your mother, she is so slim, so beautiful! Does she eat?" The daughter, giggling, replies: "Silly, just not so much," and displays her mother's helper, a bottle of FibreThin. "Aren't you jealous?" the friend asks. Dimpling, shy yet self-possessed, deeply knowing, the daughter answers, "Not if I know her secrets."

Admittedly, women are continually bombarded with advertisements and commercials for weight-loss products and programs, but this commercial makes many of us particularly angry. On the most obvious level, the commercial affronts with its suggestion that young girls begin early in learning to control their weight, and with its romantic mystification of diet pills as part of the obscure, eternal arsenal of feminine arts to be passed from generation to generation. This romanticization, as often is the case in American commercials, trades on our continuing infatuation with (what we imagine to be) the civility, tradition, and savoir-faire of "Europe" (seen as the stylish antithesis to our own American clumsiness,

11

aggressiveness, crudeness). The little girls are fresh and demure, in a way that is undefinably but absolutely recognizably "European"— as defined, that is, within the visual vocabulary of popular American culture. And FibreThin, in this commercial, is nothing so crass and "medical" and pragmatic (read: American) as a diet pill, but a mysterious, prized (and, it is implied, age-old) "secret," known only to those with both history and taste.

But we expect such hype from contemporary advertisements. Far more unnerving is the psychological acuity of the ad's focus, not on the size and shape of bodies, but on a certain *subjectivity*, represented by the absent but central figure of the mother, the woman who eats, only "not so much." We never see her picture; we are left to imagine her ideal beauty and slenderness. But what she looks like is not important, in any case; what is important is the fact that she has achieved what we might call a "cool" (that is, casual) relation to food. She is not starving herself (an obsession, indicating the continuing power of food), but neither is she desperately and shamefully bingeing in some private corner. Eating has become, for her, no big deal. In its evocation of the lovely French mother who doesn't eat much, the commercial's metaphor of European "difference" reveals itself as a means of representing that enviable and truly foreign "other": the woman for whom food is merely ordinary, who can take it or leave it.

Another version, this time embodied by a sleek, fashionable African American woman, playfully promotes Virginia Slims Menthol. This ad, which appeared in *Essence* magazine, is one of a series specifically targeted at the African American female consumer. In contrast to the Virginia Slims series concurrently appearing in *Cosmo* and *People,* a series which continues to associate the product with historically expanded opportunities for women ("You've come a long way, baby" remains the motif and slogan), Virginia Slims pitches to the *Essence* reader by mocking solemnity and self-importance *after* the realization of those opportunities: "Why climb the ladder if you're not going to enjoy the view?" "Big girls don't cry. They go shopping." And, in the variant, "Decisions are easy. When I get to a fork in the road, I eat."

Arguably, the general subtext meant to be evoked by these ads is the failure of the dominant, white culture (those who *don't* "enjoy the view") to relax and take pleasure in success. The upwardly mobile black consumer, it is suggested, will do it with more panache, with more cool—and of course with a cool, Virginia Slims Menthol in hand. In this particular ad, the speaker scorns obsessiveness, not only over professional or interpersonal decision-making, but over food as well. Implicitly contrasting herself to those who worry and fret, she presents herself as utterly "easy" in her relationship with food. Unlike the FibreThin mother, she eats anytime she wants. But *like* the FibreThin mother (and this is the key similarity for my purposes), she has achieved a state beyond craving. Undominated by unsatisfied, internal need, she eats not only freely but without deep desire and without apparent consequence. It's "easy," she says. Presumably, without those forks in the road she might forget about food entirely.

The Virginia Slims woman is a fantasy figure, her cool attitude toward food as remote from the lives of most contemporary African American women as from any others. True, if we survey cultural attitudes toward women's appetites and body size, we find great variety—a variety shaped by ethnic, national, historical, class, and other factors. My eighty-year-old father, the child of immigrants, asks at the end of every meal if I "got enough to eat"; he considers me skinny unless I am plump by my own standards. His attitude reflects not only memories of economic struggle and a heritage of Jewish-Russian preference for zaftig women, but the lingering, well into this century, of a once more general Anglo-Saxon cultural appreciation for the buxom woman. In the mid-nineteenth century, hotels and bars were adorned with Bouguereau-inspired paintings of voluptuous female nudes; Lillian Russell, the most photographed woman in America in 1890, was known and admired for her hearty appetite, ample body (over two hundred pounds at the height of her popularity), and "challenging, fleshly arresting" beauty.[1] Even as such fleshly challenges became less widely appreciated in the twentieth century, men of Greek, Italian, Eastern European, and African descent, influenced by their own distinctive cultural heritages, were still likely to find female voluptuousness appealing. And even in the late 1960s and early 1970s, as Twiggy and Jean Shrimpton began to set a new norm for ultra-slenderness, lesbian cultures in the United States continued to be accepting—even celebrating—of fleshy, space-claiming female bodies.

Even more examples could be produced, of course, if we cast our glance more widely over the globe and back through history. Many cultures, clearly, have revered expansiveness in women's bodies and appetites. Some still do. But in the 1980s and 1990s an increasingly universal equation of slenderness with beauty and success has rendered the competing claims of cultural diversity ever feebler. Men who were teenagers from the mid-seventies on, whatever their ethnic roots or economic class, are likely to view long, slim legs, a flat stomach, and a firm rear end as essentials of female beauty. Unmuscled heft is no longer as acceptable as it once was in lesbian communities. Even Miss Soviet Union has become lean and tight, and the robust, earthy actresses who used to star in Russian films have been replaced by slender, Westernized types.

Arguably, a case could once be made for a contrast between (middle-class, heterosexual) white women's obsessive relations with food and a more accepting attitude toward women's appetites within African American communities. But in the nineties, features on diet, exercise, and body-image problems have grown increasingly prominent in magazines aimed at African American readers, reflecting the cultural reality that for most women today—whatever their racial or ethnic identity, and increasingly across class and sexual-orientation differences as well—free and easy relations with food are at best a relic of the past. (More frequently in *Essence* than in *Cosmo*, there may be a focus on health problems associated with overweight among African Americans, in addition to the glamorization of slenderness.) Almost all of us who can afford to be eating well are dieting—and hungry—almost all of the time.

It is thus Dexatrim, not Virginia Slims, that constructs the more realistic representation of women's subjective relations with food. In Dexatrim's commercial that shows a woman, her appetite-suppressant worn off, hurtling across the room, drawn like a living magnet to the breathing, menacing refrigerator, hunger is represented as an insistent, powerful force with a life of its own. This construction reflects the physiological reality of dieting, a state the body is unable to distinguish from starvation.[2] And it reflects its psychological reality as well; for dieters, who live in a state of constant denial, food is a perpetually beckoning presence, its power growing ever greater as the sanctions against gratification become more stringent. A slender body may be attainable through hard work, but a "cool" relation to food, the true "secret" of the beautiful "other" in the FibreThin commercial, is a tantalizing reminder of what lies beyond the reach of the inadequate and hungry self. (Of course, as the ads suggest, a psychocultural transformation remains possible, through FibreThin and Virginia Slims.)

Psyching Out the Female Consumer

Sometimes, when I am analyzing and interpreting advertisements and commercials in class, students accuse me of a kind of paranoia about the significance of these representations as carriers and reproducers of culture. After all, they insist, these are just images, not "real life"; any fool knows that advertisers manipulate reality in the service of selling their products. I agree that on some level we "know" this. However, were it a meaningful or *usable* knowledge, it is unlikely that we would be witnessing the current spread of diet and exercise mania across racial and ethnic groups, or the explosion of technologies aimed at bodily "correction" and "enhancement."

Jean Baudrillard offers a more accurate description of our cultural estimation of the relation and relative importance of image and "reality." In *Simulations,* he recalls the Borges fable in which the cartographers of a mighty empire draw up a map so detailed that it ends up exactly covering the territory of the empire, a map which then frays and disintegrates as a symbol of the coming decline of the empire it perfectly represents. Today, Baudrillard suggests, the fable might be inverted: it is no longer the territory that provides the model for the map, but the map that defines the territory; and it is the *territory* "whose shreds are slowly rotting across the map." Thinking further, however, he declares even the inverted fable to be "useless." For what it still assumes is precisely that which is being lost today—namely, the distinction between the territory and its map, between reality and appearance. Today, all that we experience as meaningful are appearances.[3]

Thus, we all "know" that Cher and virtually every other female star over the age of twenty-five is the plastic product of numerous cosmetic surgeries on face and body. But, in the era of the "hyperreal" (as Baudrillard calls it), such "knowledge" is as faded and frayed as the old map in the Borges tale, unable to cast a shadow of doubt over the dazzling, compelling, authoritative images themselves. Like the knowledge of our own mortality when we are young and healthy, the knowledge that Cher's physical appearance is fabricated is an empty abstraction; it simply does not compute. It is the created image that has the hold on our most vibrant, immediate sense of what *is*, of what matters, of what we must pursue for ourselves.

In *constructing* the images, of course, continual use is made of knowledge (or at least what is imagined to be knowledge) of consumers' lives. Indeed, a careful reading of contemporary advertisements reveals continual and astute manipulation of problems that psychology and the popular media have targeted as characteristic dilemmas of the "contemporary woman," who is beset by conflicting role demands and pressures on her time. "Control"—a word that rarely used to appear in commercial contexts—has become a common trope in advertisements for products as disparate as mascara ("Perfect Pen Eyeliner. Puts *you* in control. And isn't that nice for a change?") and cat-box deodorant ("Control. I strive for it. My cat achieves it"). *"Soft felt tip gives you absolute control of your line."* It is virtually impossible to glance casually at this ad without reading "line" as "life"—which is, of course, the subliminal coding such ads intend. "Mastery" also frequently figures in ads for cosmetics and hair products: "Master your curls with new Adaptable Perm." The rhetoric of these ads is interestingly contrasted to the rhetoric of mastery and control directed at male consumers. Here, the message is almost always one of mastery and control over *others* rather than the self: "Now it's easier than ever to achieve a position of power in Manhattan" (an ad for a Manhattan health club), or "Don't just serve. Rule" (an ad for Speedo tennis shoes).

Advertisers are aware, too, of more specific *ways* in which women's lives are out of control, including our well-documented food disorders; they frequently incorporate the theme of food obsession into their pitch. The Sugar Free Jell-O Pudding campaign exemplifies a typical commercial strategy for exploiting women's eating problems while obscuring their dark realities. (The advertisers themselves would put this differently, of course.) In the "tip of my tongue" ad, the obsessive mental state of the compulsive eater is depicted fairly accurately, guaranteeing recognition from people with that problem: "If I'm not eating dessert, I'm talking about it. If I'm not talking about, I'm eating it. And I'm always thinking about it. . . . It's just always on my mind."

These thoughts, however, belong to a slender, confident, and—most important—decidedly not depressed individual, whose up-beat, open, and accepting attitude toward her constant hunger is far from that of most women who eat compulsively. "The inside of a binge," Geneen Roth writes, "is deep and dark. At the core . . . is deprivation, scarcity, a feeling that you can never get enough."[4] A student described her hunger as "a black hole that I had to fill up." In the Sugar Free Jell-O ad, by contrast, the mental state depicted is most like that of a growing teenage boy; to be continually hungry is represented as a normal, if somewhat humorous and occasionally annoying, state with no disastrous physical or emotional consequences.

The use of a male figure is one strategy, in contemporary ads, for representing compulsive eating as "natural" and even lovable. Men are *supposed* to have hearty, even voracious, appetites. It is a mark of the manly to eat spontaneously and expansively, and manliness is a frequent commercial code for amply portioned products: "Manwich," "Hungry Man Dinners," "Manhandlers." Even when men advertise diet products (as they more frequently do, now that physical perfection is increasingly being demanded of men as well as women), they brag about their appetites, as in the Tommy Lasorda commercials for Slim-Fast, which feature three burly football players (their masculinity beyond reproach) declaring that if Slim-Fast can satisfy *their* appetites, it can satisfy anyone's. The displacement of the female by a male (displacement when the targeted consumer is in fact a woman) thus dispels thoughts of addiction, danger, unhappiness, and replaces them with a construction of compulsive eating (or thinking about food) as benign indulgence of a "natural" inclination. Consider the ad depicting a male figure diving with abandon into the "tempered-to-full-flavor-consistency" joys of Häagen-Dazs deep chocolate.

Emotional heights, intensity, love, and thrills: it is women who habitually seek such experiences from food and who are most likely to be overwhelmed by their relationship to food, to find it dangerous and frightening (especially rich, fattening, soothing food like ice cream). The marketers of Häagen-Dazs know this; they are aware of the well-publicized prevalence of compulsive eating and binge behaviors among women. Indeed, this ad exploits, with artful precision, exactly the sorts of associations that are likely to resonate with a person for whom eating is invested with deep emotional meaning. Why, then, a male diver? In part, as I have been arguing, the displacement is necessary to insure that the grim actualities of women's eating problems remain obscured; the point, after all, is to sell ice cream, not to remind people of how dangerous food actually *is* for women. Too, the advertisers may reckon that women might enjoy seeing a man depicted in swooning surrender to ice cream, as a metaphor for the emotional surrender that so many women crave from their husbands and lovers.

Food, Sexuality, and Desire

I would argue, however, that more than a purely profit-maximizing, ideologically neutral, Madison Avenue mentality is at work in these ads. They must also be considered as gender ideology— that is, as specifically (consciously or unconsciously) servicing the cultural reproduction of gender difference and gender inequality, quite independent of (although at times coinciding with) marketing concerns. As gender ideology, the ads I have been discussing are not distinctively contemporary but continue a well-worn represen-tational tradition, arguably inaugurated in the Victorian era, in which the depiction of women eating, particularly in sensuous surrender to rich, exciting food, is taboo.[5]

In exploring this dimension, we might begin by attempting to imagine an advertisement depicting a young, attractive woman indulging as freely, as salaciously as the man in the Post cereal ad. Such an image would violate deeply sedimented expectations, would be experienced by many as disgusting and transgressive. When women are positively depicted as sensuously voracious about food (almost never in commercials, and only very rarely in movies and novels), their hunger for food is employed solely as a metaphor for their sexual appetite. In the eating scenes in *Tom Jones* and *Flashdance*, for example, the heroines' unrestrained delight in eat-ing operates as sexual foreplay, a way of prefiguring the abandon that will shortly be expressed in bed. Women are permitted to lust for food itself only when they are pregnant or when it is clear they have been near starvation—as, for example, in *McCabe and Mrs. Miller*, in the scene in which Mrs. Miller, played by Julie Christie, wolfs down half a dozen eggs and a bowl of beef stew before the amazed eyes of McCabe. Significantly, the scene serves to establish Mrs. Miller's "manliness"; a woman who eats like this is to be taken seriously, is not to be trifled with, the movie suggests.

The metaphorical situation is virtually inverted in the repre-sentation of male eaters. Although voracious eating may occasion-ally code male sexual appetite (as in *Tom Jones*), we frequently also find *sexual* appetite operating as a metaphor for eating pleasure. In. commercials that feature male eaters, the men are shown in a state of wild, sensual transport over heavily frosted, rich, gooey desserts. Their total lack of control is portrayed as appropriate, even ador-able; the language of the background jingle is unashamedly aroused, sexual and desiring:

> I'm thinking about you the whole day through [crooned to a Pillsbury cake]. I've got a passion for you.
>
> You're my one and only, my creamy deluxe [Betty Crocker frosting].
>
> You butter me up, I can't resist, you leave me breathless [Betty Crocker frosting].

Your brownies give me fever. Your cake gives me chills [assorted Betty Crocker mixes].

I'm a fool for your chocolate. I'm wild, crazy, out of control [assorted Betty Crocker mixes].

I've got it bad, and I should know, 'cause I crave it from my head right down to my potato [for Pillsbury Potatoes Au Gratin].

Can't help myself. It's Duncan Hines [assorted cake mixes] and nobody else.

In these commercials food is constructed as a sexual object of desire, and eating is legitimated as much more than a purely nutritive activity. Rather, food is *supposed* to supply sensual delight and succor—not as metaphorically standing for something else, but as an erotic experience in itself. Women are permitted such gratification from food only in measured doses. In another ad from the Diet Jell-O series, eating is metaphorically sexualized: "I'm a girl who just can't say no. I insist on dessert," admits the innocently dressed but flirtatiously posed model. But at the same time that eating is mildly sexualized in this ad, it is also contained. She is permitted to "feel good about saying 'Yes' "—but ever so demurely, and to a harmless low-calorie product. Transgression beyond such limits is floridly sexualized, as an act of "cheating." Women may be encouraged (like the man on the Häagen-Dazs high board) to "dive in"—not, however, into a dangerous pool of Häagen-Dazs Deep Chocolate, but for a "refreshing dip" into Weight Watchers linguini. Targeted at the working woman ("Just what you need to revive yourself from the workday routine"), this ad also exploits the aquatic metaphor to conjure up images of female independence and liberation ("Isn't it just like us to make waves?").

All of this may seem peculiarly contemporary, revolving as it does around the mass marketing of diet products. But in fact the same metaphorical universe, as well as the same practical prohibitions against female indulgence (for, of course, these ads are not only selling products but teaching appropriate behavior) were characteristic of Victorian gender ideology. Victorians did not have *Cosmo* and television, of course. But they did have conduct manuals, which warned elite women of the dangers of indulgent and over-stimulating eating and advised how to consume in a feminine way (as little as possible and with the utmost precaution against unseemly show of desire). *Godey's Lady's Book* warned that it was vulgar for women to load their plates; young girls were admonished to "be frugal and plain in your tastes." Detailed lexicons offered comparisons of the erotic and cooling effects of various foods, often with specific prescriptions for each sex.[7] Sexual metaphors permeate descriptions of potential transgression:

> Every luxurious table is a scene of temptation, which it requires fixed principles and an enlightened mind to withstand. . . . Nothing can be more seducing to the appetite than this arrangement of the viands which compose a feast; as the stomach is filled, and the natural desire for food subsides, the palate is tickled by more delicate and relishing dishes until it is betrayed into excess.[8]

Today, the same metaphors of temptation and fall appear frequently in advertisements for diet products. And in the Victorian era, as today, the forbiddenness of rich food often resulted in private binge behavior, described in *The Bazaar Book of Decorum* (1870) as the "secret luncheon," at which "many of the most abstemious at the open dinner are the most voracious . . . swallowing cream tarts by the dozen, and caramels and chocolate drops by the pound's weight."[9]

The emergence of such rigid and highly moralized restrictions on female appetite and eating are, arguably, part of what Bram Dijkstra has interpreted as a nineteenth-century "cultural ideological counter-offensive" against the "new woman" and her challenge to prevailing gender arrangements and their constraints on women.[10] Mythological, artistic, polemical, and scientific discourses from many cultures and eras certainly suggest the symbolic potency of female hunger as a cultural metaphor for unleashed female power and desire, from the blood-craving Kali (who in one representation is shown eating her own entrails) to the *Malleus Malificarum* ("For the sake of fulfilling the mouth of the womb, [witches] consort even with the devil") to Hall and Oates's contemporary rock lyrics: "Oh, oh, here she comes, watch out boys, she'll chew you up."[11]

In *Tom Jones* and *Flashdance,* the trope of female hunger as female sexuality is embodied in attractive female characters; more frequently, however, female hunger as sexuality is represented by Western culture in misogynist images permeated with terror and loathing rather than affection or admiration. In the figure of the man-eater the metaphor of the devouring woman reveals its deep psychological underpinnings. Eating is not really a metaphor for the sexual act; rather, the sexual act, when initiated and desired by a woman, is imagined as itself an act of eating, of incorporation and destruction of the object of desire. Thus, women's sexual appetites must be curtailed and controlled, because they threaten to deplete and consume the body and soul of the male. Such imagery, as Dijkstra has demonstrated, flourishes in the West in the art of the late nineteenth century. Arguably, the same cultural backlash (if not in the same form) operates today—for example, in the ascendancy of popular films that punish female sexuality and independence by rape and dismemberment (as in numerous slasher films), loss of family and children *(The Good Mother)*, madness and death *(Fatal Attraction, Presumed Innocent)*, and public humiliation and disgrace *(Dangerous Liaisons)*.

Of course, Victorian prohibitions against women eating were not *only* about the ideology of gender. Or, perhaps better put, the ideology of gender contained other dimensions as well. The construction of "femininity" had not only a significant moral and sexual aspect (femininity as sexual passivity, timidity, purity, innocence) but a class dimension. In the reigning body symbolism of the day, a frail frame and lack of appetite signified not only spiritual transcendence of the desires of the flesh but *social* transcendence of the laboring, striving "economic" body. Then, as today, to be aristocratically cool and unconcerned with the mere facts of material survival was highly fashionable. The hungering bourgeois wished to appear, like the aristocrat, above the material desires that in fact ruled his life. The closest he could come was to possess a wife whose ethereal body became a sort of fashion statement of *his* aristocratic tastes. If he could not be or marry an aristocrat, he could have a wife who looked like one, a wife whose non-robust beauty and delicate appetite signified her lack of participation in the taxing "public sphere."[12]

Men Eat and Women Prepare

The metaphorical dualities at work here, whatever their class meanings, presuppose an idealized (and rarely actualized) gendered division of labor in which men strive, compete, and exert themselves in the public sphere while women are cocooned in the domestic arena (which is romanticized and mystified as a place of peace and leisure, and hence connotes transcendence of the laboring, bourgeois body). In the necessity to make such a division of labor appear natural we find another powerful ideological underpinning (perhaps the most important in the context of industrialized society) for the cultural containment of female appetite: the notion that women are most gratified by feeding and nourishing *others,* not themselves. As a literal activity, of course, women fed others long before the "home" came to be identified as women's special place; Caroline Bynum argues that there is reason to believe that food preparation was already a stereotypically female activity in the European Middle Ages.[13] But it was in the industrial era, with its idealization of the domestic arena as a place of nurture and comfort for men and children, that feeding others acquired the extended emotional meaning it has today.

In "An Ode to Mothers" columnist Bud Poloquin defines *Moms* as "those folks who, upon seeing there are only four pieces of pie for five people, promptly announce they never did care for the stuff."[14] Denial of self and the feeding of others are hopelessly enmeshed in this construction of the ideal mother, as they are in the nineteenth-century version of the ideal wife as "she who stands . . . famished before her husband, while he devours, stretched at ease, the produce of her exertions; waits his tardy permission without a word or a look of impatience, and feeds, with the humblest gratitude, and the shortest intermission of labor, on the scraps and offals which he disdains."[15] None of this self-sacrifice, however, is felt as such by the "paragon of womanhood" (as Charles Butler calls her), for it is here, in the care and feeding of others, that woman experiences the one form of desire that is appropriately hers: as Elias Canetti so succinctly puts it, "Her passion is to give food."[16]

Over a decade ago, John Berger trenchantly encapsulated the standard formula he saw as regulating the representation of gender difference, both throughout the history of art and in contemporary advertising: "Men act, and women appear."[17] Today, that opposition no longer seems to hold quite as rigidly as it once did (women are indeed objectified more than ever, but, in this image-dominated culture, men increasingly are too). But if this duality no longer strictly applies, the resilience of others is all the more instructive. Let me replace Berger's formulation with another, apparently more enduring one: "Men eat and women prepare." At least in the sphere of popular representations, this division of labor is as prescriptive in 1991 as in 1891. Despite the increasing participation of women of all ages and classes in the "public" sphere, her "private" role of nurturer remains ideologically intact.

To be sure, we have inherited some of these representations from a former era—for example, the plump, generous Mammies and Grandmas who symbolically have prepared so many products:

Aunt Jemima, Mrs. Smith, Mrs. Paul, Grandma Brown. But our cultural penchant for nostalgia does not get us off the hook here. At the start of the 1990s (and this seems to be even more striking now than five years ago), popular representations almost never depict a man *preparing* food as an everyday activity, routinely performed in the unpaid service of others. Occasionally, men *are* shown serving food—in the role of butler or waiter. They may be depicted roasting various items around a campfire, barbecuing meat, preparing a salad for a special company dinner, or making *instant* coffee (usually in a getaway cabin or vacation boat). But all of these are nonroutine, and their exceptional nature is frequently underscored in the ad. In one commercial, a man fixes instant coffee to serve to his wife in bed on her birthday. "How tough can it be?" he asks. "She makes breakfast every morning." In another ad, a man is shown preparing pancakes for his son's breakfast. "My pancakes deserve the rich maple flavor of Log Cabin Syrup," reads the bold type, suggesting ("my pancakes") male proprietorship and ease in the kitchen. The visual image of the father lovingly serving the son undoubtedly destabilizes cultural stereotypes (racial as well as gendered). But in the smaller print below the image we are told that this is a "special moment" with his son. Immediately the destabilizing image reconfigures into a familiar one: like Dad's secret recipe for barbecue sauce, this father's pancakes make their appearance only on special occasions. Or perhaps it is the very fact that Dad is doing the cooking that *makes* this a significant, intimate occasion for sharing. (Imagine a woman instead of a man in the ad; would "special moment" not then seem odd?)

Continually, in representations that depict men preparing food, there will be a conspicuously absent wife or mother (for instance, in the hospital having a baby) who, it is implied, is *normally* responsible for the daily labor of food preparation and service. Even when men or boys are used to advertise convenience foods, the product has usually been left for them with expert instructions added by Mom. In the Jell-O Heritage ad, this absent maternal figure (whether mother or grandmother is not clear) appears in the small insert to the upper right of the larger image, which depicts a young man away at college, well supplied with Jell-O pudding snacks. Significantly (although somewhat absurdly), she is associated with the provision of a "strong foundation" by virtue of the fact that *she* prepares instant pudding from a mix rather than merely opening up an already prepared pudding snack. Jell-O, of course, could not present nostalgic images of Grandma preparing *real* "scratch" pudding, since it does not want to evoke longing for a time when women did not depend on its products. But in terms of the oppositions exploited in this ad, instant pudding works just as well; compared to flipping the lid off a pudding snack, preparing instant pudding *is* a laborious task. It thus belongs to women's world. Men are almost *never* shown lavishing time on cooking. *Real* coffee is always prepared by women, as are all the cakes and casseroles that require more than a moment to put together. When men *are* shown cooking an elaborate meal, it is always *with* one or two other yuppie men, converting the activity from an act of everyday service into a festive, "Big Chill" occasion. But even these representations are rare. In all the many dinner parties that Hope and Michael hosted on "Thirtysomething," no man has ever appeared in the kitchen except to sneak a bit of the meal being prepared by Hope, Nancy, and Melissa.

Food and Love

At the beginning of the 1992 U.S. presidential campaign, Hillary Clinton, badgered by reporters' endless questions concerning her pursuit of a professional career, shot back defensively and sarcastically: "Well, I suppose I could have stayed home and baked cookies and had teas. . . . " Media audiences never got to hear the end of her remark (or the questioning that preceded it); the "cookies and teas" sound-bite became *the* gender-transgression of the campaign, replayed over and over, and presented by opponents as evidence of Hillary's rabid feminism and disdain for traditional maternal values. Rightly protesting this interpretation, Hillary Clinton tried to prove her true womanhood by producing her favorite recipe for oatmeal chocolate chip cookies. Barbara Bush, apparently feeling that a gauntlet had been thrown down, responded in kind with a richer, less fiber-conscious recipe of her own. Newspapers across the country asked readers to prepare both and vote on which First Lady had the better cookie.

That the cookie itself should have become the symbol and center of the national debate about Hillary Clinton's adequacy as wife and mother is not surprising. Food is equated with maternal and wifely love throughout our culture. In nearly all commercials that feature men eating—such as the cake commercials whose sexualized rhetoric was quoted earlier—there is a woman in the background (either visible or implied) who has *prepared* the food. (The "Betty Crocker, You Sweet Talker" series has two women: the possessor of the clearly feminine hands offering the cakes, and Betty Crocker herself, to whom all the passionate croonings—"I'm a fool for your chocolate. I'm wild, crazy, out of control"—are addressed.) Most significantly, *always*, the woman in the background speaks the language of love and care through the offering of food: "Nothin' says lovin' like something from the oven"; "Give me that great taste of love"; "Nothing says 'Cookie, I love you' like Nestle's Toll House Cookies Do." In these commercials, male eating is inextricably tied to female offerings of love. This is not represented, however, as female self-abnegation. Rather, it is suggested that women receive *their* gratification through nourishing others, either in the old-fashioned way (taste and emotional pleasure) or in the health-conscious mode:

> *Her voice, heard off:* He's like a little boy—normally serious, *then* he eats English muffins with butter [shot of man's face transported with childlike delight] and *I* get to enjoy watching him. A little butter brings a lot of joy.
> *He:* What are you doing?
> *She:* I'm listening to your heart.
> *He:* What does it say?
> *She:* It says that it's glad that you've started jogging, and that you're eating healthier. It's happy that I'm giving us new Promise margarine. Eating foods low in cholesterol is good for you and your heart.
> *He:* Know what else is good for me?
> *She:* What?
> *He:* You.
> *She beams, snuggling deeper into man's chest.*

My analysis, I want to emphasize, is not meant to disparage caring for the physical and emotional well-being of others, "maternal" work that has been scandalously socially undervalued even as it has been idealized and sanctified. Nor am I counterposing to the argument of these ads the construction that women are simply oppressed by such roles. This would be untrue to the personal experiences of many women, including myself. I remember the pride and pleasure that radiated from my mother, who was anxious and unhappy in most other areas of her life, when her famous stuffed cabbage was devoured enthusiastically and in voluminous quantities by my father, my sisters, and me. As a little girl, I loved watching her roll each piece, enclosing just the right amount of filling, skillfully avoiding tearing the tender cabbage leaves as she folded them around the meat. I never felt so safe and secure as at those moments. She was visibly pleased when I asked her to teach me exactly how to make the dish and thrilled when I even went so far as to write the quantities and instructions down as she tried to formulate them into an official recipe (until then, it had been passed through demonstration from mother to daughter, and my mother considered that in writing it down I was conferring a higher status on it). Those periods in my life when I have found myself too busy writing, teaching, and traveling to find the time and energy to prepare special meals for people that I love have been periods when a deep aspect of my self has felt deprived, depressed.

Nor would I want my critique to be interpreted as effacing the collective, historical experiences of those groups, forced into servitude for the families of others, who have been systematically deprived of the freedom *to* care for their own families. Bell hooks points out, for example, that black women's creation of "homeplace," of fragile and hard-won "spaces of care and nurturance" for the healing of deep wounds made by racism, sexism, and poverty, was less a matter of obedience to a tyrannical gender-norm than the construction of a "site of cultural resistance."[18] With this in mind, it is clear that the Jell-O Heritage ad discussed earlier is more complex than my interpretation has thus far allowed. Part of an extensive General Foods series aimed at the African American consumer and promoting America's historically black colleges, the ad's association of the maternal figure with "strong foundations" runs far deeper than a nostalgic evocation of Mom's traditional cooking. In this ad, the maternal figure is linked with a black "heritage," with the preservation and communication of culture.

However, at the same time that hooks urges that contemporary black culture should honor the black woman's history of service to her family and her community, she also cautions against the ideological construction of such service as woman's natural role. (Despite the pleasure I take in cooking, in relationships where it has been expected of me I have resented it deeply.) It is this construction that is reinforced in the representations I have been examining, through their failure to depict males as "naturally" fulfilling that role, and—more perniciously—through their failure to depict females as appropriate *recipients* of such care. Only occasionally are little girls represented as being *fed;* more often, they (but never little boys) are shown learning how to feed others. In this way, caring is representationally "reproduced" as a quintessentially and exclusively female activity. It is significant and disquieting that the General Foods series does not include any ads that portray female students discovering their black heritage (or learning how to rely on convenience foods!) at college. It is possible that the ad series is very deliberate here, exploiting contemporary notions that the "crisis in black manhood" is the fault of black women and identifying its products with an imagined world in which opportunities for black men go hand in hand with "natural," prefeminist gender relations. Black men will find their way to college, it is suggested, so long as women remain in the background, encouraging and supporting rather than competing and undermining.

The ubiquitous configuration of woman-food-man, with food expressing the woman's love for the man and at the same time satisfying the woman's desire to bestow love, establishes male hunger as thoroughly socially integrated into the network of heterosexual family and love relations. Men can eat *and* be loved; indeed, a central mode by which they receive love is through food from women. For women, by contrast (who are almost never shown being fed by others), eating—in the form of private, *self*-feeding— is represented as a *substitute* for human love. Weight Watchers transparently offers itself as such in its "Who says you can't live on love?" ad. In other ads, it offers its low-cal spaghetti sauce as "A Friend." Diet Coke, emphasizing the sexual, insists that "sometimes the best relationships are purely fizzical." Miracle Whip Light offers itself as "a light that turns you on."

Notice that in these ads there is no partner, visible or implied, offering the food and thus operating as the true bestower of "love." In many ads—virtually a genre, in fact—the absence of the partner is explicitly thematized, a central aspect of the narrative of the ad. One commercial features a woman in bed, on the phone, refusing date after date in favor of an evening alone with her ice-cream bon bons: "Your Highness? Not tonight!" "The inauguration? Another year!" In another, a woman admits to spending a lot of time alone with her "latest obsession," a chocolate drink, because it gives her "the same feeling as being in love" and "satisfies her innermost cravings anytime [she] wants." She pleads with us, the viewers, not to tell Michael, her boyfriend.

These commercials hit a painful nerve for women. The bon bon commercial may seem merely silly, but the chocolate drink ad begins to evoke, darkly and disturbingly, the psychological and material realities of women's food problems. The talk of "obsession" and "innermost cravings," the furtiveness, the secrecy, the use of food to satisfy emotional needs, all suggest central elements of binge behavior. Frusen Glädjé supplies another piece and gives an important lie to the other, more upbeat commercials: "He never called. So, Ben and I went out for a walk to pick up a pint of Frusen Glädjé. Ben's better looking anyway." Frusen Glädjé: "It feels so good." Here, as in the Häagen-Dazs ad discussed earlier, the sensuousness of the ice-cream experience is emphasized; unlike the Häagen-Dazs ad, however, Frusen Glädjé offers solace from emotional depths rather than the thrill of emotional heights. This is, indeed, the prevailing gender reality. For women, the emotional comfort of self-feeding is rarely turned to in a state of pleasure and independence, but in despair, emptiness, loneliness, and desperation. Food is, as one woman put it, "the only thing that will take care of *me*."[19]

Food as Transgression

An extremely interesting fact about male bulimics: they rarely binge alone. They tend to binge at mealtime and in public places, whereas women almost always eat minimally at meals and gorge later, in private.[20] Even in our disorders (or perhaps especially in our disorders) we follow the gender rules. In the commercials I have been discussing, female eating is virtually always represented as private, secretive, illicit. The woman has stolen away from the world of husband, family, friends to a secret corner where she and the food can be alone. A "Do Not Disturb" sign hangs on the door to the room where the woman sits munching on her "purple passion," New York Deli Potato Chips. A husband returns home to discover that in his absence his wife, sitting on the floor, has eaten all the Frusen Glädjé; her voice is mildly defiant, although soft— "I ate all the Frusen Glädjé"—but her face is sheepish and her glance averted. Men sing openly of their wild cravings for Betty Crocker cakes; women's cravings are a dirty, shameful secret, to be indulged in only when no one is looking.

More often than not, however, women are not even permitted, even in private, indulgences so extravagant in scope as the full satisfaction of their hungers. Most commonly, women are used to advertise, *not* ice cream and potato chips (foods whose intake is very difficult to contain and control), but individually wrapped pieces of tiny, bite-size candies: Andes candies, Hershey's kisses, Mon Cheri bon bons. Instead of the mounds of cake and oozing frosting typical of commercials featuring male eaters, women are confined to a "tiny scoop" of flavor, a "tiny piece" of chocolate. As in the Weight Watchers linguini advertisement ("Dive in"), the rhetoric of indulgence is invoked, only to be contained by the product itself: "Indulge a little," urges Andes Candies. "Satisfy your urge to splurge in five delicious bite-size ways." The littleness of the candy and the amount of taste that is packed within its tiny boundaries are frequently emphasized: "Each bite-size piece packs a wallop of milk chocolate crunch." Instead of the emphasis on undifferentiated feelings of sensuous delight that we see in commercials showing men, the pitch aimed at women stresses the exquisite pleasure to be had from a sensually focused and limited experience. The message to women is explicit: "Indulge a *little.*" (And only out of sight; even these minuscule bon bons are eaten privately, in isolation, behind closed doors.)

If one genre or commercials hints at the dark secrets of binge behavior—the refusal of female desire to remain circumscribed and repressed; the frustrations of "feeding" others and never being fed yourself—the "bite-size" candy genre represents female hunger as successfully contained within the bounds of appropriate feminine behavior. It is significant, surely, that in all these commercials the woman is found "indulging" only after a day spent serving others. In these commercials, it is permissible for women to feed the self (if such dainty nibbling merits this description) only after first feeding others:

For my angel, I sewed for days. Now I deserve a little praise. I thank me very much with Andes Candies.

Chances are you spent the day doing things for others. Don't you deserve something for yourself? Try a Mon Cheri. [The woman is in the bathtub; in the background, dimly heard are the voices of the day gone by: "Honey, did you pick up my dry cleaning?" "Mrs. Jones, will you type this letter?" "Mommy, we want to go to the park!" She sinks down into the tub, unwrapping the candy, in exquisite anticipation.]

These commercials, no less than the Victorian conduct manuals, offer a virtual blueprint for disordered relations to food and hunger. The representation of unrestrained appetite as inappropriate for women, the depiction of female eating as a private, transgressive act, make restriction and denial of hunger central features of the construction of femininity and set up the compensatory

binge as a virtual inevitability. Such restrictions on appetite, moreover, are not merely about food intake. Rather, the social control
of female hunger operates as a practical "discipline" (to use
Foucault's term) that trains female bodies in the knowledge of their
limits and possibilities. Denying oneself food becomes the central
micro-practice in the education of feminine self-restraint and containment of impulse.

Victorian women were told that it was vulgar to load their
plates; in 1990, women students of mine complain of the tortures
of the cafeteria—the embarrassment of eating ice cream in front of
the male students, the pressure to take just a salad or, better yet,
refuse food altogether. Later at night, when they are alone, they
confront the deprived and empty feeling left in the wake of such a
regimen. As in the commercials, the self-reward and solace is food.
The problem, however, after a day of restraint is the requirement
for any further containment of the now ravenous self. Unlike the
women in the Andes candy commercials, few women who have
spent the day submerging their desires, either for the sake of their
families or to project the appropriately attractive lack of appetite to
a cafeteria full of adolescent boys, really feel rewarded by a bite-
size piece of candy, no matter how much chocolate "wallop" it
packs. In private, shamefully and furtively, we binge.

Destabilizing Images?

When, in my classes, we discuss contemporary representations, I encourage my students to bring in examples that appear to
violate traditional gender-dualities and the ideological messages
contained in them. Frequently, my students view our examination
of these "subversive" representations as an investigation and determination of whether or not "progress" has been made. My students
want very much to believe that progress is being made, and so do
I. But "progress" is not an adequate description of the cultural
status of the counter-examples they bring me. Rather, they almost
always display a complicated and bewitching tangle of new possibilities and old patterns of representation. They reflect the insta-
bilities that trouble the continued reproduction of the old dualities
and ideologies, but they do not show clearly just where we are
going.

A television commercial for Hormel microwaveable Kid's
Kitchen Meals, for example, opens with two young girls trying to

fix a bicycle. A little boy, watching them, offers to help, claiming that "I can fix anything. My dad lets me fix his car. My mom lets me fix dinner." When the girls are skeptical ("Yeah? Well, prove it!"), he fixes a Hormel's Kid's Kitchen Meal for them. Utterly impressed with his culinary skill and on the basis of this ready to trust his mechanical aptitude, they ask, "You know how to fix a bike?" "What? Yeah, I do!" he eagerly replies. Now, is this ad "progressive" or "regressive"? The little girls cannot fix their own bike, a highly traditional, "feminine" limitation. Yet they do not behave in helpless or coquettish ways in the commercial. Far from it. They speak in rough voices and challenging words to the boy, who is physically smaller (and, it appears, younger) than they; "Give me a break!" they mutter scornfully when he claims he can "fix anything." Despite their mechanical inability, they do not act deferential, and in a curious way this neutralizes the gendered meanings of the activities depicted. Not being able to fix a bike is something that could happen to anyone, they seem to believe. And so we may begin to see it this way too.

Then, too, there is the unusual representation of the male cooking for and serving the females. True, it only required a touch of the microwave panel. But this is, after all, only a little boy. One message this commercial may be delivering is that males can engage in traditionally "feminine" activities without threat to their manhood. Cooking for a woman does not mean that she won't respect you in the morning. She will still recognize your authority to fix her bike (indeed, she may become further convinced of it precisely by your mastery of "her" domain). The expansion of possibilities for boys thus extracts from girls the price of continued ineptitude in certain areas (or at least the show of it) and dependence on males. Yet, in an era in which most working women find themselves with two full-time jobs—their second shift beginning at five o'clock, when they return from work to meet their husband's expectations of dinner, a clean and comfortable home, a sympathetic ear—the message that cooking and serving others is not "sissy," though it may be problematic and nonprogressive in many ways, is perhaps the single most *practically* beneficial (to women) message we can convey to little boys.

In its provision of ambiguous and destabilizing imagery, the influx of women into the professional arena has had a significant effect on the representation of gender. Seeking to appeal to a population that wishes to be regarded (at least while on the job) as equal in power and ability to the men with whom they work, advertisers have tried to establish gender symmetry in those representations that depict or evoke the lives of professional couples. Minute Rice thus has two versions of its "I wonder what 'Minute' is cookin' up for dinner tonight?" commercial. In one, father and children come home from work and school to find mother "cookin' up" an elaborate chicken stir-fry to serve over Minute Rice. In the other, a working woman returns to find her male partner "cookin' up" the dinner. The configuration is indeed destabilizing, if only because it makes us aware of how very rare it is to see. But, significantly, there are no children in this commercial, as there are in the more traditional version; the absence of children codes the fact that this is a yuppie couple, the group to which this version is designed to appeal.

And now Häagen-Dazs, the original yuppie ice cream, has designed an ad series for this market. These ads perfectly illustrate the unstable location of contemporary gender advertisements: they attempt to satisfy representational conventions that still have a deep psychic grip on Western culture, while at the same time registering every new rhythm of the social heartbeat. "Enter the State of Häagen-Dazs"—a clear invocation of the public world rather than the domestic domain. The man and woman are dressed virtually identically (making small allowances for gender-tailoring) in equally no-nonsense, dark business suits, styled for power. Their hair-styles are equivalent, brushed back from the face, clipped short but not punky. They have similar expressions: slightly playful, caught in the act but certainly not feeling guilty. They appear to be indulging in their ice-cream break in the middle of a workday; this sets up both the fetching representational incongruity of the ad and its realism. Ice cream has always been represented as relaxation food, to be *indulged* in; it belongs to a different universe than the work ethic, performance principle, or spirit of competition. To eat it in a business suit is like having "quickie" sex in the office, irregular and naughty. Yet everyone knows that people *do* eat ice cream on their breaks and during their lunch hours. The ad thus appears both realistic and *representationally* odd; we realize that we are seeing images we have not seen before *except* in real life. And, of course, in real life, women *do* eat Häagen-Dazs, as much as, if not more than, men.

And yet, intruding into this world of gender equality and eating realism that is designed to appeal to the sensibilities of "progressive" young men and women is the inescapable disparity in how much and how the man and woman are eating. He: an entire pint of vanilla fudge, with sufficient abandon to topple the carton, and greedy enough to suck the spoon. She: a restrained Eve-bite (already taken; no licks or sucks in process here), out of a single brittle bar (aestheticized as "artfully" nutty, in contrast to his bold, unaccessorized "Vanilla Fudge." Whether unconsciously reproduced or deliberately crafted to appeal to the psychic contradictions and ambivalence of its intended audience, the disparity comes from the recesses of our most sedimented, unquestioned notions about gender.

Notes

This essay grew out of a shorter piece, "How Television Teaches Women to Hate Their Hungers," in *Mirror Images* (Newsletter of Anorexia Bulimia Support, Syracuse, N.Y.) 4, no. 1 (1986): 8–9. An earlier version was delivered at the 1990 meetings of the New York State Sociological Association, and some of the analysis has been presented in various talks at Le Moyne and other colleges and community organizations. I owe thanks to all my students who supplied examples.

1. Journalist Beatrice Fairfax, quoted in Lois Banner, *American Beauty* (Chicago: University of Chicago Press, 1984), p. 136.

2. "Starvation Stages in Weight-loss Patients Similar to Famine Victims," *International Obesity Newsletter* 3 (April 1989).

3. Jean Baudrillard, *Simulations* (New York: Semiotext(e), 1983), pp. 1–3; quotation is on p. 2.

4. Geneen Roth, *Feeding the Hungry Heart* (New York: New American Library, 1982), p. 15.

5. See Helena Mitchie, *The Flesh Made Word* (New York: Oxford University Press, 1987), for an extremely interesting discussion of this taboo in Victorian literature.

6. Quoted from *Godey's* by Joan Jacobs Brumberg, *Fasting Girls* (Cambridge: Harvard University Press, 1988), p. 179.

7. Mitchie, *The Flesh Made Word*, p. 15. Not surprisingly, red meat came under especial suspicion as a source of erotic inflammation. As was typical for the era, such anxieties were rigorously scientized: for example, in terms of the heat-producing capacities of red meat and its effects on the development of the sexual organs and menstrual flow. But, clearly, an irresistible associational overdetermination—meat as the beast, the raw, the primitive, the masculine—was the true inflammatory agent here. These associations survive today, put to commercial use by the American Beef

Association, whose television ads feature James Garner and Cybil Shepard promoting "Beef: Real Food for Real People." Here the nineteenth-century link between meat aversion, delicacy, and refinement is exploited, this time in favor of the meat-eater, whose down-to-earth gutsiness is implicitly contrasted to the prissiness of the weak-blooded vegetarian.

8. Mrs. H. O. Ward, *The Young Lady's Friend* (Philadelphia: Porter and Coates, 1880), p. 162, quoted in Mitchie, *The Flesh Made Word*, pp. 16–17.

9. Quoted in Mitchie, *The Flesh Made Word*, p. 193.

10. Bram Dijkstra, *Idols of Perversity* (New York: Oxford University Press, 1986), pp. 30–31.

11. *Malleus Malificarum* quoted in Brian Easlea, *Witch-Hunting, Magic, and the New Philosophy* (Atlantic Highlands, N.J.: Humanities Press, 1980), p. 8; Hall and Oates, "Man-Eater."

12. Women were thus warned that "gluttonous habits of life" would degrade their physical appearance and ruin their marriageability. "Gross eaters" could develop thick skin, broken blood vessels on the nose, cracked lips, and an unattractively "superanimal" facial expression (Brumberg, *Fasting Girls*, p. 179). Of course, the degree to which actual women were able to enact any part of these idealized and idolized constructions was highly variable (as it always is); but *all* women, of all classes and races, felt their effects as the normalizing measuring rods against which their own adequacy was judged (and, usually, found wanting).

13. Caroline Walker Bynum, *Holy Feast and Holy Fast: The Religious Significance of Food to Medieval Women* (Berkeley: University of California Press, 1987), p. 191.

14. *Syracuse Herald-American*, May 8, 1988, p. D1.

15. Charles Butler, *The American Lady*, quoted in Dijkstra, *Idols of Perversity*, p. 18. Margery Spring Rice noted this same pattern of self-sacrifice among British working-class housewives in the 1930s. Faced with the task of feeding a family on an inadequate budget and cooking in cramped conditions, the housewife, according to Rice, often "takes one comparatively easy way out by eating much less than any other member of her family." She gives a multitude of examples from social workers' records, including " 'Her food is quite insufficient owing to the claims of the family' "; " 'She is . . . a good mother spending most of the housekeeping money on suitable food for the children and often goes without proper food for herself' "; " 'Mrs. A . . . gives her family of eight children an excellent diet . . . but cannot eat herself as she is so exhausted by the time she has prepared the family meals' "; and, interestingly, " 'the children look well fed and one cannot help believing that Mrs. F. is starving herself unneces-

sarily' " (*Working-Class Wives: Their Health and Conditions* [London: Virago, 1989; orig. pub. 1939], pp. 157, 160, 162, 167).

16. Elias Canetti, *Crowds and Power* (New York: Viking, 1962), p. 221.

17. John Berger, *Ways of Seeing* (London: Penguin, 1977).

18. bell hooks, *Yearning* (Boston: South End Press, 1990), p. 42.

19. Marcia Millman, *Such a Pretty Face: Being Fat in America* (New York: Norton, 1980), p. 106.

20. John Schneider and W. Stewart Agras, "Bulimia in Males: A Matched Comparison with Females," *International Journal of Eating Disorders* 6, no. 2 (March 1987): 235–42.

Chapter 2

"GET FAT, Don't Die!":
Eating and AIDS in Gay Men's Culture

Steven F. Kruger

> *To explain a wonder is to risk taking from it, making it prosaic, but I wished that Dominic had seen, as I did, that in the act of writing our menu in French, putting it down in dark red ink, in fountain pen, on fine gray paper that I had bought for him in Paris, at Papier Plus, Jasper was making a dinner, and the simple act of our eating it together, an occasion, an event, and that it is by gestures like this that daily life is made less daily. This by itself, making daily life less daily, strikes me as being an enterprise worth saluting.*
>
> —Christopher Coe, Such Times *(33–34)*

> *My life is a series of restaurants and meals. My mother's letters are always filled with buffets and dinners, wedding spreads and Jewish Home Volunteer banquets. When I go on trips, I consider sending her menus in lieu of postcards. Gallagher, a tobacco-chewing transplanted Texan whom I met in California, has a basic philosophy about food: Fill the hole. As for me, any orifice is open and waiting—like the pegs and the board, the blocks and the hole. Bend over and fill the hole.*
>
> —David B. Feinberg, Eighty-Sixed *(216)*

Body, Sex, Food

What does it mean in 1990s American culture to lose 20 or 40 or 100 pounds? Putting our trust in the ubiquitous ads for "weight loss clinics" and "health clubs"—and putting aside, as the culture

36

most often puts aside, the recognition that American conceptions of beauty and thinness are hazardous to our health, and particularly to the health of young women—we would have to conclude that weight loss is still generally taken to mean something good. *Before:* fat, unattractive, slovenly, unhealthy, unhappy. *After:* slim, fit, well-dressed, vital, successful, lucky-in-love.

But what does it mean, in the same cultural context, for a gay man to lose weight? At a moment when to define oneself as gay is simultaneously to be defined by the possibility of AIDS (even if one has practiced only safe[r] sex, even if one tests negative for antibodies to HIV), at a moment when AIDS is still stubbornly imagined to be a "gay plague" (despite demographic changes in the pandemic, despite the increasingly common insistence that "AIDS does not discriminate"), at a moment when the most pervasive image of AIDS remains the bedridden, emaciated "homosexual body," weight loss means something very different in American culture when its subject is a gay man.[1] *Before:* gym-sculpted, hunky body. *After:* AIDS.

We must resist the easy identification of AIDS with gayness and challenge depictions that would draw a simple equation between living with HIV or AIDS and an inexorable process of "wasting away." Losing weight can mean as many different things for gay men as it does for others. And while severe weight loss does often accompany HIV illness, it does not do so in any necessary or even predictable way.

Still, we need to recognize the power that ideas and images clustered around AIDS have had in reshaping conceptions of the body and of such bodily functions as eating and not least for gay men ourselves. As at least one cultural critic has suggested, AIDS has meant a thorough revision of gay bodily styles, with "the [old] clone look" implicated in some people's thinking "in the spread of AIDS" and "the new boy look" that partly replaces it taken to represent "bodies and lives that [are] nondiseased":

> The boy look emphasizes youth and health. It implies that the "boy" was just not around during the era of intense [HIV] transmission. Features that would read "no AIDS here" are emphasized. Since weight loss is a sign of AIDS, it is *de rigueur* not to be too thin, just a little plump. Clothes are worn loosely; a washboard tummy is not the treasure it once was. . . . Another sign of AIDS is losing hair luster, so although hair may be cut short at the nape, some length is usually left on top. This hair should be rich and shiny; sometimes it is even oiled to add

more luster. Of course there is the bicycle or baseball cap worn backwards, which covers most of the top of the head. But see, the cap is worn *backwards,* so that a little tuft of obstinate curls can fight through in the front.

Youth represents innocence, and innocence is a major agenda in the conversation of the boy look. When we are told that our sperm is poison, our saliva treacherous, our sweat suspect, it seems liberating to be released from culpability at the site of our bodies. Appearance tensely plays with fact: boys can have HIV, too. (Leger 44)

Even as we intervene against homophobic depictions of the "gay body" as a "body of illness," and even as we resist impulses both from within and from outside gay culture that would stigmatize certain "looks" as diseased, we need also to recognize that the AIDS pandemic has meant real and pervasive changes in gay men's relations to our own bodies, to the bodies of lovers and friends, and perhaps to the idea of body itself.

Such changes are of course most obvious in the realm of sex, where body parts, fluids, functions, acts, excitements all take on new meanings in light of the possibility of HIV transmission, and where modifications of the body—condoms, dental dams, finger cots, gloves—and of its acts take on a "life or death" significance. While such changes are not limited to gay men, at least in American culture where the burden of sexual adjustment to HIV transmission—for instance, the development and initial deployment of safe(r) sex guidelines—has been largely placed on the gay community, changes in the meaning of the sexual body have been especially emphatic among gay men. (One might look, for one instance, at how gay pornography—though not always produced by gay men—has changed in the course of the past thirteen years, if slowly and resistantly, in ways that straight pornography has not.)

But while the sexual body has been most deeply implicated in the changes attendant upon AIDS, the meaning of the whole body has in fact shifted. AIDS, after all, is constructed as an illness that, in affecting immunity, challenges the body's "defenses" and thus radically alters its relation to the threatening realm of "not-self" that the immune system properly "polices." The intact "fortress" of the body is weakened, made susceptible to "attack" and "invasion." That the transmission of HIV is itself associated with "breachings" of bodily integrity—the "exchanges of bodily fluids" attendant upon penetrative, unprotected sex, intravenous drug use, blood transfusion—reinforces the construction of AIDS as a breakdown of firm boundaries between the body and the outside world.

Other challenges to bodily integrity—dental and medical procedures, blood donations, cuts and scratches, tattooing, piercing, shaving, even manicures—have all become part of the public discourse on AIDS, and it should be no surprise that the most persistent, daily reminder of the body's permeability, eating, is itself intimately involved in the full reconception of body entailed by AIDS. Of course, eating and drinking are persistently imagined—despite reliable evidence to the contrary—as possible routes of HIV transmission. Thus, to cite one of the most striking examples, in the mid-1980s, there was a lively and anxious debate, among Christians, about the wisdom, in the midst of an epidemic, of drinking the wine of communion from a common cup (see, for instance, "Parishioners"). Also in the early years of the pandemic, people worried about the safety of eating out—especially in large urban centers like New York and San Francisco where, rightly or not, they imagined that the staff of restaurants was likely to include a large number of gay men. And in a countermovement within gay culture, eating or drinking from common utensils has become an important sign of community in the face of HIV and AIDS: "People who may be HIV positive inevitably offer you a drink out of their glass. It's a test of loyalty to see if you're prejudiced or not, to see if you are informed enough to know that you can't get it that way" (Schulman 201).

Food, eating, and their effects on the body are in fact ubiquitous in thinking about AIDS, given roles, in both popular and medical understandings, at every possible stage of the body's interaction with HIV. Thus, weight loss is often scrutinized as a sign of HIV illness, and the recognition that one has lost weight becomes, in fictional and nonfictional accounts alike, a common *topos* in the discovery of one's HIV status:

> From one of the earliest medical reports of "a new acquired cellular immunodeficiency": "A 30-year-old, previously healthy, homosexual man was admitted to the UCLA Medical Center with a one-month history of pain on swallowing, oral thrush, leukopenia, and a weight loss of 12 kg. . . . A 29-year-old homosexual man was referred to UCLA Medical Center on June 5, 1981, with an eight-month history of high fever, lymphadenopathy, fatigue, and a weight loss of 11 kg." (Gottlieb et al. 1427)

From an "AIDS diary": "My appetite is showing no sign of returning. Even though I've gained a little weight, I'm still only 162 pounds. Down from a normal weight of close to 180 or so. Something isn't right here. This is no normal flu." (Burrell 122)

From one of the first novels about AIDS: "Usually quite robust and muscular, Andy now looked extremely tired, pale, and much thinner." (Reed, _Facing It_ 11)

Once HIV illness has been diagnosed, scrutiny of the body's intake and output becomes especially careful. Infections associated with immune suppression—thrush, cryptosporidiosis, cytomegalovirus, _Mycobacterium avium_ complex—affect eating at all its stages: appetite, ingestion, digestion, absorption, excretion. Thus, one overview lists diseases of the esophagus, stomach, liver, gall bladder, bile duct, small intestine, colon, and rectum among the possible "gastrointestinal manifestations of HIV" (Roland). Symptoms accompanying HIV illness range from loss of appetite to nausea and vomiting to diarrhea to "wasting syndrome." And not only are the _effects_ of HIV illness intimately involved with eating; diet and nutrition also play significant roles in one's susceptibility to the action of HIV and the opportunistic infections associated with HIV illness. In the words of one physician, "It is well known that the function of the immune system is influenced by the nutritional status" (Heyman 3), and studies have suggested that "nutrient supplementation can be an effective prophylaxis against many kinds of infection" (Heyman 1), that "a number of nutrients, whether obtained from food or nutritional supplements, might reduce progression to AIDS in persons with HIV" (James, "Six-Year Diet Study" 3), and that "[n]utrition can . . . alter the efficacy of other treatments" for HIV illness such as AZT (Heyman 2). Dietary regimes designed to counter the effects of HIV have been common and have ranged from macrobiotic diets to herbal preparations to more medicalized regimens like the "protocol of nutritional supplements"— "vitamin C; vitamin A (beta carotene); vitamin E; NAC [N-acetylcysteine]; multivitamin/mineral (Jarrow Pack); quercetin; evening primrose oil; garlic; SSKI (potassium iodide); and B-complex injections"—developed by Dr. Joan C. Priestly (James, "Nutrition" 4). One of the "centerfold boys" in the comic _'zine Diseased Pariah News_, parodying _Playboy_ centerfolds, lists his "medications" as "AZT, ddC, Bactrim[R], and Ben & Jerry's chocolate fudge brownie ice cream" ("Letter" 23). And not only do foods, nutrients, and vitamins become "medications"; those drugs that are now standard in the treatment and prophylaxis of HIV and its attendant infections become an intimate part of eating for people living with HIV and AIDS:

> From a non-fictional account: "Each day I take three capsules of AZT, along with six Zovirax, three Trental, two multiple antioxidant vitamins, one lysine, and one aspirin." (Feinberg, "HIV + Me" 94)

> From a short story by the same author: "At the time of my visit I was on several antibiotics for the sore throat, with varying schedules. One was to be taken every six hours on an empty stomach for ten days; another, with milk, every four hours for twenty days; and a third, twice daily, while reading the *Encyclopaedia Brittanica.* I had taken the liberty of signing out a Toshiba portable computer from work to aid in my dosage calculations. This was all in addition to the dread zidovudine. Every fifteen minutes (the greatest common divisor of the least common multiple), I would dash off to my room for another dose of snake oil." (Feinberg, *Spontaneous Combustion* 147)

The borderline between food and drug is often blurred, with potentially promising drugs derived from foodstuffs like the Chinese cucumber (compound Q; see Reed, *The Q Journal*) or the common spice turmeric (see James, "Curcumin"). On the other hand, food also becomes a potentially dangerous source of infection for the person whose immune system has been compromised, and careful food preparation, with the avoidance of such microorganisms as salmonella, becomes particularly important: "There are a number of opportunistic infections that could be prevented if food safety were higher on people's lists" (Gilden 5). The whole range of possible foods is scrutinized not just for taste or nutrition but for medicinal value and for possible danger: substances like alcohol, thought to suppress the immune system, are to be avoided, while a substance like marijuana, "bring[ing] relief from nausea or poor appetite almost immediately" (Smith 4), may be prescribed (in smoked or ingested form).

The possible connections between HIV illness and eating are thus complicated, indeed disorientingly so. For the person living with HIV, they may entail a full reassessment of eating habits—and a reassessment guided only by incomplete, and sometimes even contradictory, information on how HIV and nutrition interact. For communities like American gay communities in which HIV and AIDS have become a defining part of everyday experience, there have been major changes in the overall culture of food and eating. Those changes, however, are not easy to delineate or codify, and a full assessment of them would require sociological and anthropological work that I am not prepared to perform. As the epigraphs from Christopher Coe and David B. Feinberg that begin this essay would suggest, the relations between gay men's culture, both pre- and post-AIDS, and eating are not simple, and in fact encompass positions as different as those expressed by Feinberg's narrator B. J.—with his emphasis on a voracious, and not very picky, appetite that is simultaneously culinary and sexual—and by Coe's Timothy—with his attention to the aestheticizing acts by which "daily life" may be "made less daily."

In this essay, rather than try to capture the full details and complexities of a gay culture of eating that has changed in response to AIDS, I will look closely at just one literary work in which food and eating play integral parts, the ongoing column "GET FAT, don't die!" from the 'zine *DPN (Diseased Pariah News)*. This represents an unusual, and perhaps unique, product of the AIDS crisis, but, as I will suggest, it also, in important ways, participates in a larger American gay response to living with HIV and AIDS.

How to Eat in an Epidemic

In a certain sense, "GET FAT, don't die!"—despite its outrageous title and despite its appearance in the purposely outrageous *Diseased Pariah News*—is serious self-help literature. As such, it participates in an impulse that, originating within the gay community in the early 1980s, moved from a recognition of broad societal and governmental silence and inaction in the face of AIDS toward a breaking of silences and an involvement in direct action. The early reporting on AIDS in the *New York Native;* the formation of such service, support, and advocacy organizations as Gay Men's Health Crisis (GMHC), the San Francisco AIDS Foundation, and the People With AIDS Coalition; the activism of ACT UP; community-based research and drug testing initiatives; informational publications like *AIDS Treatment News*—all have been part of a broad activist/self-empowerment movement important to many of the most striking successes in the fight against AIDS, thus, the strong treatment activism of ACT UP and others has resulted in the development of a "parallel track" in drug testing, the revision of the CDC definition of AIDS, and movement toward broader health care reform.

Though groups and publications like GMHC, ACT UP, and *AIDS Treatment News* are not *exclusively* products of gay community organizing, and though all have, since their formation, made serious attempts to reach out to a broader, not just gay, "AIDS community," all grew at least partly out of gay political and social movements, and all have become an intimate and important part of current gay men's culture. The relation of *DPN* to gay culture is similar. Tracing its ancestry self-consciously to another, explicitly gay 'zine, *GAWK, a Fagazine of the Yarts* (S[hcarcr], "Welcome" 2), *DPN* is nevertheless careful to express an openness to nongay material: admitting that "DPN's been fairly boy oriented so far," but insisting that "we love girlie pariahs too, yes we do" ("THAT'S 'puh-RYE-uh' "); later proclaiming that "AIDS is a global problem. . . . Fags are no longer It, boys and girls. The whole world has it" ([Shearer], "Hostess" 6); and publishing, for instance, a nongay feature like "Letter from an Innocent Victim/DPN Centerfold Boy, Kevin Irvine" (of course, presenting a straight man as "centerfold boy" in a 'zine with a largely gay readership cannot be seen simply as a "nongay" gesture). *DPN* has remained, however, largely gay in its orientation, and in issue 4, responding to readers' suggestions, Tom Ace defends the 'zine's gayness while simultaneously calling for material written from other perspectives: "We write about what we understand best; we use so many gay male themes because we're homo boys. 'Put up or shut up' is the operating philosophy here at DPN. You want to see stuff written from a different point of view? Send us some" ("Pontifications" 5).

DPN thus positions itself like many other groups and publications as most specifically concerned with HIV and AIDS, but also as intimately invested in "gay male themes." And since its beginning in 1990, *DPN* has self-consciously recognized its place within a tradition of gay-originated self-help organizations and publications, even as it strongly evokes other, perhaps less serious, traditions: comic books, gay pornography, humor writing (like that found in *Mad* or *National Lampoon*), and desk-top publishing, with the attendant phenomenon of 'zines. *DPN* announces itself, in each issue, as "a quarterly publication of, by, and for people with HIV disease" (in issue 8) this has changed to "an increasingly wayward publication of, by, and for people with HIV disease [and their friends and loved ones]"), a self-definition that places it firmly alongside such publications as *PWA Newsline,* the journal of the People With AIDS Coalition, "Published By and For People With AIDS and AIDS Related Conditions," and *The Body Positive,* the journal of a "community-centered, not-for-profit, self-help organization" (*Body Positive* 4.7, 2), which is subtitled "A Magazine By and For People Affected by HIV/AIDS."[2] Indeed, several of *DPN's* regular features overlap with the kinds of material included in such publications. "Condom Corner" provides detailed information not just about condoms but about lubricants, dental dams, finger cots, dildos, and poppers. "The DPN Meat Market," while evoking the personal ad columns of pornographic and mainstream publications, also echoes the HIV self-help literature—for instance, the column "Positive+ Connections," "an opportunity for people to meet people," in *The Body Positive.* And "The DPN Resource Guide" calls to mind such regular columns as "Resources" in *The Body Positive* and "PWA Coalition Resource Directory" in *PWA Newsline;* like other such columns, *DPN's* "Resource Guide" tends to appear at or near the end of the journal, referring readers to further publications and organizations that provide services and information for people living with HIV (the placement of "The DPN Resource Guide," on the last page of issues 1–4, begins to vary with issue 5; the column is absent, as is "Condom Corner," in issue 7). And from its beginning, *DPN* has explicitly acknowledged its admiration for the sort of self-help publications it often echoes: "Our vote for most important HIV publication goes to John James' AIDS Treatment News. Every two weeks a new helping of rational, intelligent, apparently unbiased analysis of new developments, promising treatments, political issues, and stuff like that. . . . Don't depend on newspaper articles written by scientifically illiterate nincompoops for this vital information" ("DPN Resource Guide," *DPN* 1, 30).

    Community-based publications like *AIDS Treatment News, The Body Positive,* and *PWA Newsline* have been particularly important in focusing attention on issues that receive little attention from the medical and scientific establishment or in the mainstream media— and this includes the recognition of food and eating as important factors in HIV illness. There has been relatively little organized research into the connections between HIV and nutrition. Dietary and nutritional therapies are generally consigned to the category of "alternative treatment"—as opposed to those more "standard treatments" that involve the prescription of (lucrative) pharmaceuticals— and information about them tends to be scattered and unsystematized.

Much of the information that *has* become available on the nutritional involvements of HIV illness derives from the work of individual doctors engaged in large clinical practices and from community-based research (often closely linked to gay communities). And this information is often most fully systematized and publicized by community groups in their publications. Thus, *AIDS Treatment News*, researched, written, and published in San Francisco by a small staff under the direction of John S. James with the intention of "report[ing] on experimental and standard treatments, especially those available now"—"We interview physicians, scientists, other health professionals, and persons with AIDS or HIV; we also collect information from meetings and conferences, medical journals, and computer databases. Long-term survivors have usually tried many different treatments, and found combinations which work for them" ("Statement of Purpose")—reports frequently on the gastrointestinal and nutritional implications of HIV. Pragmatic advice about eating and nutrition is often provided in *PWA Newsline* and *The Body Positive*, for instance, in the series of articles entitled "Food for Healing," written by members of one community-based group—the Whole Foods Program of the Manhattan Center for Living ("a resource center for people dealing with life-challenging illness" [Pierce and Donnelly, *Body Positive* 5:3, 16])—and published by another in *The Body Positive*. And in part through community-based service and activist groups, "alternative therapies," including an increased awareness of the importance of nutritional support, have begun to make their way into more mainstream medical contexts. "For over a year we [at the Whole Foods Project] have been working with members of the ACT-UP Alternative and Holistic Committee and other nonprofit organizations to make some changes in the nutritional services being brought to AIDS patients at Bellevue Hospital (the third largest in New York City, with over 1200 beds)" (Pierce and Donnelly, *Body Positive* 5:8, 21).

It is out of such work in discovering and publicizing dietary information for people with HIV and AIDS that *DPN*'s "GET FAT, don't die!" has grown, and this column treats a range of topics related to eating, nutrition, and gastrointestinal problems similar to that addressed in publications like *AIDS Treatment News* and *The Body Positive* (though "GET FAT, don't die!" takes a much less "whole/organic foods" approach than does Pierce and Donnelly's "Food for Healing"). The first "GET FAT, don't die!" column presents general "strategies for dealing with HIV- and AIDS-related dietary problems," particularly "[m]alnutrition and weight loss . . .

due to some nasty infection . . . [or] being too tired to cook or changes in taste perception due to certain medications (including our favorite, AZT)":

> A high-fat, high-protein diet is recommended for people with AIDS.[3] There are a couple of reasons for this. First of all, when you suddenly drop weight, you tend to lose about 10 to 15 percent of what you originally weighed, regardless of what your original weight was. If you are already underweight, this is even more dangerous, so it's best to be at or a little over what the insurance company's charts say you should weigh. Secondly, a fortified diet will help you recover from a bout of illness. This is especially true if your appetite is weak, and every bit of food you can choke down must work to its full advantage.

The column then presents a list of particular recommendations for "boost[ing] calories and protein," while warning against "snarf[ing] those marshmallow pies and Ho-Ho's at the expense of good nutrition." And this first column, like most subsequent ones, ends with the advice to "check with your physician before making any radical changes to your diet" (T[horne], *DPN* 1, 23).

Having thus provided some general nutritional advice to its readers, subsequent installments of "GET FAT, don't die!" focus in on a variety of more specific problems, presenting overviews of those problems and their implications as well as detailed suggestions for pragmatic behavioral responses. The column in issue 2 focuses on nausea and diarrhea—"everyday menace[s] . . . caused by germs, medications for those germs, or both"—and provides a long list of ways to reduce nausea and prevent the weight loss and dehydration that may result from persistent diarrhea (T[horne], *DPN* 2, 23). The following column similarly examines two HIV-related phenomena that adversely affect eating—oral thrush ("it can make trying to eat a living horror") and "taste perversions" (not "the same as your best friend suddenly deciding to redecorate with Sears mock-opulent furniture,"[4] but rather medication- or illness-related changes in "the way we taste foods")—and provides a list of "some things to do" "if eating has become a gruesome experience" (T[horne], *DPN* 3, 15). The column in *DPN* 4 "revisits" nausea, looking particularly at marijuana and its active ingredient THC as antinausea (and appetite-stimulating) drugs, while warning that the side effects of THC "includ[e] immunosuppression, fatigue, and photophobia"; the column provides practical instructions for "leaching" the THC from marijuana into butter that can then be used in cooking—"The food will taste much better than cooking with leaf marijuana directly" and "your medicine is distributed throughout the plate of confections, so you can control the dosage" (T[horne], *DPN* 4, 23). *DPN* 5 presents a taste test of commonly recommended nutritional supplements—Ensure, Ensure Plus, Nutrament, Sustacal, Meritene, Enrich (with Carnation Instant Breakfast "included as a control")—concluding, in "[o]ur entirely objective opinion," that "they stink":

> Overall, we cannot recommend food supplements as the first line of offense for any dedicated calorie packer. They are, essentially, typical medical scams, and their high prices reflect the ruthless markup of anything connected to the wonderful world of medicine. They get recommended because they are covered by insurance, as a prescribed medical intervention. . . . [M]ost of us would be better off with a real milk-shake and a One-A-Day supplement. (B[otkin], *DPN* 5, 19–21)

(A later issue of *DPN* returns to this taste test, adding the product ReGain to the nutritional supplements tested earlier [T(horne], "Great DPN Taste Challenge"].) "GET FAT, don't die!" next takes on sushi and the dangers—parasites, salmonella—posed by eating raw fish; the column provides a guide to "safe sushi," items that include only rice, vegetables, and cooked fish (T[horne], *DPN* 6, 17–18). The column in issue 7 moves somewhat beyond the strict realm of food and eating, providing advice for how to remove "those nasty little . . . STAINS" of blood, shit, cum, egg, milk, sweat, vomit, piss, ink, gravy, salad dressing, lipstick, wine, coffee, soft drinks, juice, and booze (T[horne], *DPN* 7, 11). And finally, in the most extensive "GET FAT, don't die!" to date, *DPN* 8 looks at the special needs of vegetarians, presenting discussions of "Protein," "Philosophy," "Tofu," "Beans" (with a side column on "Flatulence"), "Taste Perversions," and "The Official Truth" ("Don't feel guilty about eating foods that orthodox vegetarian guidelines might frown at. If you're getting all of your nutrients and staying fat, that's what's important") (T[horne], *DPN* 8, 34).

"GET FAT, don't die!" thus focuses consistently on issues that are real and often pressing for people living with HIV; in addition, each installment of the column presents a variety of recipes, some sent in by readers, with pragmatic instructions for preparing foods that put into action the column's more general advice. (This too is part of the self-help tradition; there are recipes published, for instance, as part of Pierce and Donnelly's series of articles in *The Body Positive*.) These recipes, presented in the first four issues of *DPN* as a kind of appendix to the main "GET FAT, don't die!" column, become a more and more prominent feature of *DPN* from issue 5 on. There they begin to be distributed throughout the magazine, and in issues 7 and 8 a separate table of contents is provided for the recipes themselves.

"To spite you, I lived!"

But while *DPN*'s "GET FAT, don't die!" thus fits firmly into a tradition of self-help writing, it also strongly resists certain aspects of that tradition. Announcing itself in each issue as "a forum for infected people to share their thoughts, feelings, art, writing, and brownie recipes in an atmosphere free of teddy bears, magic rocks, and seronegative guilt," it embraces an approach where people with HIV are themselves the authorities but at the same time attacks a "teddy-bear," "feel-good," "New Age" self-help approach to living with HIV:

> We should warn you that our editorial policy does not include the concept that AIDS is a Wonderful Learning Opportunity and Spiritual Gift From Above. Or a punishment for our Previous Badness. Nor are we much interested in being icons of noble tragedy, brave and true, stiff upper lips gleaming under our oxygen hoses. . . . We are not saints nor devils, just a couple-o-guys who ran into a Danger Penis and caught something we don't like very much. And we HATE teddy bears. (S[hearer], "Welcome" 2)

This sort of attack becomes a regular part of *DPN*, developed in features like "Zen and the Art of Teddy Bear Burning" or "Haywire: Louise, the Morning After," a critique of the "New Age" self-help "philosophy" of Louise Hay (A[ce]).

DPN in fact approaches HIV and AIDS very differently from most self-help publications, even those like *AIDS Treatment News* that it explicitly admires. Introducing itself in 1990, the *'zine* made it clear that, no matter how serious the topics it might address and no matter how useful the information it might provide, it would approach its subjects with an attitude very different from that of most other HIV-oriented publications:

> And now for Something Different. Not something completely different, 'cos many publications address the HIV epidemic, and not all of them are sanctimonious teddybear droolbuckets, but we are certainly breaking new ground approaching the plague of the century from the angle of *humor*. . . . What's so damn funny about a pandemic devastating the world? Well, *we* have it and sometimes we find it amusing. After all, life itself kills *everybody*, and there's much about life that is purty darn funny. . . . Besides, who wants to be serious all the time, even about fatal illness? So what we're hoping to do here is bring some much-needed levity to the experience of HIV infection. (S[hearer], "Welcome" 2)

DPN's prime mode is in fact humor, but from the beginning it is clear that that humor will not be simple "levity" but instead will have a biting, even a bitter, edge. The cover of *DPN* 1, in a parody of Palmolive's television commercials, shows the hand of a manicurist soaking another hand in a bowl of liquid. The caption reads, "The blood of over 100,000 Americans who have died of AIDS, Mr. President? You're soaking in it!"

The humor of *DPN* and of "GET FAT, don't die!" most obviously arises from a desire to outrage and shock: such a desire is clearly at the heart of the *'zine's* founding gesture, its embracing of the label "diseased pariah." Like the recent activist claiming of words like "queer" and "dyke" and "fag," the use of "diseased pariah" represents the rejection of a particular stance where the political goal for lesbian/gay or AIDS activism would be "tolerance" or "acceptance" *within* a societal and cultural "mainstream." Defining oneself as "queer" or "diseased pariah" involves taking and claiming a linguistic term of exclusion for oneself, and, by that action, insisting that definition of the stigmatizing term proceed not from within the "mainstream" where it originates but rather from within the group of people it defines. As Shearer suggests in explaining the origin of *DPN*'s title, such a procedure is bound and intended to shake people up, and precisely because it does disturb comfortable understandings of social positioning it may be a way to force a real reconsideration of who gets to define the roles of marginalized and stigmatized people:

> A few years before I had seen a bitter little cartoon. An airline had refused passage to a person with AIDS, and there was a

big stink about it. The cartoon showed a man at the airline counter, and the clerk was saying "And would you like the smoking, non-smoking, or diseased pariah section?" Mr. Tom was much impressed by this terminology and began to refer to himself as a diseased pariah, to much dismayed fluttering from his friends. At this time, remember, the only acceptable role for an infected person was Languishing Saint and Hug Object. (S[hearer], "Welcome" 2)

DPN thus accepts as its starting point a stigmatizing name for people with HIV and AIDS, but it moves even as it embraces that name to rewrite its significance, to make the marginalized and stigmatized "diseased pariah" a *central* and self-speaking consciousness. Named by others as outlaws, "diseased pariahs" take on that name not to validate its common understanding but to focus attention on the act of exclusion that that naming involves and to turn the exclusionary act back on the dominant group that performs the naming: you call us outlaws, and we gladly claim that status since we do not wish to be within the law that would insist that we, by our very nature, stand outside the law.

The kind of impulse thus enacted in the naming of *DPN* informs much of the work it publishes, including features like "GET FAT, don't die!" that are not explicitly political or engaged in overt discussion of the social positioning of people with HIV and AIDS. "GET FAT, don't die!," even at its lightest moments, often expresses the desire to outrage, to ridicule and resist conventional pieties and tastes—as, for instance, in a recipe for rabbit mole entitled "Rhietta Lou's Chocolate-Covered Easter Bunny": "This traditional holiday meal is so tasty it's almost sinful! . . . While the bunny bakes, make 3–4 batches of colored water, and dye the peeled, hardboiled eggs. Remove the rabbit from the oven, garnish with the colored eggs, and serve. Goes best with a tomato aspic in the shape of a crucifix. Mmm, tastes just like chicken!" (B[otkin], *DPN* 5, 20).

Relations between eating and HIV in fact lend themselves easily to the critique of conventional stances and understandings that is central to *DPN*. As the first "GET FAT, don't die!" notes, "classic dietary guidelines often fail to address the specific needs of people living with HIV and AIDS" (T[horne], *DPN* 1, 23), and the reevaluation of eating habits entailed by the AIDS crisis means, as seen above, that much conventional wisdom about eating and the body is overturned or reversed: "The famous expression 'you can't be too thin or too rich' was obviously coined before the AIDS epidemic" (B[otkin], *DPN* 5, 19). "GET FAT, don't die!," rather than lament such overturnings and reversals, embraces them with a certain manic energy:

> In this world obsessed with fiber [because of diarrhea] you have permission to eat low fiber foods, including white rice, white bread, and cooked vegetables and fruit without the skin. (T[horne], *DPN* 2, 23)

> [T]he serum cholesterol of HIVers tends to be significantly lower than our seronegative comrades, so there's little worry about arteriosclerosis twenty years down the road. (Twenty years? We should be so lucky.) (T[horne], *DPN* 8, 31)

> Mmm-mmm! Feel those arteries harden! Serve with whipped cream. (T[horne], *DPN* 6, 4)

The recipes presented in "GET FAT, don't die!" are consistently and systematically unconcerned with the usual worries of American diet; high caloric value is in fact the prime *desideratum* in the food world of the "diseased pariah."

The flaunting of a freedom from dietary constraints provides a certain (small) compensation for the many worries about food and eating that the person with HIV or AIDS confronts and that "GET FAT, don't die!" is primarily concerned with addressing. It also participates in an expression of anger and hostility toward a world that would exclude people with HIV and AIDS, putting into operation a counterexclusion (like that involved in the act of claiming the name "diseased pariah") that rereads the position of people with HIV and AIDS not as a margin to which they have been consigned but rather as a center from which they might speak their own experience—and speak not just horror and suffering, but also humor and enjoyment.

The attacks on an outside, conventional world that the writing in *DPN* often performs are thus not simply hostile; they also participate in the creation of a certain intimacy, a community of those affected by illness, those disaffected with others' (even well-intentioned) insistence that living with HIV means taking on particular consigned roles ("Languishing Saint and Hug Object"), and those set apart by stigma. This creation of intimacy depends partly on the very shocking and outrageous quality of the writing in *DPN*: those who can't "take" this are excluded from the circle of intimacy; those who can—those willing to wear the mantle of "diseased pariah" and see the potential power of that gesture—are included. Ultimately, then, "GET FAT, don't die!" develops a simultaneously exclusive and inclusive, hostile and loving, voice—a voice that, even in the title of the column, announces itself, with the combative "GET FAT," as imperative, strong, and angry, at the same time that, in the explanatory "don't die!," it shows itself to be caring and protective.

Such a voice, as I have suggested above, participates in the current queer political moment, with its confrontational stance ("We're here, we're queer, get used to it") and its community building ("Queer Nation"). It also draws heavily—as does queer activism itself—on older gay traditions of humor based in resistance to societal conventions and norms. Most strikingly, "GET FAT, don't die!" makes extensive use of camp: the author of seven of the eight columns—co-founder of *DPN*, "Cranky Editor & Irresistible Force," Beowulf Thorne—takes on the drag identity of "Biffy Mae" for the purposes of the column. This gesture is a complicated one, involving not just gender bending but also specific class references. Biffy Mae's name, stereotypically Appalachian or southern, evokes "poor white trash," and many of the low-budget, antigourmet recipes presented— "Biffy Mae's Totally Amazing Gumbo" (T[horne], *DPN* 2, 24), "Betty Ann Mae's Pork Chops with Campbell's™ Cream of Mushroom Soup," (B[otkin], *DPN* 5, 6), "Biffy Mae's White Trash Chicken" (B[otkin], *DPN* 5, 8)—call to mind a similar class stereotype. One way to read "GET FAT, don't die!" is in fact as an extended parody of the already parodic *White Trash Cooking:*

> Lightly brown the pork chops. The hard part's over now, it gets easy from here on. . . . (If you're a real gourmet kind of cook, arrange the Actual Mushrooms on top and around. This goes against every tenet of trash cuisine, but the kids'll love 'em.) . . . Remember: *'Trashy people cook with Campbell's™ Cream of Mushroom Soup!'* (B[otkin], *DPN* 5, 6)

Such a parody of a parody enables the development of a double critique, addressed both against the "gourmet" cooking that *White Trash Cooking* "trashes" and against "trashy" American cooking itself, and this critique fits easily into *DPN*'s larger attack on the "mainstreams" of American culture. While providing real and useful recipes to its readers, "GET FAT, don't die!" makes those recipes part of a comic cultural criticism.

But the strongest force of Biffy Mae's drag identity rests in the realm of gender, depending on the specifically gay traditions it evokes.

Most particularly, Biffy Mae takes on the role of an older "girlfriend" or "mother." Such a figure—protective and even overbearing like a certain stereotype of "real" mothers, but wise in the ways of the world, and particularly the sexual world, in a manner one's "real-life" mother "should not" be—has a long history within gay culture, from the angry, street-smart drag queens of John Rechy's *City of Night* to characters like Keller and Mother in Joey Manley's *The Death of Donna-May Dean* and Neil Bartlett's *Ready to Catch Him Should He Fall*. Biffy Mae plays this role to the hilt. She proclaims her "femininity" at the same time that she calls attention to its constructedness—"Special thanks to the women who invited Biffy Mae to a Lesbian sex party. The gesture was sincerely appreciated, even if not entirely appropriate" (T[horne], *DPN* 3, 15–16)—and she defends her "womanliness" in a mock serious way: responding to a letter from "Elsie Borden" that accuses her of being a "carnivorous pig," Biffy Mae responds, "that's 'carnivorous *sow*,' dear" (T[horne], *DPN* 8, 30). The voice in which Thorne's drag persona speaks is sometimes a parody of the "hysterical" voice of a stereotypical panicky woman—"Eeek! The executor of your boyfriend's estate is coming over and you haven't a thing for dinner!" (T[horne], *DPN* 8, 34)—but usually it is the knowing, protective, opinionated, somewhat world-weary voice of an older, more experienced woman:

> Not only does being undernourished reduce your chances of getting lucky at that next orgy, it can make you much more susceptible to illness, and we'll have none of that. (T[horne], *DPN* 1, 23)

> Remove the stubby little tail [of the chicken], for all the evils of the world dwell there. If you want to cook the heart, gizzard, etc., too bad, because I think they're disgusting. (T[horne], *DPN* 2, 24)

> Oh, wipe that shocked look off of your face! (T[horne], *DPN* 4, 23)

> Biffy Mae strongly urges you to use frozen pie pastry, which is the pinnacle of Western civilization. (T[horne], *DPN* 7, 25)

> Cut [the tofu] up and put it in the stir-fry that we cast aspersions on earlier (Biffy Mae suggests getting the extra firm kind

which won't fall apart), drop it in soups, or put it in a pilaf, but never ever make a cheesecake with it. Some things are sacred. (T[horne], *DPN* 8, 32)

Biffy Mae's advice is practical and no-nonsense (and again often mock serious): "The idea here is to take all of those nasty food scraps remaining from last night's poker party and transform them into the perfect brunch centerpiece for the annual Palo Alto Blue-Hairs Lawn Bowling Cotillion" (T[horne], *DPN* 7, 25). And she scolds and cajoles "her boys" for their own good:

> Now, about those recipes: don't be shy! Danny-Mae was the only one who sent anything in. Shame on the rest of you! (T[horne], *DPN* 2, 23)

> Take the time to clean up, you've made a terrible mess! (T[horne], *DPN* 2, 24)

> As I said before, I won't tolerate any of my boys getting skinny without putting up a fight. (T[horne], *DPN* 3, 15)

The persona thus imagined for Biffy Mae plays an important part in the development of the simultaneously angry and caring voice of *DPN*. Speaking out of a sad knowledge of what HIV and AIDS can mean in people's lives—just as the camp voice of gay tradition speaks from sad experience of the pain that being gay has meant for many gay men—Biffy Mae speaks, nevertheless, not with resignation but with a determination to fight for life and for the pleasures of life. She speaks with a clear anger, but also with love for "my boys."

⋖◇⋗⋖◇⋗⋖◇⋗

It would be too simple, finally, to classify "GET FAT, don't die!" as a self-help column, though it certainly functions to provide useful information and advice. Nor would it be accurate to see the column as "just" humorous. "GET FAT, don't die!" is, rather, survival literature, writing that insists on the possibility of *living* with HIV and AIDS, and of living with as much pleasure as possible. But while it is thus in a certain sense optimistic, it refuses to turn away from the horrors of the epidemic, or to see AIDS as something positive, "a Wonderful Learning Opportunity and Spiritual Gift From Above" (S[hearer], "Welcome" 2):

> [T]here isn't much commonality between these folks [long-term survivors of AIDS], except that they are committed to life, aggressively so. . . . When I say "good attitude" I don't mean hug your teddy, Louise Puke-Puke Hay stuff. I mean like I said before, aggressive commitment to life. Some of these people are angry as hell. See the marginal quote below ["Fuck You! Fuck You! Fuck You! To spite you, I lived!"] for a ferinstance. ([Shearer], "Hostess" 5–6)

"GET FAT, don't die!" also refuses to see AIDS as "a punishment for our Previous Badness," as an imperative to reject a previous gay life. Rather, it embraces gay traditions like camp, mining those traditions, developed in resistance to longstanding hatred and persecution, for the strength they might provide. Here, "GET FAT, don't die!" shares much with the most powerful of contemporary gay political and literary responses to the AIDS crisis:

> ACT UP's humor is no joke. It has given us the courage to maintain our exuberant sense of life while every day coping with disease and death. . . . Because being queer is an identity most of us share, one of our happiest affinities is camp. (Crimp and Ralston 20, 22)

> I'm frightened, I . . . no, no fear, find the anger, find the . . . anger, my blood is clean, my brain is fine, I can handle pressure, I am a gay man and I am used to pressure, to trouble, I am tough and strong and. . . . (Kushner 117)

Notes

1. For an early use of the phrase "gay plague," see VerMeulen. The phrase "homosexual body" is used by Watney.

2. The subtitle of *The Body Positive* was changed in September 1992 from "A Magazine About HIV/AIDS."

3. A later column warns against excessive fat intake, while still touting the usefulness of a high-fat diet for gaining weight: *"Danger, Will Robinson!* Fat can be hard to digest, and many of us Diseased Pariahs have

G.I. problems. If your innards have trouble digesting fat, keep away. . . . But if ol' Mr. Stomach and Mr. Bowel can handle it, then nothing'll put on the weight faster than Fatty Mae's Bacon 'n Egg Sandwich" (B[otkin], *DPN* 5, 8).

4. This joke is similar to Feinberg's in *Spontaneous Combustion:* "Attached to each bottle [of AZT] was a highly-technical five-hundred page pamphlet too depressing for words, listing warnings, precautions, contraindications, adverse reactions, dosage and administration instructions, and approximately 16,457 side effects, of which my favorite was 'taste perversion,' which I interpreted as a strong predilection for chintz and black velvet paintings of nude large-breasted women" (133).

Works Cited

A[ce], T[om]. "Haywire: Louise, the Morning After." *DPN [Diseased Pariah News]* 7 (1992), 13–14.

————. "Pontifications: The Readers Write Back!" *DPN* 4 (1991), 3–5.

Bartlett, Neil. *Ready to Catch Him Should He Fall.* New York: Plume, 1992 [1990].

The Body Positive 4:7 (July/Aug. 1991), 2 [fund-raising notice].

B[otkin], M[ichael]. "GET FAT, don't die!: Taste Challenge." *DPN* 5 (1992), 6, 8, 10, 19–21.

Burrell, Walter Rico. "*The Scarlet Letter,* revisited: A very different AIDS diary." In *Brother to Brother: New Writings by Black Gay Men.* Ed. Essex Hemphill. Conceived by Joseph Beam. Boston: Alyson, 1991. 121–35.

Coe, Christopher. *Such Times.* New York: Harcourt Brace, 1993.

"Condom Corner." *DPN* [regular column].

Crimp, Douglas, and Adam Ralston. *AIDS demo graphics.* Seattle: Bay Press, 1990.

"The DPN Meat Market." *DPN* [regular column].

"The DPN Resource Guide." *DPN* [regular column].

"The DPN Resource Guide." *DPN* 1 (1990), 30.

Feinberg, David B. *Eighty-Sixed.* New York: Viking, 1989.

————. "HIV + Me." *Details* 12:8 (Jan. 1994), 92–95, 128.

————. *Spontaneous Combustion.* New York: Viking, 1991.

Gilden, Dave. "Protecting Body Composition in HIV Infection: Interview with Nutritionist Cade Fields Newman." *AIDS Treatment News* 163 (20 Nov. 1992), 4–8.

Gottlieb, Michael S., Robert Schroff, Howard M. Schanker, Joel D. Weisman, Peng Thim Fan, Robert A. Wolf, and Andrew Saxon. "*Pneumocystis Carinii* Pneumonia and Mucosal Candidiasis in Previously Healthy Homosexual Men: Evidence of a New Acquired Cellular Immunodeficiency." *The New England Journal of Medicine* 305:24 (10 Dec. 1981), 1425–31.

Heyman, Jason. "Nutrition at VIII International Conference on AIDS." *AIDS Treatment News* 158 (4 Sept. 1992), 1–3.

James, John S. "Curcumin Update: Could Food Spice Be Low-Cost Antiviral?" *AIDS Treatment News* 176 (4 June 1993), 1–3.

———. "Nutrition and AIDS: Some Information Sources." *AIDS Treatment News* 134 (6 Sept. 1991), 1–5.

———. "Six-Year Diet Study: Nutrients May Reduce AIDS Risk." *AIDS Treatment News* 181 (20 Aug. 1993), 3–4.

Kushner, Tony. *Angels in America: A Gay Fantasia on National Themes. Part One: Millennium Approaches.* New York: Theatre Communications Group, 1993.

Leger, Mark. "The Boy Look." *OUT/LOOK, National Lesbian and Gay Quarterly* 1:4 (Winter 1989), 44–45.

"Letter from an Innocent Victim/DPN Centerfold Boy, Kevin Irvine." *DPN* 6 (1992), 21–24.

Manley, Joey. *The Death of Donna-May Dean.* New York: St. Martin's Press, 1991.

Mickler, Ernest Matthew. *White Trash Cooking.* Winston-Salem: Jargon Society; Berkeley: Ten Speed Press, 1986.

"Parishioners See AIDS Peril in Communion." *New York Times* 8 Dec. 1985, I.46.

Pierce, Richard, and Patrick Donnelly. "Food for Healing: The Whole Foods Perspective." *The Body Positive* 5:3 (March 1992), 16–17.

Pierce, Richard, and Patrick Donnelly. "Food for Healing: Whole Foods on the Move." *The Body Positive* 5:8 (Sept. 1992), 21–24.

"Positive+Connections." *The Body Positive* [regular column].

"PWA Coalition Resource Directory." *PWA Newsline* [regular column].

Rechy, John. *City of Night.* New York: Grove Press, 1963.

Reed, Paul. *Facing It: A Novel of AIDS.* San Francisco: Gay Sunshine Press, 1984.

———. *The Q Journal: A Treatment Diary.* Berkeley: Celestial Arts, 1991.

"Resources." *The Body Positive* [regular column].

Roland, Michelle. "Gastrointestinal Manifestations of HIV: Diagnosis and Treatment." *AIDS Treatment News* 133 (23 Aug. 1991), 1–7.

Schulman, Sarah. *People in Trouble.* New York: E. P. Dutton, 1990.

[Shearer, Tom]. "Hostess With the Toxoplasmostest: *Surviving AIDS* by Michael Callen." *DPN* 2 (1991), 5–6.

———. "Welcome to Our Brave New World!" *DPN* 1 (1990), 2.

Smith, Denny. "Marijuana: Therapeutic Access Threatened." *AIDS Treatment News* 131 (27 July 1991), 4.

"Statement of Purpose." *AIDS Treatment News* [reproduced in each issue].

"THAT'S 'puh-RYE-uh.' " *DPN* 5 (1992), 4.

T[horne], B[eowulf]. "GET FAT, don't die!: High Calorie Cooking with Biffy Mae." *DPN* 1 (1990), 23–24.

———. "GET FAT, don't die!: High Calorie Cooking with Biffy Mae." *DPN* 2 (1991), 23–24.

———. "GET FAT, don't die!: High Calorie Cooking with Biffy Mae." *DPN* 3 (1991), 15–16.

———. "GET FAT, don't die!: High Calorie Cooking with Biffy Mae." *DPN* 4 (1991), 23–24.

———. "GET FAT, don't die!: Sushi and the Seropositive." *DPN* 6 (1992), 4, 5, 7, 13, 17–18.

———. "GET FAT, don't die!: [special report]." *DPN* 7 (1992), 11, 15, 24, 25, 26, 27.

———. "GET FAT, don't die!: Come All Ye to Vega!" *DPN* 8 (1993), 3, 4, 5, 14, 30–34, 38.

———. "The Great DPN Taste Challenge, Revisited." *DPN* 8 (1993), 31.

VerMeulen, Michael. "The Gay Plague." *New York* 15:22 (31 May 1982), 52–54, 56–62.

Watney, Simon. "The Spectacle of AIDS." In *AIDS: Cultural Analysis/ Cultural Activism*. Ed. Douglas Crimp. Cambridge: MIT Press, 1988 [1987], 71–86.

"Zen and the Art of Teddy Bear Burning." *DPN* 3 (1991), 17–18.

Chapter 3

Eating Animals

Carol J. Adams

Introduction

When we talk of eating animals, we are referring to eating nonhuman, rather than human, animals. But then, we rarely talk of eating (dead) animals at all. We talk of eating "meat." And once we begin talking about eating "meat," we are in the realm of cultural production that poses as individual decision. Herein lies the problem. For what "meat" eaters see as "a nagging moralistic tone" in vegetarians (as one philosopher puts it)[1] might actually reflect the response that "meat" eaters bring to any attempt to expose the cultural construction of the eating of animals' corpses. As another philosopher retorts: "There can be no doubt that almost all people in Western countries have a vested interest in maintaining the *status quo* because they are strongly identified with the taste for meat .... [T]he identification promotes a stream of self-supporting arguments."[2] Is the vegetarian voice a judgmental one or is the "meat" eating listener defensive? Will any discussion that names the raw material—the living animal—and exposes the manner of "meat" production and the accompanying production of "meat's" meaning face a problem of tone and voice? We will see.

For this (supposed) nagging tone, this (perhaps) resistant response, the admitted self-interest of all involved in the debate, is not without effect on the writer and reader of this essay. Either one consumes cooked animal flesh (do you?) or one does not (I don't). There is no neutral ground from which to survey this activity and the debates about it.

Complicating this contested terrain is a startling but little acknowledged fact: most abstainers from flesh know a great deal more about "its" production than do most consumers of dead animals. Since "meat" is from once-living animals, I question whether the word "it" is appropriate to use about them once dead.[3] Ethical vegetarians know (often by heart): the size of a veal crate (22" × 54"), a hen's cage (4 in a 12" by 18" cage); the ingenious contraptions for controlling birth mothers' reproductive activities ("rape rack" for inseminating, "iron maiden" for delivery); the amount of topsoil erosion caused by cattle (85%); or the amount of all raw materials consumed in this country for livestock foods (one-third).[4]

While abstainers generally know a great deal more about the production of "meat" than the consumers, discursive power resides in those with the least knowledge. When former President Reagan (who did not know French) met François Mitterand (who knew both English and French) what language do you think they spoke?[5] In our culture, bilingual vegetarians must always speak English. Indeed, because of the discursive control exercised by the dominant "meat" advocating culture, it is when vegetarians attempt to speak "French" (that is, reporting on slaughterhouses, "factory" farms, the threat of e-coli from eating dead bodies) that they are accused of having a nagging moralistic tone.

Vegetarians and "meat" eaters approach the same phenomenon—the consumption of dead animals—and come to opposite opinions: is it "meat" or flesh? life or death? humane slaughter or murder? delicious or repulsive? nutritious or fat-laden? departure from tradition or return to tradition? "Meat" eaters see vegetarianism as a fad; vegetarians see "meat" eating as larger fad. "Meat" eaters see vegetarians as Puritans, legislating others' enjoyments; vegetarians see "meat" eaters as resisting awareness, indulging in fantasy about where "meat" comes from. "Meat" eaters generally accept the cultural construction of the farm as benign, friendly, and family-based. Vegetarians see an alternate view: industry-owned, cruel, and factorylike. "Meat" eaters ask "Why did you stop eating animals?" Vegetarians respond with Plutarch, saying, "You ought rather, in my opinion, to have enquired who first began this practice, than who of late times left it off."[6] While vegetarians regard the word *vegetable* with respect (it's life-giving, the purported root of the name vegetarian), "meat" advocating cultures see it as an appropriate term for brain-dead individuals.

The "moralistic" vegetarian and the "vested interest" flesh eater cannot meet on neutral ground to examine their conflict over what appropriately should be consumed by human animals and the facts that inform this debate. Not only is there no disinterested observer to this tradition—i.e., one is implicated either by choice of "meat" or resistance to flesh—but there is no impartial semantic or cultural space in which to hold a discussion.

We live in a "meat" advocating culture. One version of reality appears to be the only version, and in this claims its own comprehensiveness. Conflicts in meaning are resolved in favor of the dominant culture. Thus, vegetarians face the problem of making their meanings understood within the dominant "meat" advocating culture. As the feminist detective in Lynn Meyer's *Paperback Thriller* remarks early in the novel, "I could tell you now that I'm a vegetarian, but let's just leave it at that. I won't go into the reasons. If you don't understand them, there's not much I can say; and if you do, there's no need for me to say anything."[7]

The battle for interpretation is evident as the dominant culture attempts to redefine even the notion of vegetarianism. Can one eat a dead fish or a dead chicken and be a vegetarian? Yes, according to the American Society for the Prevention of Cruelty to Animals, who coined the words pesco-vegetarian and pollo-vegetarian.[8] The dominant culture eviscerates the critique of its diet by absorbing it, implying that a dead cow, rather than any animal's corpse, is the problem. In the face of "vegetarians" who eat dead chicken and fish,[9] people who don't eat anything with eyes (except potatoes) must search for other terms. What is literally transpiring in the widening of the *meaning* of vegetarianism is the weakening of the *concept* of vegetarianism by including within it some living creatures who were killed to become food.

The Case of the False Mass Term

In the use of the term "meat" we have a clue to the cultural hegemony achieved for the eating of animals. We also witness the production of meaning and the actual production of (what some see as) food. The term "meat" represents what Quine calls a "mass term."[10]

Mass terms refer to things like water or colors; no matter how much you have of it, or what type of container it is in, water is still water. You can add a bucket of water to a pool of water without changing it at all. Objects referred to by mass terms have no individuality, no uniqueness, no specificity, no particularity.

When we turn an animal into "meat," someone who has a very particular, situated life, a unique being, is converted into something that has no distinctiveness, no uniqueness, no individuality. When you add five pounds of hamburger to a plate of hamburger, it is more of the same thing; nothing is changed. But if you have a living cow in front of you, and you kill that cow, and butcher that cow, and grind up her flesh, you have not added a mass term to a mass term; and ended up with more of the same.[11]

Because of the reign of "meat" as a mass term, it is not often while eating "meat" that one thinks: "I am now interacting with an animal." We do not see our own personal "meat" eating as contact with animals (in the lifetime of an average animal eater that would be 984 chickens, 37 turkeys, 29 pigs, 12 cattle, two lambs, one calf, and more than 1,000 fish) because it has been renamed as contact with food. But what is on the plate in front of us is *not* devoid of specificity. It is the dead flesh of what was once a living, feeling being. The crucial point here is that we make some*one* who is a unique being and therefore not the appropriate referent of a mass term into some*thing* that is the appropriate referent of a mass term. We do so by removing any associations that might make it difficult to accept the activity of rendering a unique individual into a consummable thing. Not wanting to be aware of this activity, we accept this disassociation, this distancing device, of the mass term "meat."[12]

We can observe just how "meat" becomes a mass term: "Someone kills an animal so I can eat her or his corpse as 'meat'," becomes "an animal is killed to be eaten as 'meat'," then "an animal is 'meat'," and finally "meat animal," thus "meat." With the mass term of "meat" the agency of the consumer is consummately elided.

Mass terms also function when a specific term is being used ambiguously, such as chicken, lamb, turkey.[13] In accepting their presentation in saran wrap packages as mass entities and calling this "chicken," perhaps it becomes easier for creophagists to acquiesce to gathering 80,000 chickens together when alive in one warehouse. Just as our language denies them individuality, the institutions created to hold them while alive denies them the opportunity to the expressive gestures that characterize and give meaning to their individual lives. Pigs cannot root; chickens cannot peck; calves cannot nurse. These activities do not fit into the profit requirements. "The 'meat' industry is a high-volume, low-profit-margin business, and it is structured to raise, fatten, slaughter, and merchandise its product as quickly and cheaply as possible."[14]

In essence we are to view the living animal as though already dead, already a mass term (this may explain the existence of the redundant term *dead 'meat'*: through warehousing of animals we now have *living 'meat'*). We are encouraged to "forget the pig [or a cow, a chicken, etc.] is an animal." Instead, call her and view her as "a machine in a factory."[15] She becomes a food-producing unit, a protein harvester, an object, product, computerized unit in a factory environment, egg-producing machine, converting machine, a biomachine, a crop. A recent example of erasure of animals can be found in the United States Department of Agriculture's description of cows, pigs, and chickens as "grain-consuming animal units."[16] As Colman McCarthy points out, this makes people "animal-consuming human units."[17]

Using "meat" as a mass term implies its own comprehensiveness though it only transmits a partial reality. It appears to represent the sole meaning, but instead it represents one of many competing meanings. Not only does it require all to speak English, it implies that there is no other language, such as French, in which to converse. The conflict in interpretation that besets the vegetarian-"meat" eater debate occurs in part because of the false comprehensiveness accorded to the "meat" advocating perspective. A term such as this essay's "flesh eater" (creophagist) may feel judgmental rather than accurate, while the term "meat eater" appears neutral rather than evasive.

Athough "meat" is accepted as a mass term, it is not one. Production of "meat" can occur only with individuals (six billion of them a year). Since mass terms require no modifiers (we do not have to say *extremely wet* water), appropriate and informative modifiers that might challenge "meat's" neutral associations are omitted—such as *recently-butchered, individual cow*-meat. Indeed, an animal's name modifies the word "meat" *only* when that form of animal flesh is not consumed. As Paul Postal describes it, we form compounds with the word *meat* [such as horsemeat, dogmeat] "where the first element is the name of an animal type [such as horse, dog] only if American culture does not sanction the eating of that animal."[18] Thus we have *wombatmeat* but not *sheepmeat*, *dogmeat* but not *chickenmeat*, *horsemeat* but not *cowmeat*. Instead, *sheepmeat* becomes *mutton, cowmeat* undergoes numerous changes depending on the location from which the "meat" was derived *(chuck*, etc.) or the form *(hamburger)*.

Accepting the premise that "meat" is a mass term, we assume that it is accurate and adequate. As a result the rendering of animals as consumable bodies is a given rather than a problem. But none of us chooses "meat's" meanings, we either adhere to them or reject them.[19]

And in rejecting "meat" as a mass term, renaming occurs. One begins to speak French. One does not reorient one's relationship with the dominant culture without also reevaluating that culture's language. Where "meat" eaters see "complete protein," "iron-rich food," "life-giving food," "delectable," or "strength-inducing food," vegetarians see "partly cremated portions of dead animals," or "slaughtered nonhumans," or in Bernard Shaw's words, "scorched corpses of animals." Like Benjamin Franklin, they consider fishing "unprovok'd murder" or refer, like Harriet Shelley to "murdered chicken."[20] Language about "meat eating" normalizes the eating of dead bodies. As Colman McCarthy observes, "Such words as meat, beef, pork, veal or poultry are the Adolph's Tenderizers of language: They make gruesomeness palatable."[21]

If the dominant language breaks the association between dead bodies and "meat"—gruesomeness and palatability—does that mean that to rejoin them automatically brings about a vegetarian consciousness? Not necessarily. But what is curious about the dominant discourse is that it goes to such lengths to maintain the disassociations; "sanitized, cosmetized viands lull us into forgetting their bloody origins."[22] The absence of awareness of the origins, and the energy that is used to maintain disassociations, suggest that a rigid separation between the appetitive and awareness must be maintained for much "meat" eating to continue. As the hero of "Get a Life," a recent television comedy show, observed: "There are certain questions that should go unanswered, like where does meat come from?" The appetitive (especially as it desires flesh) is a drive we do not necessarily deal with, or want to deal with, on a cognitive level. The common response when the issue of flesh eating is brought up over a meal confirms this: "Let's not talk about it, it will ruin my dinner."

As a result, the cultural concepts and presentations by which we know "meat" rely on fantasy, rather than reality. Charlie the Tuna begs to be caught and eaten; an animated hot dog desires nothing more than to be an Oscar Meyer wiener. When lamb chops are discontinued from the menu of hotels because Shari Lewis and "Lamb Chop" are visiting, the unreality of our associations become clear. Or when a newspaper's headline announces that reindeer-meat sausages have received USDA-approval for interstate shipping by proclaiming "On Dasher, on Dancer, on toast"—the unreality is promoted. After all, Dasher, Dancer, and Lamp Chop represent fantasies, not flesh and blood animals.

This fantasy is encouraged by "meat" promoters. "My chickens live in a house that's just chicken heaven," according to Frank

Perdue—all 25,000 of them in each darkened "house." The 1985 "Beef Gives Strength" promotional campaign was pulled when the New York state attorney general's office called it "deceptive."[23] 150 years ago, Henry David Thoreau exposed the homeopathic fantasy in the belief that flesh gave strength as he walked alongside a man plowing a field with an ox. Despite the fact that he relied on the strength of a vegetarian animal, the farmer protested that he needed "meat" for strength.

The Sexual Politics of Meat[24]

Perpetuating the fantasy minimizes awareness, appealing instead directly to the appetite: "Somehow, nothing satisfies like beef."[25] And the appetite being appealed to is constructed as male. Masculinity appears to require both satisfaction *and* beef. In a *New York Times* story about the opening of a new men's store, we learn: "In keeping with the masculine spirit of the evening, the hors d'oeuvres were beefy. Roast beef on toast. Chunk chicken in pastry shells. Salmon and saucisson. None of that asparagus and cucumber fluff here."[26] We are told that "meat" eating societies gain male identification by their choice of food, and "meat" textbooks heartily endorse this association. *The Meat We Eat* proclaims "meat" to be "A Virile and Protective Food," thus "a liberal 'meat' supply has always been associated with a happy and virile people."[27] *Meat Technology* informs us that "the virile Australian race is a typical example of heavy "meat"-eaters."[28] Leading gourmands refer "to the virile ordeal of spooning the brains directly out of a barbecued calf's head."[29] *Virile: of or having the characteristics of an adult male,* from *vir* meaning *man*.

Meat eating demarcates individual and societal virility. Men who decide to eschew "meat" eating are deemed effeminate; failure of men to eat "meat" announces that they are not masculine. Nutritionist Jean Mayer suggested that "the more men sit at their desks all day, the more they want to be reassured about their maleness in eating those large slabs of bleeding meat which are the last symbol of machismo."[30] The late Marty Feldman observed, "It has to do with the function of the male within our society. Football players drink beer because it's a man's drink, and eat steak because it's a man's meal. The emphasis is on 'man-sized portions,' 'hero' sandwiches; the whole terminology of 'meat'-eating reflects this masculine bias."[31] "Meat"-and-potatoes men are our stereotypical strong and hearty, rough and ready, able males. Hearty beef stews are named "Manhandlers." Chicago Bears head football coach, Mike Ditka, operates a restaurant that features "he-man food" such as steaks and chops. A chain of French restaurants in the Dallas-Fort Worth area added rotisserie (dead) chicken "to satisfy the hunger of male patrons for something meaty."[32]

When an advertisement claims that "meat" is "real food for real people," the implications are obvious. We want to be included; we want to be real people; and so we are absorbed into the dominant viewpoint. To resist the eating of animals causes one to be excluded from the culturally constructed "we," and to announce one's difference. If I do not see "meat" as a real food, than I am not a real person. The subtext here is, "If I am not real, I am not male." Inevitably, cultural images of "meat" appeal to male-identified appetitive desires. Thus, Gretchen Polhemus was hired by the Nebraska Beef Board because her presence "adds a unique and attractive element that embodies 'The New Beauty of Beef.' "[33] The association between attractive human female bodies and delectable, attractive "meat" appeals to the appetitive desires as they have been constructed in our culture in which we interpret images from a stance of male identification and human-centeredness.

In an article on a low-fat, low-cholesterol ground "meat," the *New York Times* featured an image of a cow's head on top of a slim human female body, whose arms and legs ended in hoofs.[34] Combining human femaleness with cow femaleness (though the udders and breasts are invisible or underemphasized), it glorifies the anorexic, female body while positing a feminine sex object, seductress image. All this to represent a story about *beef*, which does not come from cows but from steers.[35]

Or consider a kitchen tool called the "turkey hooker." Designed to be used to move a cooked turkey corpse from the cooking pan to the serving plate, it hooks into the gaping hole that was once the neck. Accompanying an image that shows the "turkey hooker" in use, is a fantasy image of a turkey in high-heeled shoes, one wing placed seductively, invitingly, behind her head, hints of breasts showing. In large print, we are told: "AN EASY PICK UP FROM PAN TO PLATTER."[36]

A healthy sexual being poses near her drink: she wears bikini panties only and luxuriates on a large chair with her head rested seductively on an elegant lace doily. Her inviting drink with a twist of lemon awaits on the table. Her eyes are closed; her facial expression beams pleasure, relaxation, enticement. She is touching her crotch in an attentive, masturbatory action. Anatomy of seduction: sex object, drink, inviting room, sexual activity. The formula is complete. But a woman does not beckon. A pig—Ursula Hamdress by assigned name—does. Is she inviting someone to eat her or rape her?

The Hustler, prior to its incarnation as a pornographic magazine, was a Cleveland restaurant whose menu presented a woman's buttocks on the cover and proclaimed, "We serve the best 'meat' in town!" Who?

An article about "How to Kill a Chicken" describes the look of dead chickens after their blood stops flowing, and they are scalded to remove their feathers:

> Skinny, absurdly skinny, a characteristic withheld from the patrons of supermarkets, where the chickens are sold sans feet, their necks jammed inside the body cavity and their scrawny carcasses squeezed into spurious plumpness by tight fitting paper tubs tightened even further by tough plastic wrappers. Miller's back room employs no such cosmetics, and for the [dead] chicken lover the result is an appalling and funny overdose of truth, sort of like a centerfold feature showing the Playmate of the Month undergoing a gynecological exam.[37]

"Vanitas: Flesh Dress for an Albino Anorectic" by Jana Sterbak was displayed on a mannequin in a Montreal gallery in the early 1990s. It would remain undisturbed until the 50 pounds of salted flank steak decomposed, then another $260 worth of fresh flesh would be added.[38]

Frank Perdue asks "Are you a breast man or a leg man?"

In the construction of these images, the consumer is presumed to be a human male who consumes both images of female beauty and large hunks of dead animals. Many ironies are contained within this camouflage of reality by fantasy: the fat-laden "meat" portrayed by aneroxic, white, human female bodies; the butchered, fragmented, bleeding flesh of dead animals presented as beautiful; male animal flesh (such as beef) paraded as human female flesh; the equation of prostitution and flesh eating; the pornographic imaging of animals and women. We should not be surprised that Meat is the name of a sex club in Manhattan.

When "meat" is claimed as "real food for real people," the message is that vegetarians are unreal people, "they" but not "we," "sissies" or "fruits" but not "he-men" or Iron Johns.

The Trojan Horse of the Nutrition Community

The coercive nature of our "meat" advocating culture is further evidenced by the traditional nutritional approach to flesh eating. The framing of the question of eating dead animals as a question of nutrition regularizes "meat" eating. Although it is one of many discourses available, the four basic food groups—"the Trojan Horse of the nutrition community"[39]—has been the nutritional discourse assigned to us for debating the eating of animals.

Until 1956, there was no basic four food groups (milk, "meat", vegetable-fruit, and bread-cereal). Before that, "meat" and dairy industries spent millions of dollars in advertisements that advised us to "eat more 'meat'" and "drink more milk." The "Basic Seven" had been introduced during World War II, supplanting the "Twelve Food Groups" used as a guideline during the 1930s. According to the American "Meat" Institute, from 1938 to 1956, there was a declining rate of "meat" consumption. While the introduction of the four basic food groups is often cast as an important nutritional device created to aid people, it is clear that the dairy and "meat" industries were alarmed by the instability of their market. Working closely with the government United States Department of Agriculture (USDA), they reduced the number of food groups while alloting greater space to their specific products.

The Four Basic Food Groups is a literal representation of how a question of production and promotion becomes a nutritional question. The reason for the four basic food groups, we are told, is to insure that we are getting our recommended daily amounts of protein, calcium, vitamins, and iron. The Basic Four Food poster that inculcated generations from 1956 until recently indicated that "meat" and dairy products were an excellent source of these items. It made this claim because it measured these products from a *producer's* point of view (nutrients per *weight* ratio) rather than a *consumer's* point of view (nutrients per *calories* ratio). Examining this choice of measurement, it appears curiously unhelpful to consumers—"people do not eat until a certain weight of food has been consumed but rather until Caloric requirements are satisfied"[40]—while extremely favorable for producers: foods high in fat like "meat" fare better when measured by weight rather than calorie. Turkey flesh can be claimed to be 96% fat-free when measured by weight, although 28.6% of the calorie content is fat.

Although there is no Recommended Daily Allowance for weight in the diet, foods are interpreted according to weight in these charts to hide a consumer's concern—concern about fat and calories. "Fat is lighter (specific gravity .913-.945) than water, the chief constituent of fruits and vegetables, so fatty foods will show up well in a nutrient/weight sort; but since fat is high in calories these foods do poorly in a nutrient/calorie sort."[41] As a result, "if foods are sorted and preferenced by nutrient/Calorie rather than nutrient/weight ratios, animal foods lose their clout and the whole 'Basic Four' concept evaporates." It evaporates because excessive intake of protein and fat, fostered by the traditional basic four food groups, poses a greater health risk, then the obtaining of calcium, protein, and iron from vegetables, grains, and fruits. The typical Western flesh indulger's diet is high in animal fat and protein, while lacking in fiber. This diet is associated with increased risk of cancer, heart disease, obesity, diabetes, and osteoporosis.[42] In fact, some vegetable foods protect against diseases such as arterosclerosis and cancer, while high-fat foods increase risk for these diseases.

In April 1991, the Physician's Committee for Responsible Medicine introduced a new four food groups of whole grains, vegetables, legumes, fruits. This proposal from a group who might generally be marginalized by the dominant discourse garnered quite a bit of media attention.[43] But soon its radical evisceration of a "meat" diet seemed unimportant, because—perhaps to confuse matters—lower-echelon USDA staff unveiled a new representation of the four basic food groups.[44] No longer contained within a wheel that imparted fifty percent of its space to dairy and "meat," the four basic food groups were to be illustrated through a New Age pyramid, with "meat" and dairy products toward the apex, though now inhabiting less space. This diminishment in space, though counteracted by the placement of "meat" and dairy in hierarchically superior locations, was not acceptable to the beef and dairy industries. In encapsulating their space, the pyramid appeared to shrink their nutritional importance as well. Protesting this to the USDA—the pyramid was "confusing," it "stigmatized" their products, both by the reduction of size, and by their placement next to that of fats and sweets—the "meat" and dairy industries succeeded in having the new image withdrawn. As one newspaper reported, "Industry Beefs, USDA cowed."[45]

The pyramid survived, however, and was reintroduced to the public in 1992 (after a series of consumer surveys, costing $855,000, showed that it was not confusing). However, while realigning them from circle to pyramid, it does not destablize the concept of the four basic food groups. In fact, it continues to reinforce the idea that dairy products—what I call "feminized" protein—are essential to a diet.

When analyzed as an industry rather than a food product, the dairy industry cannot be so easily separated from meat production: it supplies "veal" calves, chickens for soup and stock, exhausted cows for "burgers" and other "meat." Remember, too, that milk is produced in surplus in our country, and having a government image and concept that assures a market for its product is a great boon.

Just as the traditional nutritional measurement of "meat" by weight instead of calories ignored its serious health implications, so constructing the argument about eating animals in solely nutritional terms—no matter what the shape—ignores the context for the nutritional debate. When we are talking about the "meat" and dairy industries, we are talking about the second largest industry in the United States. Through the USDA's Four Basic Food Groups we have government sponsorship of an animal-based food diet. Instead of being seen as industry-sponsored propaganda, it can be viewed neutrally as government-sponsored education, lifting cultural promotion to an even greater coercive dimension. The Four Food Groups might be called not the Queen's English, but the government's English.

During the 1993 e-coli scare, in which at least two children died as a result of undercooked "meat," and many more became sick, the focus of debate was not "why do we continue to eat dead bodies?" but "how should dead bodies be cooked so that we do not die from them?" Vegetarians around the country listened with ears that heard repeated evidence for the need to abandon the eating of flesh. "Meat" eaters listened with anxiety for assurance that they could continue to eat flesh. Not surprisingly, the dominant culture determined the focus of the debate, all kept respectfully within the confines of government English. New labels to appear on all dead flesh will warn of the need to cook dead bodies completely before consuming them. If the labels were in vegetarian "French" they might say: "Warning: This is a dead body. Recently executed, the decaying process has already begun. You do not need to eat dead animals to stay healthy. Reduce your risk of getting six out of ten diseases that cripple and kill Americans: boycott this product and choose vegetarianism."

Conclusion

If the words favored for insulting others are any sign, the animals whom humans consume do not figure grandly in any hierarchy of value: "you cow," "eating like a pig," "chicken-brained," "chicken-hearted," "turkey." One commentator has suggested that "in coming days we may marvel at the strange phenonmenon of constituting ourselves by the intimate act of eating beings we despise."[46] But can the dominant discourse allow for such marveling, such introspection, when it comes to eating animals?

In a sense, vegetarians are no more biased than flesh eaters about their choice of food; the former, however, do not benefit as do the latter from having their biases actually approved of by the dominant culture through the coercive effects of a government-sponsored "meat" diet. As a result, in this culture, it requires less energy, less knowledge, less concern, less awareness, to continue eating animals than to stop. Yet it may be that the unexamined meal is not worth eating.

Notes

1. Cora Diamond, "Eating Meat and Eating People," *Philosophy* 53 (1978), p. 469.

2. Stewart Richards, "Forethoughts for Carnivores," *Philosophy* 56 (1981), p. 86.

3. See Carol J. Adams, *The Sexual Politics of Meat: A Feminist-Vegetarian Critical Theory* (New York: Continuum, 1990).

4. For a summary of the environmental consequences of eating dead animals, see Alan B. Durning, "Fat of the Land," *World Watch*, 4, no. 3: 11–17.

5. On discursive control, see Eve Kosofsky Sedgwick, *Epistemology of the Closet* (Berkeley and Los Angeles: University of California Press, 1990).

6. Plutarch, "Of Eating of Flesh," in *Animal Rights and Human Obligations*, ed. Tom Regan and Peter Singer (Englewood Cliffs, N.J.: Prentice-Hall, 1976), p. 111.

7. Lynn Meyer, *Paperback Thriller* (New York: Random House, 1975), pp. 4–5.

8. Cited in Peter Sinclair, "Carrots and Sticks," *Vegetarian Times*, #167 (July 1991) p. 68.

9. See, for instance, Kathryn Paxton George, forthcoming, *Signs*, who defines vegetarians as people who eat chicken and fish.

10. Willard Van Orman Quine, *Word and Object* (Cambridge: M.I.T. Press, 1960), pp. 99ff. Nancy Tuana pointed out that Quine's explanation of "mass term" was applicable to the cultural construction of animals as edible. Her interpretation of his work has greatly influenced my description in this article.

11. This example is based on an explanation offered by Nancy Tuana.

12. This idea is developed and applied in Carol J. Adams, "The Feminist Traffic in Animals," in *Ecofeminism: Women, Animals, Nature*, Greta Gaard, ed. (Philadelphia: Temple University Press, 1993), 195–218. It complements the concept of the absent referent, which I introduced and defined in *The Sexual Politics of Meat*.

13. Insight of Nancy Tuana.

14. Wayne Swanson and George Schultz, *Prime Rip* (Englewood Cliffs, N.J.: Prentice-Hall, 1982), p. 24.

15. J. Byrnes, "Raising Pigs by the Calendar at Maplewood Farm," *Hog Farm Management*, September 1976, p. 30, quoted in Jim Mason and Peter Singer, *Animal Factories* (New York: Crown Publishers, 1980), p. 1.

16. "Doublespeak awards don't mince words," *Dallas Morning News* 20 November 1988, p. 4a.

17. Colman McCarthy, "Sins of the Flesh," *Washington Post*, March 1990.

18. Paul M. Postal, "Anaphoric Islands," in *Papers from the Fifth Regional Meeting of the Chicago Linguistic Society, April 18–19, 1969*, ed. Robert I. Binnick, Alice Davison, Georgia M. Green, Jerry L. Morgan (Chicago: Department of Linguistics, University of Chicago, 1969), p. 235.

19. It could be argued that stalking and killing an animal and then eating that animal's dead flesh is an alternative to this commodification of the other animals. It is beyond the scope of this paper to explore this claim, except to identify that whether one posits animals as mass terms and mass produces "meat" or as an individual hunts individual animals, both activities ontologize animals as edible. Moreover, this argument often includes an appeal to the idea that life is tragic, pointing to the fact that some animals kill and eat other animals. It is interesting that our species, which exerts so much energy demarcating differences between us and other species, often appeals to the fact of carnivorousness in other species to justify our own peculiar forms of flesh eating. Yet our flesh eating has little resemblance to that of the carnivorous animals. On hunting, please see Marti Kheel, "Environmental Ethics as the License to Kill: An Ecofeminist Critique of Hunter's Discourse," forthcoming in *Animals*

and Women: Theorizing the Feminist Connection, ed. Carol J. Adams, Josephine Donovan, and Susanne Kappeler; and Carol J. Adams, "Ecofeminism and the Eating of Animals," in which I address the question "Can Hunting Be Reconciled to Ecofeminist Ethics?" In *Hypatia: A Journal of Feminist Philosophy*, 6, no. 1: 125–45.

20. Geoffrey L. Rudd, *Why Kill for Food?* (Madras, India: The Indian Vegetarian Congress, 1973), p. 77; Peter Singer, *Animal Liberation*, p. xii; Bernard Shaw quoted in Dudley Giehl, *Vegetarianism: A Way of Life* (New York: Harper & Row, 1979), p. 137; *The Autobiography of Benjamin Franklin*, ed. Leonard W. Labaree, Ralph L. Ketcham, Helen Boatfield, and Helene Fineman (New Haven: Yale University Press, 1964), p. 87; Richard Holmes, *Shelley: The Pursuit* (New York: E. P. Dutton and Co., 1975), p. 129. This may have been tongue-in-cheek, yet as she and Percy Shelley were attempting vegetarianism at this time, Harriet reveals the attitudes that they associated with vegetarianism.

21. MacCarthy, "Sins."

22. Steven G. Kellman, "Green Freedom for the Cockatoo," *The Gettysburg Review* (1991), p. 152.

23. Karen L.T. Iacobbo, "Advertising: Making risk acceptable," *Vegetarian Voice*, 1991, p. 9.

24. This section draws on examples found in my book *The Sexual Politics of Meat*, as well as material that has been sent to me subsequent to that book's publication.

25. Bernice Kanner, "The Ways of All Flesh: The New Marketing of Meat," *New York*, November 22, 1982, p. 20.

26. "Scotch and Beef are served in a new shrine to trousers and $1000 suits," *New York Times*, 1990. Thanks to Ken Reichley for sending me this clipping.

27. P. Thomas Ziegler, *The Meat We Eat* (Danville, Ill.: The Interstate Printers and Publishers, 1966), pp. 5, 1.

28. Frank Gerrard, *Meat Technology: A Practical Textbook for Student and Butcher* (London: Northwood Publications, 1945, 1977), p. 348.

29. Waverley Root and Richard de Rochemont, *Eating in America: A History* (New York: William Morrow, 1976), p. 279.

30. Quoted in "Red Meat: American Man's Last Symbol of Machismo," *National Observer* July 10, 1976, p. 13.

31. Marty Feldman, quoted in Rynn Berry Jr., *The Vegetarians* (Brookline, Mass.: Autumn Press, 1979), p. 32.

32. Article on La Madeline, *Dallas Observer*, June 10, 1993–June 16, 1993, p. 21.

33. Helen Bryant, *The Dallas Times-Herald*, n.d.

34. Denise Webb, "Eating Well," *New York Times*, January 23, 1991, p. C3.

35. Thanks to Emily Culpepper and her friend for calling this image and its feminist implications to my attention.

36. Thanks to Hilary Martinson and Ingrid Newkirk of People for the Ethical Treatment of Animals for sending me one.

37. F. K. Plous Jr. "How to Kill a Chicken," *Reader: Chicago's Free Weekly* (January 18, 1980), p. 24. Thanks to Karen Davis for discovering this metaphor and sending it to me.

38. "Political art critics fed more raw meat," *Washington Times*, April 4, 1991.

39. Greg Moyer, "School Daze," *Nutrition Action* (September 1982), p. 7.

40. William Harris, M.D., "Hype Parades as Science" *Ahisma*, 31, no. 3 (July/September 1990), p. 6.

41. Ibid., p. 5.

42. See John Robbins, *Diet for a New America* (Stillpoint), and "The New Four Food Groups: Summary," Physicians Committee for Responsible Medicine, April 1991.

43. See Marian Burros, "Rethinking 4 Food Groups, Doctors Tell U.S.," *New York Times*, April 10, 1991.

44. The reason I wonder whether the PCRM proposal prompted a premature release by the USDA Health and Nutrition Service is because the USDA had printer's proofs of brochures, but had planned to release the graphic later in the spring. See Carole Sugarman and Malcolm Gladwell, "Pyramid deserted as symbol of foods," *Buffalo Evening News* [originally in the *Washington Post*], April 26, 1991, p. A4.

45. *Dallas Times-Herald*, editorial, May 5, 1991.

46. Karen Davis, "Chickens reign a la King, not peasant poultry," *Montgomery Journal* (Sept. 17, 1992), A3.

Chapter 4

Eating Out: Voluptuosity for Dessert

David Farrell Krell

Although Novalis will be our gourmet guide throughout, let us begin perversely, cunningly, with Nietzsche's apotropaic dessert, if only in order to alter his recipe:

"But what happened to you?"—"I don't know," he muttered hesitantly. "Perhaps the Harpies flew over my table."—Today it occasionally happens that a mild-mannered, reserved, reticent human being suddenly goes berserk, smashes dinnerware, overturns the table, screams, runs amok, insults everyone present—only in the end to turn aside in shame, furious with himself. To what end? On account of what? In order to starve in isolation, in order to suffocate under the weight of his memory?—Whoever knows the cravings of an elevated and selective soul, one who only rarely finds his table set and his meal prepared, will be in grave danger at all times. Today, however, that danger is extraordinary. Thrown into a noisy and motley age, in which one does not wish to share one's bowl, one can easily perish of hunger and thirst. Or, if one finally does "dig in," one can perish due to an attack of nausea. We have probably all sat down at a table where we didn't belong; and precisely the most alert of us [*die Geistigsten*], who are most difficult to nourish, know of that menacing dyspepsia that arises from sudden insight into and regret concerning our victuals and our messmates—*nausea for dessert.* (*Beyond Good and Evil*, no. 282)[1]

76

Having begun with nausea for dessert, we shall now go backwards, working our way, perversely, linguistically, toward the canapé of cosmic creation, then back again in the direction of Romanticism and Post-modernity. And voluptuosity. Our just desserts.

⌗⌗⌗

In Plato's *Timaeus*—the archival belly and bowel of the Occidental mind—the Pythagorean astronomer explains that the universe was created as a living sphere complete unto itself. It possessed no organs of any kind, certainly no organs of ingestion and excretion. For when there is no *other* for organs to work on, no *other* to incorporate and excrete, organs are superfluous. Here is but one detail from Timaeus's portrait of the world (at 33c–d): "Nor would there have been use of organs by which it might receive its food or get rid of what it had already digested, since there was nothing that went from it or came into it, for there was nothing besides it. By design [ἐκ τέχνης] it was created thus, its own waste [φθίσις] providing its own food [τροφή], and all that it did or suffered taking place in and by itself." Centuries later, Novalis overhears Timaeus talking to Socrates. He interjects: "If every organic part had the life-duration of eternity, it would need no nourishment in the stricter sense of the word, no renovation, no elimination" (Novalis, 563).[2]

Timaeus talks so smoothly that we are likely to swallow whole what is most puzzling about his remarks. Not even Novalis's shy intervention disturbs our devouring ears. There *was* nothing besides the universe, nothing it could have eaten even if it had desired to eat. Hence no organs of ingestion, digestion, and elimination. Yet by the demiurge's design (for the demiurge *is,* and is outside the sphere, as are also the εἴδη "up to" which the demiurge "looks"), universal waste provides cosmic food. Perhaps the sphere could have eaten the demiurge? Perhaps it could have munched on Forms and sucked out the marrow of god? But no. Timaeus says that the sphere's "waste" (waste? whence?) provided its own "food" (why food?). If there is no food taken in from outside, whence the waste to satisfy cosmic coprophagia? Why food at all for a blessedly self-sufficient economy? Acting and suffering "in and by itself," present to no *other,* an other it could eat or be eaten by, Timaeus's universe is in no comprehensible sense *alive.* It is instead smothered in its own surfeit, pickled in its own toxins.

Manger l'autre. "Eating the other." That was the title of Jacques Derrida's lecture course in Paris during the autumn of 1990. (The title is particularly difficult to render in English: it did not contain the word *autrui,* the existential and ethical Other that has been the rage for decades now, but the neuter/neutral word *l'autre,* other with a small "o.") The course was not principally about cannibalism, except in a metaphysical sense. It all turned about a conundrum: all one can eat *is* something *other*—not just any other, of course, but the *nourishing* other. Yet all ingestion of nourishment is followed by excretion, the elimination of what even in the nourishing other could not be assimilated. One can eat only the other, but the other can be consumed only with remnants, residues, excrement, and leftovers—*les restes.* There are always bits and scraps of *caput mortuum* and effluvium to be purged and hidden away, buried or burned by lime or by fire, or washed away into someone else's back yard.

    Yet what is the *system* of such waste production and management? Does this system have anything to do with the other systems of the mouth—all of them touched by Gödel's theorem—systems such as speech and kissing? What would be the remnant of a pristine kiss? What would bring kissing into the proximity of waste? "I would wish that my readers could read my observation—that the beginning of philosophy is a first kiss—at the precise instant when they were listening to Mozart's *Wenn die Liebe in Deinen* being performed with passion, if indeed they were unable to be in tremulous proximity to a first kiss" (Novalis, 331).[2] Is every aspect of the oral system assimilated in the kiss? Is every aspect of the kiss consonant with the other systems of the mouth? Or are there residue and waste products even here? If so, can there be a wasting of waste, a perfect elimination of all that is unassimilable? Would such wastage be what philosophers pursue when they dream of the *absolute* and the *system*—and even when they dream of the *fragment* or the *aphorism,* which aspire to wholeness as much as any encyclopedia of philosophical sciences does?

    I will not be able to pursue Derrida's questions here, although anyone who has dined out will understand the proximity of the question of waste to all these systems. For every *rest*aurant has its *rest*erooms. Indeed, where does waste begin? With fermentation? With the controlled spoilage of grape juice, beet juice, salted cabbage, cows' and sheep's milk? Consider cheese for dessert, as in France, where a native will demand *un fromage qui put,* a cheese that evokes a horrified "P. U." from an innocent abroad, a wedge of blessed corruption ("Blessed are the cheesemakers. . .") produced by cows who laugh. If you can get it past your nose, your mouth will thank you. *Pour rire, Pourrir.*

Eating out? In these United States? Promiscuous junk food and fear of contamination by salmonella and worse have made eating out all but impossible in our time. People used to go out if only to gaze at the others, just as one went to the zoo to observe the comical cageless animals observing the caged animals. Some even went out solely in order to eat. For a while, a brief while, eating out seemed the sensual nub of our culture. Indeed, Christopher Lasch decried it as the sexual sacrament of *narcissism,* and thus a perversion of the home, of the bustling Norman Rockwell kitchen. Now, thanks to universal anxiety concerning infection—a modest proposal to eat out is now regarded as a death threat—all are under the lash, forty lashes for anyone who eats out, and so no one dares. The gods are flown and communion impossible. Each mortal glowers at the other as a possible font of contagion, and each invents or embraces an ism that prohibits the pleasures of eating out. Never mind that such isms are fueled by the only source of energy available to Americans, the puritanism. Oh, that savory meat, ah, that luscious fruit, and oh, the shellfish so dainty and mucous. Forty lashes!

Not even a picnic. In the old days a man and a woman who succumbed to love would share a bite in the great outdoors. Languorously, longingly, never simultaneously but always alternately, in order not to break their concentration on one another, in order not to miss a trick. They would seek out a place in the hills by the sea, near scrub pine and olive, or by kelp and clam, and devote hours to it, as though the workaday world could wait forever—Freud was right: they were subversive of civilization and all its discontents, for they were content. They were more than content. They were *erhaben, erhoben,* sublime without sublimation, elevated without footwear, ecstatic without the static. It was like a religion to them, their First Communion, except that they were always laughing in church.

> The shared meal is a deed symbolic of unification. . . . All enjoyment, appropriation, and assimilation is an eating; or rather, eating is nothing other than appropriation. All

spiritual enjoyment can therefore be expressed as eating. In
friendship, one eats of one's friend, lives on one's friend. To
substitute the body for the spirit is a genuine trope, and the
commemorative meal for a friend enjoys his flesh in every
bite with a keen supersensuous imagination, enjoys his blood
in every draft. To our effete age, this seems barbaric—but who
says that they have to think of raw, corruptible flesh and
blood? Corporeal appropriation is mysterious enough to be a
lovely image of the way I make something *mine* in spirit. And
then, are flesh and blood in fact so repulsive and low? Truly
there is more here than gold and diamonds, and the time is
not far when one will have a more elevated concept of the
organic body. . . . Thus we enjoy the genius of nature daily,
and every meal is a Mass—an agency for the nourishment of
soul and maintenance of body, a mysterious means of
transfiguration and deification on earth, an animating intercourse with what is absolutely alive. We enjoy what is name-
less in slumber. We waken as a child wakens on its mother's
breast, and we know that all this replenishment and nourishment came to us as a free bestowal out of love. We know that
air, drink, and food are the constituents of an ineffably loving
person. (Novalis, 409–10)

Thomas Aquinas knows that people are better than trees. Trees
stand on their heads and suck the earth, baring their nether parts
as leaves to the sky. Humans are higher up on the stairway to
heaven, their heads closer to what Timaeus called the circles of the
same. Unless of course they go down, in which case they are closer
to hell than even the oaks. Which reminds me of an old story that
comes from Umbria during the Late High Middle Ages.

Guillermo knew that the Father Superior's accusation against
the two friars—Brother Felice and Brother Beatus—was too far-
fetched to be true. Even so, he had to investigate. That was his job.
And so he made the two days' journey from Rome. The two portly
friars were accused of mocking the Eucharist. The fact that they
were simple men of the countryside, earthy but pious, and entirely
submissive, only increased their superior's suspicion that it was
diabolical possession.

Guillermo had heard of similar cases of possession, sometimes mass possession, evidenced by fits of uncontrollable laughter

and lewd dancing. His interview with the two, hardly an inquest, occurred in the cell of Father Superior. It was a corner room of the monastery, with the lemon yellow light of the Umbrian morning entering through the two barred windows high overhead. The emaciated Father Superior sat wordless and unmoving in his high-back chair. Felice and Beatus shifted from foot to foot, sweat pouring from their brows.

"My dear brothers in Christ," began Guillermo softly. "Perhaps it would be best if you told me in your own words what has happened to you."

Silence.

Then Beatus mumbled something in the dialect of his country, his gravelly voice scarcely audible, his eyes fixed on the stone floor, his mouth working against the guilt of the past and the catastrophe of the imminent future.

"It . . . happens . . . always at chapel, always at Holy Mass. . . . When the celebrant says *Take ye and eat!*"

Without warning, Brother Felice, at the side of Beatus, released a fearful snort. It was more a sneeze or a stifled cry for help than a laugh. He buried his face in the sleeve of his habit. Brother Beatus recoiled in horror, surprised by the inconsolable wail of a stricken cat that issued forth from his own mouth. He doubled over, as an unseen imp savaged his belly. Father Superior leapt to his feet, knocking his chair against the rear wall of the cell.

"Blasphemers! It is the most sacred doctrine of Holy Mother Church! The son of God offers himself up to you sinners for your salvation—*This is my body!*

The stricken fratres collapsed to the floor in agonies of laughter. Father Guillermo no longer had the presence of mind to compare the scene to reports he had read in the Holy Office. He had never witnessed such an attack firsthand. He tried to calm Father Superior, seeing that the two men who were rolling across the stone floor convulsed with laughter were beyond help.

However, Father Superior refused to be placated. He was mad with rage. Indeed, he raised his hand to strike a blow.

Guillermo could not have known that the blow was coming down on him. For the judicious Father Guillermo, called in to grant counsel and render judgment in the case of the errant friars, could not see his own face contorted with the most unexpected and most irreparable of grimacing grins, could not hear the belches of sacrilegious laughter that now exploded from him.

⊲◇⊳⊲◇⊳⊲◇⊳

> The philosopher lives on problems, as human beings live on foodstuffs. An unsolvable problem is an undigestible food-stuff.... A digestible means of nourishment—that's the way everything should be. As for the condiments for foodstuffs, they are the paradoxes in problems. A problem is truly dis-solved when it is annihilated as such. So it is with foodstuffs as well. The gain in both cases is the activity that is stimu-lated by both. Yet there are nourishing problems, just as there are nourishing foodstuffs—whose elements constitute an aug-mentation of my intelligence. By philosophizing ... my intel-ligence is constantly ameliorated—which is true of foodstuffs only up to a certain point. A rapid amelioration of our intel-ligence is as dubious as a sudden enhancement of our strength. The true step to health and improvement is a slow step.... Just as one does not eat in order to attain an altogether novel and foreign matter, one does not philosophize in order to find en-tirely novel and foreign truths. One philosophizes about why one is alive. If one were ever to achieve a life without any *given* means of nourishment, one would also get to the point where one would not philosophize about any *given* problems. Perhaps a few are already that far along. (Novalis, 354–55)

That is why Novalis is so clever. That is why he is so wise. Which reminds us of Nietzsche once again—Nietzsche explaining Nietzsche. Why is he so clever? On account of his wretched diet. Or on account of his *insight into* the wretchedness of his *former* diet, the diet of his youth and student days—an insight, of course, that he would still owe to a change in diet. "Indeed, well into maturity I have only eaten *badly*—in moral terms, 'unegotistically,' 'selflessly,' 'altruistically,' to the salvation of cooks and all the other fellow-Christians" (6, 279). What sins the German kitchen has on its conscience! Soup *before* the salad, meat boiled, veg-etables cooked to a tasteless pulp, dumplings like paperweights. The German spirit? Exhalations of wretched entrails, the incapac-ity to digest anything once and for all and to put it behind one, as it were.

Contra the German spirit, Nietzsche issues his precautions: no alcohol, no coffee, precious little tea. Above all, no beer. "My antipodes live in Munich" (280). Water. Water does the trick, espe-cially in locales where one can draw it from gurgling springs fed by mountain snow—Nice, Turin, Sils. "With me, the spirit hovers over the *water. . .*" (281). If there must be tea, make it strong. Better to drink cocoa, if the oil has been removed. No snacks, no café afternoons. Hearty meals, bring on the stomach juices full force, but don't overdo it.

All these precautions—for example, precautions taken *against* vegetarianism—contribute to Nietzsche's cleverness. Until in his madness they feed him cakes.

Cleverness? What is its axis? On what does it turn? Novalis has a slightly different answer:

> Les Femmes are the pole about which and for whose sake the existence and the philosophy of the clever nobility turn, because Les Femmes affect body and soul at the same time. They too love cohesive unity, and set unlimited value on this mixed enjoyment—a taste that applies to everything: the bed should be soft, its form and its embroidery should be pretty, the food they eat should be delicate but animating too. (Novalis, 392)

Les Femmes and their action at a severely reduced distance. *Actio in distans?* This dance?

⊸◇⊷⊸◇⊷⊸◇⊷

"If an organ serves another then it is, so to speak, as his *tongue*—his throat, his mouth. The tool that most willingly serves spirit, that is most readily capable of manifold modifications, is primarily the organ of speech—hence a language of mouth and fingers" (Novalis, 377). Which reminds me of another story, this one as true as the first.

The book was bound in red leather veined in black and gold. It was a book of poems that contained a poem "To Novalis." [3] It was not one of the poems he had read that night, but he read it now:

An Novalis (2. Fassung [a])

In dunkler Erde ruht der heilige Fremdling.
Es nahm von saftem Munde ihm die Klage der Gott,
Da er in seiner Blüte hinsank.
Eine blaue Blume
Fortlebt sein Lied im nächtlichen Haus der Schmerzen.

To Novalis

In dark earth the holy stranger rests.
From his soft mouth God took the lament,
When in his blossom time he wilted.
A blue flower
Lives on: his song in the nocturnal house of pain.

A book of poems for sisters and brothers and lovers in pain and joy and incense. That night he opened the book and laid it across the mountain moss, an unsteady purchase, but fragrant. He bowed his head to the sacrament, then looked up to read. Rosary bead poems. To his sister. He bowed his head again, looked up again to read to her. The letters on the page were blurred, his tongue laden exhausted paralytic, refusing to wrap around the pungent words of lament and adoration. He had to slow down, dilate the liturgy, become a lover of slow reading, one word at a time. A man who has stuffed his gob at supper slobbers over his story. The tang, the zest, burnt his eyes and blessed his palate. One mouthful of word at a time: *Gott . . . Lider . . . Sterne . . . Karfreitags-kind . . . .* Afterwards she confessed that she had never heard poetry quite like that before.

In the way that a *woman* is the *supremely visible* means of nourishment, constituting the *transition from body to soul—* so the genitals are the supreme *external* organs that constitute the transition from the visible to the invisible organs. (/) The *gaze*—speech—*holding hands—the kiss—touching the breasts—reaching down to the genitals*—the act of embrace: these are all rungs on the ladder down which the soul climbs. Facing it is a ladder up which the body clambers—to the heights of the embrace. *Premonition—sniffing out the scent—the act.* Preparing the soul and the body for the awakening of the sex drive. (/) Soul and body *touch one another* in the act. Chemically or galvanically or electrically—or *ardently*—the soul eats the body (and digests it?) instantaneously; the body conceives the soul (and gives birth to it?) instantaneously. (Novalis, 497)

It is not, as Freud would have it, the most common form of degradation in love life. It is the opportunity, for an instant or a fragment of a day, to pilot a great shuddering ship. Not with mastery, not with a license. But the chance to see what so many deny ever sets sail under the tattered flag of *pleasure*. Poor, war-torn word! To see it and to hear it. The head turning abruptly to the side, a convulsive movement of the whole body fixed in place, a gasp, and one's own name spoken as though for the first time, spoken in a way that was never spoken before, not even when a proud mother and father bent over the crib and pronounced the name tenderly through all its syllables, as though the suckling infant would already know it, were already learning it. However, the learning is postponed for years and decades, awaiting the voice of a lover who no longer looks down to see the reader of poems, but, head and eyes averted, bestows the name. Eve in Paradise, bestrewing Adam with flowers and a name. Or this same Eve on the turbulent sea, well outside of Paradise, looking to the horizon, no longer even mindful of the pilot's mouthful:

> Eating is but an accentuated living. Eating, drinking, and breathing correspond to the threefold division in the body into things firm, things fluid, and things airy. The entire body breathes—the lips alone eat and drink—they are precisely the organ that articulates in manifold tones what spirit has prepared, what it has received by means of the other senses. The lips are so important for sociality; how very much they deserve the kiss. Every soft and gentle elevation is symbolic of the wish to be touched. Thus nature invites us all, elegantly and modestly, to partake in enjoyment—and thus the whole of nature must be female, virgin and mother at once. (Novalis, 407)

Virgin and mother, or both or neither, or somewhere in between, or above and beyond them all.

⟨◇⟩⟨◇⟩⟨◇⟩

People sandwiches. On the seashore. MMR. Because of the sand which is there. The outrageous smell of fish. Outrageous because the source of lifedeath. People sandwiches. "Theory of Voluptuosity. (/) *It is amor* that presses us together. At the basis of all the functions we have been thinking about [dancing, eating, speaking, etc.], there lies voluptuosity *(sympathy)*" (Novalis, 666).

Who will write the great poem of trimethylamine? Who will dream the dream that replies to the dream of Irma's injection, putting an end to all stuttering and anxiety? The poem will draw us back to the sea, to which the metaphysical professor is inevitably drawn. We shall dive in, headlong headfirst, and put our mouth where our money is. To the thalassal regressive tug, we shall pay more than lip service.[4] Not with a cessation of consciousness, but with an enhanced awareness and alertness. Our great danger is not contamination but desiccation. Anaximander's "thorny fish" now stranded, wall-eyed, hearing only faintly the sound of pebbles receding on the shore, sensing its own decomposition and outrageous fragrance, the outrageous promise of it own body. For the moment, and perhaps for decades hence, anxious about contagion, we prefer to be walruses ("Goo goo g' joob . . .") and seals, suffering a "geotropic" regressive tug, instead. We live in memory of cataclysm, catastrophe, impending shipwreck. We shun the sea. Life is killing us. "*Life* in general is the properly absolute *Menstruum universale*— and the universal means of *cohesion*. There are infinitely many kinds of life. Every organ is *excrement* or the *product* of *life*" (Novalis, 514–15).

If the poem should involve "the age-old intimate connection between the genital impulse and intellectuality,"[5] then let us put our minds to it. Circumscribe my lips, circumscribe my heart, circumscribe my entire face:

> Our lips often show great similarity to the two will-o'-the-wisps in fairytales. The eyes are the higher pair of siblings to the lips. They close and open a holier grotto than the mouth. The ears are the serpent that hungrily swallows whatever the will-o'-the-wisps let fall. Mouth and eyes have a similar form. The lashes are the lips. The eyeball is the tongue and the gums, the pupil is the gorge. (/) The nose is the mouth's brow, and the brow is the nose of the eyes. Each eye has a cheekbone as its chin. (Novalis, 557)

If mouth and eye have a similar form, let my mouth look into the face of Medusa, lip to lip. MMR. Fra Lippo Lippi. When I was a child, I trembled as a child. Now than I am a man, I tremble as a man. When I was Empedocles—bird, bush, boy, and girl in one— I wept because the gods had flown. Now that I am Hölderlin, Novalis, and Nietzsche, I seek communion wherever I may find it. "Speaking and hearing is fecundation and conception. . . . *The Last Supper*. A shared eating and drinking is a kind of *unification*, an act of generation" (Novalis, 506).

Molluscular mussel, muscular and fine, with more gates and doors and portals and curtains and veils and folds than the many-chambered nautilus, ruddy red to purple, fine-veined, bathed in mother-of-pearl, pearl-of-mother, most beautiful articulation: sing O Musaic musky mollusc mine. No, not mine, except by generous invitation. Printed with the kind permission of. Patent applied for but not likely to be granted.

The mollusc. A mouth that sticks out its tongue but never to sneer "Nyaaaah!" It whispers lightly and sometimes laughs like a fish or an eel coming out of its cave or an eye out of slumber. All the fragility and all the muscle of the world gather here: not the death grip but the life grip, she said, or maybe the lifedeath grip: what Novalis would have called the wisdom, the Sophie, of the concept. Fragility, but not a wound, not a lesion. Like the inside of the cheek, mucous, do not bite it in your anxious hunger, do not damage what time and the moon took almost forever to weave.

And if home seems uncanny, be grateful all your life for all of life, and if you are tongue-tied in the face of life, that is to be expected, no shame in that, never read with your mouth full anyway (Emily Post) except perhaps on this one very rare occasion, always too rare, always privileged, of joy.

One could write a cook book, *The Joy of Eating Out*, doubling as a restaurant guide, three-stars, explaining all the transpositions of this singular being:

The mollusc is the mouth of the thigh, if the thigh is the gorge of the torso, the knee the dimpled chin, the calf the nape of the neck, the foot the five-nippled breast whereon I rest my case.

Let the others go agape for ἀγάπη. You go for grace. The upward curving, gentle elevation, the invitation. And no more turn aside and brood. Let there be meals on wheels out on the town, let there be underground gourmets, let there be laughter in church, and secret touches, genuine touches.

"Genuine touches are mutual excitations" (Novalis, 577).

Notes

1. I cite the Kritische-Studienausgabe (KSA) of Nietzsche's works throughout; the KSA is edited by Giorgio Colli and Mazzino Montinari (Berlin and Munich: de Gruyter and Deutscher Taschenbuch Verlag, 1980), and is cited by volume and page in the body of my text.

2. Throughout I cite Novalis, *Werke, Tagebücher und Briefe*, 3 vols., eds. Hans-Joachim Mähl and Richard Samuel (Munich: Carl Hanser, 1978), vol. 2, *Das philosophisch-theoretische Werk*, by page number in the body of my text.

3. Georg Trakl, *Dichtungen und Briefe*, eds. Walther Killy and Hans Szklenar (Salzburg: Otto Müller Verlag, 1969), p. 182.

4. Sándor Ferenczi, "Versuch einer Genitaltheorie" (1924), in *Schriften zur Psychoanalyse*, 2 vols. (Frankfurt am Main: Fischer, 1972), 2, 317–400; English translation by Henry Alden Bunker, *Thalassa: A Theory of Genitality* (New York: W. W. Norton, 1968), passim.

5. Ferenczi, 2, 379; English, 71.

Chapter 5

Only Food

Marianna Beck

She finished licking the last of the béchamel sauce from his armpit and looked at him, sadly. In his horned rimmed glasses and thick uncombed hair sticking up in large kinetic clumps—no doubt a result of his chef's hat—he reminded her of crazed-looking James Joyce. She moved to cradle his head, pulling him closer to kiss all the large parts of his face—his jutting brow, his Aquiline nose gone German, his Dudley-Do-Right chin. Ursula was about to tell him it was curtains, *finita la musica*. Since hiring him as her sous chef six months before, she had put on twenty-seven pounds.

The problem was food, naturally; specifically *his* food. He kept insisting she eat it, lick it, nibble it—off his body. She ate knowing he was bad for her.

"Here, my ramekin," he'd order, "lick this!" And he'd drop his white pants, invariably covered in flour so that a small cloud of white dust enveloped him, giving the illusion that he was some sort of genie rising out of the white-tiled kitchen floor. He would pour some delicious elixir from a small silver pipkin over his penis and well, it was difficult to deny him.

Ursula didn't necessarily want to give up the wild, and at-times capillary-bursting sex, but she faced two dilemmas. As owner of a small restaurant in the Village currently blessed by the trendy, she feared looking like the Venus of Willendorf in relation to the fashionable, stick bodies who swallowed fistfuls of antioxidants for breakfast and fasted until dinner. Secondly, she needed to make a living. She was dependent upon Wolfie. His culinary genius had catapulted her restaurant from a little known bistro to "a gastronomic nirvana," where one critic wafted: "it's manna for Everyman!" Unfortunately, in order for Wolfie to both create *and* rise to the occasion, as it were, he demanded some sort of oral approval from Ursula.

He forced her to repeat the little gratified noises she made everytime she sampled his cuisine, her tongue swirling in and out of any number of crevices. "Do you think it needs more saffron?" he'd suddenly ask about the sauce he'd slowly poured in a thin stream from his chest to his now slowly rising baguette. Ursula lapped ceremoniously, then stopped. "I really can't taste the saffron. It's something more subtle, more aromatic. Did you add basil my concubone?" He grew more excited. "Of course! Yes! Yes? And what else? Can you guess?" After three or four more such exchanges, he grew as hard as a marble rolling pin and she straddled him for the roiling romp that inevitably followed these culinary forays.

For her birthday, he actually wore a *schwartzwälderkirschtorte.* Ursula had just closed the restaurant and gone to switch on the alarm system when she found him in the nearly dark kitchen, reclining on one of the prep tables, a miniature cake impaled on his penis *complete with candles.* Nobody had ever done anything like this for her before.

"Now, come here and blow them out and tell me if there's too much kirsch," he commanded. How could Ursula resist such attentions? Despite her fatigue and the late hour, she found herself moistening at the prospect of taking her first, tentative nibble. Her nipples hardened in the wet, warm, air blowing from the three nearby dishwashers.

"I thought about a pistachio soufflé, but then changed my mind," he whispered. Ursula bent over him to make a wish and blew out the candles. He took her hand and drew her closer. "Or would you have wanted a delicate crème anglaise. Or perhaps a penuche icing instead?"

"No, my sweet, it would have fought the cherry taste. This is perfection," she said, pulling out the candles and allowing the aroma of chocolate and cherry to permeate her nostrils. From what she remembered now, she ate until she found the tip of his penis; shiny, taut and ready to be sprung from its gooey prison. It was the first time Ursula remembered eating an entire cake. She wasn't sure whether she'd enjoyed it because it was good or because she suffered from false consciousness.

But now, six months later with her triglycerides at an all time high, enough was enough. No more scurrying her tongue over his well-defined gluteals and down his crack in search of that last little taste of clarified curry butter. Or lapping the remains of babas au rhum from behind his knees. Or foraging for the lobster rumaki he claimed to have buried inside his tiny Calvins.

Ursula needed to find a way to loosen his gustatory grip and stop feeling harassed by food. *His* idea of food. She stroked her puffy mons, contemplating a bleak return to boiled chicken breasts. With her thighs around his neck, she watched him gazing at her lips just inches away, close enough so that he could see through the tufts of her red-tinged bush, and observe the changes in color of her lips—from dark brown at the edges to that lighter, pinkier hue they took on when excitement forced them to part all on their own. She knew he was as intoxicated by her aroma as he was by certain Chinese restaurants. A delicate sweet and sour piquancy found its way to his nose and made his eyes water.

"Wolfie," she began, "I've been thinking about the menu. We should spice it up—add some Thai and Szechuan dishes. We could start out with that dish called Tiger Cries." She had suddenly remembered reading how cayenne purifies the blood and removes toxins. If she adopted a diet high in capsicum, telling him she needed peppers to stimulate her metabolism, he might relent. Perhaps the thought of a peppery epiphany in his tenderer parts would send him in search of occluding some other woman's arteries.

Wolfie traced the outline of her burgeoning belly and sighed the way he always did when Ursula contemplated a change in major food groups. "Maybe I should just go back to reading porn," he said, his voice as thin as phyllo dough.

Chapter 6

The Careers of Chefs

Priscilla Parkhurst Ferguson and Sharon Zukin

The past twenty-five years in the United States have seen enormous investment in the food business. Reacting, no doubt, to the industrialization of food production and the depersonalization of comprehensive food delivery systems, American consumers have rediscovered the elemental delights of fresh, varied cooked-to-order dishes. Although health factors—nutrition and pollution—frequently influence individual selection or avoidance of specific foods, social and cultural processes account for most of the prominence of the contemporary culinary field. If the basic fodder of human existence has long served as a marker of social identity and social status, consumption of foodstuffs has acquired in recent years an exceptional presence in American society.

To a great extent this promotion of food is connected to eating outside the home. The rise of the restaurant industry during the 1980s reflects not only an enormous growth in the mass market for standardized food, but also a new focus on an individualized experience of "fine dining" in comfortable, even luxurious, surroundings. The theatricality of food presentation in these spaces of consumption is a self-conscious production of the waiters and the chefs, with the willing collaboration of customers who, it is said, subordinate their true social identity to roles scripted by the restaurant.[1] Even in France, where classical high-status Western cuisine developed, restaurants are attracting scholarly interest because of a new social, economic, and ideological significance.[2]

While self-consciously "gastronomic" restaurants in Paris embody "the spirit . . . of young restaurateurs who are conscious of their social, economic, and cultural role," they also provide a launching pad for a star system of new French chefs who are no longer crafts "workers," or even "artists," in a time-honored production system, but media stars.[3] This " 'creative' dimension is so exacerbated today that we have entered a period of chefs as 'show business stars' or 'haute-couture' [designers], professions that offer striking parallels."[4] To a great extent, the stardom of chefs is related to an explosive expansion of "lifestyle" media and other "critical infrastructure" that disseminate, evaluate, and compare experiences of cultural consumption.[5] But chefs, and the restaurants to which they supply objects of desire, have also become investment objects in their own right. An entertainment management agency in Beverly Hills, California, recently added chefs to its more usual clientele of rock stars.[6]

Several factors contribute to the celebrity status of chefs in both France and the United States. From television and daily newspapers to travel, fashion, and other specialized magazines, the visibility of chefs and their cuisines in the mass media highlights the importance of consumption in representations of society and place. The glorification of individual chefs supports the heavy capital investment required by new restaurants. By stressing differentiation among cultural producers, it also legitimates a newly prominent cultural field. Chefs, especially those who own their restaurants, appreciate and often actively cultivate publicity to gain a competitive advantage. For their part, consumers more readily understand restaurants as social and cultural markers if they can associate them with "signature" styles of individual chefs.

Chefs' stardom also has clear connections with the self-conscious artistry of *nouvelle cuisine,* itself a beneficiary of a long-standing association of *haute cuisine* with art. The culinary mode that came to be known as *nouvelle cuisine* emerged in France in the 1960s in opposition to many of the precepts and practices of classical French cuisine. Developed at first by a young generation of chefs with roots in the provinces, *nouvelle cuisine* eventually became the basis of the culinary strategies of most ambitious chefs in France. By the mid-1970s, such highly rated chef-owners as Paul Bocuse (in Lyons), Roger Vergé (in Mougins), and the Troisgros brothers (in Roanne) had risen to the top of their profession. Often ridiculed for its pretentiousness and theatrical presentations—"the trendy affectations, the small portions, the big plates, and the even bigger bills"—*nouvelle cuisine* appealed to a well traveled, sophisticated, often health-conscious consumers intrigued by combinations of ingredients and techniques ordinarily found in separate and distinct culinary hierarchies.[7]

Nouvelle cuisine chefs blended new and old styles, exotic and commonplace ingredients, familiar and foreign cuisines. They emphasized a richness of taste derived from the freshest ingredients. They also introduced a modern wittiness about food, a new smartness that carried over to the restaurant. They were, in their way, a conceptualist avantgarde; one often went to their restaurants to enjoy "the shock of the new."

During the 1980s, *nouvelle cuisine*—sometimes called *nouvelle American cuisine*—became the established model for "designer" chefs in the United States. In contrast to France, the sources of the new culinary strategies were diverse. On the one hand, there was a new, somewhat generational awareness of the importance of good food, especially fresh food, organically grown ingredients, and native American products. On the other hand, new American chefs increasingly traveled to Europe for exposure to fine cooking and coveted ingredients. In the restaurants of *nouvelle cuisine* chefs in France, they found inspiration and work experience. Alice Waters, chef-owner of Chez Panisse in Berkeley, California, and Larry Forgione, chef-owner of An American Place in New York City, belong to that generation of American chefs who both found and founded a *nouvelle cuisine* in the late 1970s and early 1980s.

From that time, *nouvelle cuisine* has been distinguished by a rigorous, even fanatical, concern for seasonal ingredients, often especially grown for the chef, and light "natural" preparations. Steamed fish and vegetables take precedence over meat roasts or stews, while light natural juices, extending to "bouillons" and "infusions," supplant heavy, starch-thickened gravies and sauces. The purity of products and stress on freshness reflect not only a changed relation between cuisine and nature, but also a shift in the status of the chef. The new chef has "ethics" as well as technique and "respects" the ingredients.[8] *Nouvelle cuisine* resolves the old conundrum about whether the chef is an artist or a worker in favor of creative vision.[9] To the extent that economic recession has given financial and psychological impetus to a return to the simpler cooking strategies and stick-to-the-ribs dishes of *bistro* cuisine, the most inventive chefs continue to emphasize such elements of *nouvelle cuisine* as seasonality, combinations of unusual ingredients and culinary hierarchies (e.g., "peasant fare and *haute cuisine"*), and individual signature dishes.

To be sure, culinary creativity is a luxury enjoyed by only a small percentage of those who cook for a living. And the exercise of that creativity is necessarily limited by the preferences of customers, the budgets of restaurant owners, and the constraints of time. Nevertheless, at the top level of the occupation, among those chefs who aspire to invent dishes or claim to work in the tradition of a specific cuisine, artistry is sought and prized.[10]

Until recently, American-born chefs were not considered artists capable of producing a real *cuisine.* But with the rise of elegant, expensive restaurants all over the United States—featuring a self-described "American" cuisine—the very definition of an American chef has changed. From untutored "savages" who didn't know how to eat, let alone produce good food, American chefs have carved a place for themselves at the center of culinary innovation. Their careers reflect the Americanization of *nouvelle cuisine,* as well as the diverse social and economic sources of its institutionalization. In contrast to French-born chefs, who come from working-class and lower-middle-class backgrounds and apprentice their way into the center of the profession, American chefs increasingly come from the middle class and learn to eat by traveling in Europe before they learn to cook. Moreover, Americans who have become chefs since 1970 often choose this career to resist the routinization of white-collar occupations. Despite these specific American conditions, it is interesting that the careers of excellent French chefs have opened up to include work outside France, especially in the United States. Relations between French and American chefs, and French and American cuisine, are no longer characterized by "otherness." Instead, like culinary products, the careers of chefs suggest the emergence of a global profession.

Questions about the culinary field of cuisine (and a shared interest in good eating) led us, in 1991, to a series of thirty intensive interviews with twelve chefs and sous chefs, nine chef-owners, and nine owners of twenty-six well-known, high-status restaurants in Manhattan. Our respondents are, by and large, at the center of the dominant culinary world in New York City. New York is, in turn, arguably the culinary capital of the United States. At any rate, New York restaurants mediate between the old culinary hegemony of Europe and the new ingredients and preparations carried from Asia, the West Coast, and the Southwest.[11]

The "French" Chef

That only five of the twenty-one chefs and chef-owners in our study are French-born indicates a significant shift in the recruitment of chefs in the Manhattan culinary world. This shift in turn points to a host of changes in both the French and the American culinary landscapes. Indeed, the four younger French chefs in our study—all in their 30s—owe the opportunities for their creativity and mobility to those changes. Nevertheless, all five of our French respondents share the patterns of family and social class recruitment and specialized training that make up the traditional "French" model.

Until the 1980s, the production of high-class restaurant cuisine in the United States was dominated by French chefs. These chefs were usually French by birth and invariably by training, culinary sensibility, and practice. They were male, had worked in restaurant kitchens in France from an early age, and had followed the importing of French *haute cuisine* to New York by the French pavilion at the 1939 World's Fair.[12] From the 1940s to the 1960s, a handful of these chefs headed the kitchens in a small number of high-quality, high-price restaurants, including grand hotel restaurants in New York specializing in representations of French *haute cuisine.* Others founded and worked in two kinds of restaurants: those presenting medium-price, generic French cuisine (known in France as *cuisine bourgeoise* and now identified in the United States, to some extent, as "bistro food"), and those offering the hybrid, medium-to-high-price elegance of "Continental" cuisine. Neither chefs nor diners paid anything more than minimal attention to local and regional variations and accepted the necessary reliance upon American ingredients and preferences. It followed that, as several of our respondents pointed out, no one who ate in, or read about, these top restaurants during this time had any reason to know the chefs' names. French chefs of New York restaurants were definitely not stars.[13]

The route taken by a French chef typically begins with family contacts in the restaurant business, usually a modest local restaurant. A father or uncle owns a small, roadside cafe or provincial restaurant; a cousin knows the local restaurant owner. In either case, the chef starts his career around the age of 14, as soon as he finishes compulsory primary schooling. This is as true for our younger respondents as for the senior chef-owner. These French chefs all come from lower-middle-class, provincial milieux. Their fathers are artisans, restaurateurs, fishers, or farmers. As one chef puts it, there was "nothing glorious" about food. Being a chef represents a certain, but not necessarily dramatic, step up the social ladder.

Related to this matter-of-fact, early choice of a career, French chefs minimize their initial attachment to food for aesthetic or creative reasons. The oldest chef-owner whom we interviewed thought first about carpentry, but his brother became a carpenter so he switched to cooking. Another chef-owner whose innovative cuisine enabled him to take the unusual step of transplanting his restaurant from Paris to New York says that he became a chef "because of atavism." He wasn't interested in school, his father operated a small restaurant during the summers, and he was "caught up in the system." The chef at one of New York's best and most elegant restaurants was born on a farm near Lyons where *"la cuisine* was very important. . . . And outdoor work didn't interest me particularly, that's what gave me a taste for the kitchen." Another chef, whose rapid celebrity in a job in New York enabled him to find investors to open his own successful restaurant earned pocket money by helping out in his uncle's restaurant. "I liked it, but I said to myself, I would rather make the presentations [in the kitchen] than carry out the dishes."

French chefs abandon any thought of higher education for apprenticeship in the kitchen. They all describe the apprentice's life as one of Orwellian endurance—the Orwell of *Down and Out in Paris and London.* A 32-year-old chef reports that he started out in 1973 earning 50 francs [$10] a month, rose to 100 francs the second year, and 250 francs the third: "No one wants to start out like that any more. . . . Now people come straight out of school." The conventional career ladder is, nonetheless, based equally on kitchen experience and state certification. The oldest chef-owner in our study passed his examination for a *Certificat d'aptitude professionnel* (CAP) in order to assume the position of *commis* (assistant chef) in a Paris restaurant. The youngest chef-owner is exceptional because he started his first apprenticeship at the ripe age of 18, after having passed his BEPC (*Brevêt d'Études du Premier Cycle,* roughly a high school diploma), and he emphasizes that he abandoned his studies. While there are schools for professional chefs in France—in contrast to Italy, where budding restaurateurs and hoteliers typically attend hotel school—the chefs in our study did not attend them.[14]

Primarily, a chef's career demands hard work and more hard work. The first apprenticeship is followed by several others as a would-be chef learns the tasks and skills of all the kitchen stations. Moving around from kitchen to kitchen allows the young chef to move up the career ladder in prescribed stages: from *garde-manger* (cold preparations) to fish, sauces, roasts, *sous chef,* and head of a section *(chef de parti).* (Pastry is often a separate circuit). A more ambitious young chef also tries to learn different things from the chefs whose kitchens he passes through: style of presentation from one chef, organizational skills from another. While French chefs occasionally refer to recipe books—that they sometimes compile themselves from notes taken in kitchens where they have worked— they rely even more on oral precepts refined in conversation, passed on in practice, and subject to constant experimentation.[15]

For those who eventually become great French chefs themselves, the move to the center of the profession begins at the end of the first, formal apprenticeship. The older chef-owner leaped out of the provinces—first to Switzerland, and then to Paris. Not only does this show the importance, until the 1970s, of a shift to Paris, it also indicates the status that was attached, in those days, to the state-licensed examination, for this chef made the geographical leap on the basis of getting first place in the CAP exam for his region. By contrast, the younger French chefs who completed their first apprenticeships in the 1970s went on to more advanced apprenticeships in the kitchens of the most prestigious chef-owners. Thus they very quickly entered a powerful culinary world. Most of these chefs are in the provinces rather than Paris, part of a major change in the geography of French cuisine related to *nouvelle cuisine* and automobile tourism in regions off the beaten track. By doing well in their first apprenticeships and having some connection, sometimes through their first employer, to a great chef, they got the sponsorship of such restaurateurs as Roger Vergé in Mougins (the chef mentioned most as a mentor by American as well as French respondents and one of the chefs signed by the Beverly Hills management company in 1992), Paul Bocuse in Lyons, and Michel Guérard, who moved his high-class kitchen from a working-class suburb of Paris to the southwest of France. The waiting list for apprenticeships in these kitchens suggests the value attached to such sponsors. One of our French chefs did a three-year apprenticeship in the region where his father owned a bar-brasserie while waiting for an apprentice's slot to open up at the restaurant owned by the Troisgros brothers. Another apprenticed for two years in a two-star restaurant while waiting for a position at another three-star establishment. (Three stars is the highest ranking of the bible of French gastronomes, the *Guide Michelin.*)

The great chefs' superior artistry or knowledge is only one resource potentially available to the young chefs who work in their kitchen. They also enter a social network, a "mafia," as the French chefs say, that is good for a lifetime of job contacts. "I never had to write a letter to apply for a job," says the 32-year-old chef-owner who worked in two major French kitchens, Germany, Thailand, and Hong Kong before coming to the United States. As the younger generation of chefs moves about the world wherever their sponsors recommend them, they export French cuisine, as French chefs have done since the eighteenth century, but they now pay attention to local, especially Asian, cuisines and produce, which they incorporate into their repertoire.

The chefs who eventually enjoy spectacular success are a very small proportion of those who apprentice in three-star kitchens. Somehow, some chefs become conscious of the ambition to develop a personal style. As they work under great chefs, they articulate their own culinary sensibility. Suddenly there is an "explosion": "Arriving in a place like that, you are motivated, there are great things going on." What happens to their peers? They may opt for less pressure, preferring at that stage to work in a less competitive kitchen, perhaps opening a small restaurant in an out-of-the-way town or remaining in a subordinate position in a large kitchen. Ambitious young chefs, however, take full advantage of the central circuit. In recent years, this may not mean a move to Paris so much as a job in a hotel kitchen in a business capital of Asia or Africa, a major French restaurant in a European country outside France (our respondents mentioned Copenhagen, Munich, and London), an embassy kitchen in Washington, D.C., or even a French-owned restaurant in California. Work sites that once would have been considered purgatory are now steppingstones in a global career. This mobility also demonstrates the global reach of the "French" model of chefs' careers. However, it suggests, in turn, a certain denationalization of the French culinary world.

The move from France to New York occurs in different ways. A generational difference reflects the enlargement of the circuit of French chefs and the increase in outlets for French culinary strategies. Until the 1980s, French chefs were recruited directly from Paris by the few New York restaurateurs with large culinary ambitions and broad contacts. These restaurant owners, themselves Europeans by birth, may have heard of a promising young French chef and gone incognito to Paris to taste his cuisine. This was the case with our oldest chef-owner, who in his turn became a patron to a number of young French chefs who were willing to come to

New York. Over the years, social networks became even more important in recruiting French chefs to New York. In the early 1970s, when an owner in our study opened his restaurant, he went into partnership with an older French chef from one of the best restaurants in New York. When that chef retired in the late 1970s, the co-owner who was not a chef sought the advice of another very respected French chef-owner in New York (who happens to be our oldest chef-owner). This man proposed a younger French chef who had recently worked in New York, where he received the highest, four-star rating from the *New York Times*. Because the younger chef had already returned to France, the owner went overseas to see him and lured him back to New York with a high salary. When that chef moved on, he recommended the next French chef, already working in New York, who is also in our study.[16]

While the move to New York has tended to signify exclusion from the controlling French culinary world *in France,* there are indications that this is changing. In 1968 our oldest chef-owner was the first French chef working outside France to win the prestigious title of *Meilleur ouvrier de France* (MOF) in the rigorous national competition, or "cook-off," held every year in Paris. This validation in turn encouraged other French chefs with culinary rather than financial ambitions to come to New York. This same chef-owner subsequently encouraged his pastry chef to compete for the MOF, and he also won the title. (This pastry chef eventually opened his own pastry shop in New York.) Since the early 1970s, the great chefs of France have visited New York's best restaurants (as well as restaurants around the world). For French chefs now in their 30s, however, the move to New York may still preclude returning as an active chef to France. They know the market here too well, and contacts with suppliers, customers, and backers are not easy to reproduce. Even so, one of the chefs in his 30s that we interviewed hesitated a year before deciding to open a restaurant in New York rather than go back to France. That returning was a possibility at all suggests a new, geographical expansion of the French culinary world. In future, French chefs in France may well be more "American."

The "American" Chef

Even though the profession of chef in the United States is dominated by males of European origin, American chefs are more diverse than their French colleagues by gender, ethnicity, and social class background. Among the sixteen American chefs and chef-owners whom we interviewed are eleven men and five women. One of the women is a chef-owner, the other is an owner. Yet all levels, from chef-owner to sous chef, remain predominantly male.[17] We also interviewed an African American and an Asian chef, neither of whom went to cooking school or did a formal apprenticeship, and both of whom produce "French" cuisine. The absence of African Americans, Latinos, and Asians among top restaurateurs, chefs, and chef-owners in New York indicates a relative lack of access to capital and investors, as well as a very small presence in this culinary world.[18] Perhaps the greatest indication of openness, however, is the Italian *woman* who works as executive chef in a celebrated Italian restaurant in New York.[19]

With the exception of this and one other woman, who are older, nearly all the American chefs in our study (like most of the French chefs) are in their 30s. Their relative youth indicates the rapidity of restaurant and career mobility in the 1980s and the high demand for high-status chefs, even American chefs, who could make a representation of *haute cuisine*. All but three of the sixteen American chefs we interviewed work in, or own, restaurants that opened in the 1980s. Labor markets for chefs also follow immigration laws. In the 1930s, and again after 1965, changes in immigration laws restricted the entry of Europeans to the United States.

For Americans who began to work in restaurant kitchens in the 1970s and 1980s, the new visibility of chefs in France might have made the career of chef attractive. But the American chefs whom we interviewed emphasize that they were never drawn to the glamour of being a chef. Indeed, since many of them work 60 to 100 hours a week in highly competitive restaurants and spend most of that time in the kitchen, they deride the notion that being a chef is glamorous. Many of them entered the restaurant industry simply because the industry itself was expanding. As high school or college students, they may have had a first job in an uncle's catering business or a hash house, or selling fish, or even at a McDonald's. Once they were working in the restaurant industry, they either realized they had an aptitude for cooking or found that they were attracted to the taste of "real" food prepared by a senior chef.

Along with this mode of recruitment, a large number of American chefs who entered the profession in the late 1970s and 1980s came straight from college or graduate school, usually before completing a degree. Drawn to food as a cultural medium, these men and women generally knew little or nothing about *nouvelle cuisine.* They rebelled, not against a highly sophisticated and complex culinary code but rather against the standardized, bland tastes of mid-century American cooking.[20] What they knew about French cuisine, or learned during a trip to France, was that, to the French, it represented a way of life. However, the preparations that emphasized fresh ingredients, color, and placement on the plate—hallmarks of *nouvelle cuisine*—also tasted good.

The career trajectories are surprisingly similar in their variation. In contrast to the French chefs who tended to have family connections with the restaurant world, virtually all of our American chefs voiced a sense of discovery of a new world altogether. An American chef in her 30s, for example, says that she became a chef because she "was studying nutrition and decided I didn't want a job behind a desk." A more intellectual approach to food, joined by a desire for an active work life, is expressed by a chef-owner, who wanted "a balance between intellectual and physical activity." Another chef-owner left graduate work in anthropology, having done field work overseas. She speaks of being "drawn" to the food through which her foreign hosts shared their culture. She loved "tasting different things, watching people cook. . . . Then just as I started working in the [culinary] field a little bit, I was swept away." Another sous chef drifted into the profession via a vocational high school and jobs in a few bakeries, then the School of Visual Arts for film. Cooking was limited to work at summer camp. Then, after leaving school, he got a job at a highly-rated "French" restaurant (where he still works), and after a few months realized he wanted to be a chef.

Several American chefs felt comfortable with food preparation because of their family background and ethnic cooking traditions: Italian, French, or Jewish. A chef who eventually became the first American to head the kitchen in a well-established, high-class French restaurant in New York notes that growing up in a large Italian family, he was always involved with the women. "There was no such thing as an event without eating and preparing food. I felt comfortable with that." Even so, he attended college for two years, working in neighborhood coffee shops or diners. Until he worked at a Manhattan cafe he did not even think about a career as a chef: "It was the first time I really cooked in a restaurant. . . . I was still geared to college but wasn't enjoying college any more. . . . I liked working with my hands." A chef-owner celebrated for his culinary innovations speaks fondly of his French grandparents' cooking and eating style, but "cooking was never something I decided to do; rather, it was a means of developing some cash." He graduated from college with a degree in business and decided to travel. "I started to move around." He went to Paris where he studied French and took classes in photography and painting. Because he wanted to stay longer he started to work in a bistro. And there, food was really *la cuisine.* "The business there was so much more civilized, for everything the standards were much higher, there was a lot more joy and satisfaction from it. Everyone supported it, the clientele was very serious, and the growers; the whole environment was very rich."

While a growing interest in food led a small number of our American chefs to cooking school, most of them took other paths to permanent work in the kitchen. Some traveled, eating as they went and studying informally, mostly by reading culinary literature. Others sought apprenticeships with great French chefs in Europe—the first generation of Americans to do so. A very few—mostly women, the African American, and the Asian—worked through unpaid and low-paid apprenticeships in the United States, confirming the entry barriers in the profession, especially in France.

Thus in contrast to the French chefs in our study, American chefs take a variety of paths into the profession. The small number of great American restaurants in which they could have trained, including the great "French" restaurants that would not hire them, precluded a "French" apprenticeship. Although American professional cooking schools have expanded rapidly over the past ten years, graduates of these schools are not necessarily preferred candidates for jobs in the kitchen. Even chefs in our study who themselves graduated from cooking school criticize new graduates' inflated job expectations and lack of willingness to take direction: there is no substitute for training in the high pressure conditions of a working kitchen.

Further, all the American chefs speak to the importance of *eating* as a means of learning about cuisine. This is especially important for Americans not raised in the codified practices of French cuisine and not familiar with the tastes of fresh products. We thus encounter a reason for continued French, as opposed to "French," culinary authority. While basic "French" culinary techniques and repertory can be learned in any very good kitchen, only in France do these practices fit within a larger cultural context that values food.

It is just this valorization of food that a small number of the American chefs appreciated in certain classic books on food by such authors as M. F. K. Fisher, Richard Olney, and Madeleine Kammen. In these works the chefs did not look for recipes but rather for the literary evocation of a culinary sensibility. (One, who had himself worked in a Paris hotel kitchen, even cited Orwell's *Down and Out in Paris and London* as a rather frightening negative model.) More generally, especially for American chefs with some higher education, food writing reinforces what one chef called "the artistry that is for me the spiritual side [of cooking]."

Like the French chefs, the Americans are influenced by chefs whom they work with. But while younger chefs of both groups emphasize innovation, more Americans claim to be self-taught. For obvious reasons, the Americans who lack formal apprenticeships, and thus long socialization, rely most on personal inspiration—or pay the least attention to the strictures of traditional cuisine. Thus all the women, and a number of the men, say they strive to produce an idiosyncratic cuisine. One chef declined to specify influences at all: "It is not so much who [influenced me]. It is a style I developed through working in different restaurants and figuring out what I liked and disliked about them." She like most of the others makes a point of trying out new cuisines and visiting new restaurants in New York.

Two of our American chefs confirm the significance of *nouvelle cuisine* in expanding culinary horizons and developing culinary ambitions. After graduating from the Culinary Institute of America (CIA) in the 1970s, one chef who is now part owner of his own highly successful restaurant got his first job at La Côte Basque, which had just been completely renovated by its new French chef-owner, Jean-Jacques Rachou (who is still the chef-owner). It was Rachou who more or less introduced *nouvelle cuisine* to America, and his kitchen was an exciting place to be. The American chefs who worked for him learned a culinary mode that was strikingly different from the usual fare: "[Rachou] had a good philosophy of food in that era. It was very vibrant, presentation-orientation, deeply based on classical cooking, very flamboyant in colors and plates. . . . It was the state of the art. It was something no one else was doing at that scale." Although he now considers this " 'art on a plate' . . . stupid," it was an important influence at the time. This chef also made three brief working trips to restaurants in France, which in the 1970s was still unusual for Americans. Another

American chef, who has owned his own restaurant in New York since the early 1980s, also graduated from CIA in the 1970s. He wrote to a French chef in Europe for an apprenticeship and stayed with the chef more than two years.

Only two of our chefs actually held positions as chefs in Europe: one graduated from a vocational chefs' program at a technical college; the other had no cooking school education whatsoever. Both benefited from direct exposure to the work of great chefs and from access to the professional network of those chefs. The first chef was sent to work in a restaurant in Paris by a professor at the technical college. After he returned to New York, the professor convinced a Parisian restaurateur to hire him, along with several other Americans, for the kitchen of her new restaurant in New York. There the young chef met three-star French chef Michel Guérard, who was a consultant at the restaurant. Guérard brought him to work in his own restaurant-spa resort in southwestern France, then got him a job in Switzerland, where he stayed four years. He then returned to New York, where he was hired by an old-line, prestigious French restaurant, whose owner was related to the chef's first employers in Paris. This was the breakthrough to which we referred earlier: the first hiring of an American-born chef to run a New York French restaurant kitchen. But it depended entirely on breaking into the social networks of French chefs.

The other chef with long-term European experience made a more casual entry into the same career pattern. He never attended cooking school. When he went to study at the Sorbonne after college in the early 1970s, he began to work in a Parisian bistro. He took classes with the famous pastry chef Gaston Lenôtre, whom he met through a French pastry chef in America. After meeting the pastry chef of Roger Vergé at Lenôtre's, he worked with Vergé, then with Paul Bocuse, and then with Joël Robuchon in Paris (all then or subsequently three-star chefs). As the first American to work in Robuchon's kitchen, he also broke a professional barrier. Back in New York City, this chef worked under French chefs at such leading restaurants as Le Cirque and La Côte Basque, and was the first American chef hired at Le Périgord.

As one of the chefs with European training acknowledges, "There is still a good amount of worthwhile experience to be gained from working in Europe. It looks good on a resumé." He had, at the time of our interview, just arranged for one of his sous-chefs to train in one of the top French kitchens. We would say, then, that

French connections are likely to remain important in the culinary world of New York, both for the exposure to *haute cuisine* in a broad cultural context and for ties to professional networks.

Nevertheless, according to all our American respondents, training with an American chef now offers enormous credibility. A recommendation from a top American chef carries more weight in hiring than either cooking school or a French apprenticeship. Indeed, many of our chefs also rely on the sense they get from a would-be chef's presentation of self at an interview, a sense confirmed by a short trial period in the kitchen before hiring.

The fluidity of credentials, compared to the "French" model, is illustrated by a young American chef who was given an ownership share of his highly-rated restaurant shortly before our interview. He started his career in high school:

> In the country club my parents belonged to I started hanging around the kitchen and then I ran the snack bar. . . . I started busing tables in high school, and as soon as I graduated, I took a job in the kitchen. . . . I learned much of the French technique from books because the first restaurant I worked at was an American fish house. . . . I just picked up a few books and started teaching myself and knew there was something more. After four or five years, I took my first job in New York at The Quilted Giraffe [a pioneer avant-garde "French" restaurant run by an American chef-owner; it closed in 1993], and after about three months they brought me up to sous chef, at about twenty years old. It was quick.

Clearly this background formed his own hiring style:

> I hire people, I don't hire resumés. I don't even ask for resumés. If someone comes to me and tells me they can cook, I ask them what they know, how long they have been doing it. But I am more interested in them as a person. The first thing I ask is, Can you come here and try *us* out for a day?

In contrast to French chefs, most American chefs hire by talking to potential employees as well as by personal recommendation. Several chefs mention the importance they place on an individual's feeling for food. Above creativity, all emphasize qualities of level-headedness and perseverance in the kitchen—precisely those qualities that are bred in the long years of a "French" apprenticeship.

The emphasis on culinary sensibility is strengthened, and perseverance is weakened, by the presence in American restaurant kitchens of men and women who have come to professional cooking relatively late, after careers in totally unrelated fields. The kitchen of the chef who started out as a kid in a country club offers a paradigm of the importance of career-change for American chefs:

> At one point I had three M.B.A.s downstairs.... Last Wednesday night, with seven people in the kitchen, there were no Culinary [Institute] graduates on staff. Sometimes there are lots. My two sous chefs are both culinary school graduates. My saucier is a Culinary grad. My night saucier has a degree in music and is one of the best cooks I have ever worked with.... Another guy was a lighting technician for a rock and roll group. Another guy worked for a company that did mechanized window displays. Then a couple of career cooks. Another guy who played football in college.... You wouldn't expect him to be cooking. He went to Cordon Bleu in Paris for a while.

We should add that the pastry chef trained in France.

Ironically, the American chef-owner who is most "French" in terms of his work in France prefers to hire career-change people: "I find it more interesting to work with someone who has compassion for food—they've been traveling, or they've been cooking at home—than to work with students who are out of school for a few years, who have no palate of food experiences.... [With] eclectic career change people ... the success is much faster because we already communicate." Yet the other chef with several years of job experience in Europe tends to hire cooking school graduates, probably because he went to cooking school. The four chefs who had a somewhat formal training period in France use their contacts to send their best American chefs for such training, thereby providing both continuous open recruitment into, and institutional reproduction of, the profession.

The originality of American chefs cannot be emphasized too much. Beginning in the 1970s, the first generation created their own business and professional networks, often beginning with suppliers who had no concept of letting tomatoes ripen on the vine or chickens run around in the barnyard. Younger chefs, who today shop at subsidized New York City greenmarkets where regional farmers bring their produce to consumers, benefit from the innovations of earlier connections between chefs and suppliers. Indeed, the chefs who started out in America in the 1970s slowly became aware of young chefs like themselves across the country: people who had read about culinary sensibility, or had grown to like good food, and beat the bushes to find suppliers of fresh, ripe, or French-quality domestic products. This generation of American chefs created their own "nouvelle cuisine" as they worked through the principles of traditional *haute cuisine* with American products, and American employees, for American customers who increasingly traveled to Europe. "When I was in Europe," says one chef-owner:

> I came back with the idea to enlighten American cooking, to change the reputation of American cooking on a worldwide scale. When I was in Europe . . . it was a joke that an American could cook in a French kitchen. It was all right that I started out as an apprentice, but I worked my way up all the way to chef saucier and was offered the sous chef job before I left. . . . The common understanding was that as an American, I didn't even know how to eat.

Some of this, of course, was true:

> I had worked in a couple of . . . really good places [in America], and I had never seen a fresh chanterelle . . . or some of the other things that were coming into [French] kitchens every day. . . . Why do the chefs in the United States use canned chanterelles from France rather than fresh chanterelles from the United States? It is because nobody bothered to set up a network to get people to pick them. . . . And that is where the twelve or fifteen chefs I'm talking about independently got frustrated with that system and started to go to individual suppliers.

During the first half of the 1980s, much like the earlier practitioners of *nouvelle cuisine* in France, these chefs were linked by coverage in the media. Gradually, they met each other by traveling to each other's restaurants and participating in culinary events, such as collectively produced dinners, to promote new products (e.g., local wines), to raise funds for charities, and to welcome visiting French chefs on their global tours.

The development of this professional network *after* chefs began to work out their individual approaches to cuisine contrasts sharply with the "French" model. Although they were born in, and opened or continued family restaurants in different regions, the French chefs who founded *nouvelle cuisine* had ties to professional networks from young adulthood. In the late 1980s, however, American chefs increasingly associated in professional and quasi-social organizations. A New York wine supplier formed a group of American chefs for a monthly tasting luncheon. These "Chefs from Hell" were eventually written up in the media (which influenced several members to drop out), and they invited their first women members (who are among the chefs in our sample). By this point, American chefs in New York began to dominate the high-class restaurant business. Investors sought them out when they began to shine in someone else's kitchen. Young French chefs and apprentices now applied to do a training period with these American chefs. That the son of three-star chef Paul Bocuse was studying at the Culinary Institute of America in 1991 is surely the ultimate sign of American culinary power.

By the same token, both the Americanization of French chefs and the institutionalization of American chefs have a lot to do with America's market power. They may have even more to do with Asia's economic power. Foreign travel to France, and dining in fine French restaurants, have been joined by a true global market for French cuisine. With globalization, this cuisine has lost its singular geographical context. "French" cuisine now connotes a classical method of preparation, an attention to detail, a uniformity of high standards though not of culinary products. Under these conditions, the training of chefs assumes even greater importance. The expansion of transnational apprenticeships, culinary academies, and culinary publications are important ways of incorporating the Other. In time, as our New York chefs foresee, the national referent—French or American cuisine—will be replaced by the individual identity of the chef or by a new term that has not yet been devised.

Notes

1. Joanne Finkelstein, *Dining Out* (New York: New York University Press, 1989).

2. Alain Huetz de Lemps and Jean-Robert Pitte, eds., *Les Restaurants dans le monde et à travers les âges* (Grenoble: éditions Glenat, 1990).

3. François Blanchon, "A Paris," in *Les Restaurants dans le monde*, p. 188.

4. Guy Chemla, "L'évolution récente des restaurants gastronomiques parisiens," in *Les Restaurants dans le monde*, p. 46.

5. See Sharon Zukin, *Landscapes of Power: From Detroit to Disney World* (Berkeley and Los Angeles: University of California Press, 1991), pp. 202–8, 214–15.

6. See Florence Fabricant, "The Man Who Would Turn Chefs Into Household Names," *New York Times*, March 17, 1993.

7. Claude Fischler, "The Michelin Galaxy: Nouvelle Cuisine, Three-Star Restaurants, and the Culinary Revolution," *Journal of Gastronomy* 6, no. 2 (Autumn 1990), p. 79.

8. Ibid., pp. 91–92.

9. See Gary Alan Fine, "The Culture of Production: Aesthetic Choices and Constraints in Culinary Work," *American Journal of Sociology* 97 (March 1992): 1268–94.

10. Yen Peterson and Laura D. Birg, "Top Hat: The Chef as Creative Occupation," *Free Inquiry in Creative Sociology* 16 (May 1988): 67–72.

11. On French culinary hegemony, see Stephen Mennell, *All Manners of Food* (Oxford: Blackwell, 1985). Our interviews were conducted with the assistance of Jennifer Parker. The 21 chefs whom we interviewed are constantly quoted and photographed in the media, are recognized innovators, and get the highest ratings in restaurant reviews. When one of our chefs left his job to open his own restaurant, the *New York Times* ran a news article about it.

12. See "Naissance de la gastronomie française aux États-Unis" [Interview with Pierre Franey], *France-Amérique*, April 11–17, 1992. Official recognition of the contributions of French chefs based in America took time. In 1992, the Legion of Honor was awarded to Roger Fessaguet, who had been a prominent chef in New York from the 1950s to the 1980s. One prominent French chef-owner prominently displays his award of the *Ordre du Mérite* in the bar of his restaurant.

13. Craig Claiborne, former food editor and restaurant reviewer for the *New York Times*, may have been the first writer to break this barrier, in 1964, when he wrote about "the professional bloodlines" linking a new, highly regarded French restaurant in Manhattan to others—but he traced these networks of chefs, captains, waiters, and owners through those who had worked for a single French restaurant owner, Henri Soulé. Craig Claiborne, "Le Mistral Is the Newest Offshoot of Pavillon Tree," *New York Times*, December 11, 1964. By 1993, a journalist could identify a network of American chefs. Trish Hall, "Family Tree Nurtures a New Generation of Chefs," *New York Times*, April 14, 1993.

14. There are signs that this is changing in France, given the increasing complexity of the restaurant business. Three-star chef Pierre Troisgros sent all three of his children to hotel school, so that the son who is now his partner (his brother Jean having died in 1983) started his actual cooking apprenticeship at the advanced age of 20. Interview, Annie Lorenzo. *Profession? Cuisinier-restaurateur* (Paris: Charles Massin 1985), pp. 48–52. Interestingly, Pierre Troisgros's father, the original owner of the inn at Roanne, strongly opposed hotel school for his grandchildren going into the business.

15. Although the question of what chefs discuss in the kitchen does not enter into the framework of this article, our interviews with chefs at the center of the profession contradict Gary Fine's observations in "Wittgenstein in the Kitchen" in this issue. Conversation among chefs in a hegemonic culinary world often focuses on preparations they have enjoyed or have created, preparations that they theorize, and their philosophies of food.

16. Competition among high-status restaurants in New York and problems getting visas for European chefs magnified the importance of the restaurateur making the right hiring decision.

17. For reflections on the patterns of prejudice in France, see the interview with Christine Massia in Lorenzo, *Profession? Cuisinier-restaurateur*, pp. 81–96. Our female respondents also remarked upon the difficulties encountered in male-dominated kitchens.

18. During the 1980s, a noted African American chef (whose restaurant we would call hegemonic) moved from New York to open his own restaurant in Los Angeles; this restaurant subsequently closed, and he took a position in another high-status restaurant.

19. Our Italian chef was self-taught, ran her own restaurant in her home town in Italy for 10 years before working in France and now in New York. See also Marian Burros, "In the Restaurants of Italy, Women Rule the Kitchen," *New York Times*, January 6, 1993.

20. On standardization, see Waverley Root and Richard de Rochemont, *Eating in America* (New York: William Morrow, 1976) and Harvey Levenstein, *Revolution at the Table* (New York: Oxford University Press, 1988).

Chapter 7

A Place at the Counter:
The Onus of Oneness

Mary Lukanuski

Few human activities are more basic than eating. Deprived of companionship, sex, spiritual and creative outlets we may wither, but deprived of food we die.[1] We must eat. Eating is so intrinsic to our routine we are both aware and unaware of our need. We will plan elaborate meals, prepare sumptuous dishes yet forget what we had for lunch yesterday. We may forget, but our stomachs and the abundance of readily available food remind us of our need.

We may not be fully conscious of what we've eaten, but we're even less conscious of how we eat. It's such an everyday occurrence, we rarely give thought to when we eat, whom we eat with, what we eat, and where we eat. Only until the expected pattern is broken do we notice. We may become distressed with a changed mealtime, introduction of new foods, or new dining location, but we usually manage to eat. We may be sharing a meal with strangers, and, regardless of how awkward we feel, we still eat. Even if all of the expected parameters (time, situation, food) are in place, there is one situation we balk at—eating alone.

At one time or another we have eaten by ourselves. We probably did so out of situation (we didn't have anyone to eat with) or schedule (there wasn't time to invite a companion), and we probably were all too aware of how uncomfortable it felt eating by ourselves. We might have felt similar to the single diners M. F. K. Fisher observed:

At such times few men realize that they are dining with them-selves. In fact, they try to forget that rather frightening truth. They read the newspaper or turn on the radio if they are at home. More often they flee from themselves to friend-filled clubs, or to the noisiest nearby restaurant where other lone humans eat crowded together in a hungry, ugly mob and take digestive pills between their hurried courses.[2]

Why have we made eating alone so uncomfortable? Most of us like to eat, but what is it about the situation of being alone that turns our stomachs? Before we look at eating alone we have to consider the context of eating.

Food nourishes us. The need for food played a central part in the formation of social groupings. Remember the natural history dioramas with the women gathering and the men hunting. The next scene would show how the development of agricultural soci-eties gave rise to permanent communities. The focal activity of many communities was, and continues to be, food gathering and preparation.

Yet, for the fortunate foraging seems a distant necessity. Supergrocery stores pop up everywhere offering produce and prod-ucts that were once exotic and unavailable. Nevertheless, regard-less of how many grocery stores appear, we continue a practice from when foraging was a necessity: the shared meal—that is, the sharing of the communally obtained foods.

Consequently food is still prepared with the expectation that it will be shared. Daily meals are with the immediate family or companions; on holidays, with an extended gathering of friends and relatives. In the sharing of food, the sense of community is continually defined and maintained.

How food is consumed is a powerful method of further defining a community. A group who follows proscriptions forbidding certain foods, and or combinations of foods, immediately separate them-selves. A sense of order, place, and discipline is created: the tacit understanding being, beside any divine command, is that without such regulations the community would fall victim to its individual appetites. Once members of the community were pursuing their own desires, the community would disintegrate.

We speak of a "healthy appetite" always aware that there is the unhealthy appetite. Whether denied or indulged, appetite and hunger are regarded with suspicion. Appetite and hunger, because they are innate urges, are seen as mysterious and potentially dangerous. Regardless of what diet or discipline is followed, there is always the need, the hunger, that reminds us that we can never quite control our desires. Our appetite must be constantly monitored, and how we satisfy it even more carefully watched.

It's not surprising that eating is closely associated with sex: hunger and appetite becoming metaphors for sexual desire. Sex, like hunger, is regarded as a powerful urge that must be tightly controlled or society as we know it will be destroyed: paternity of children would be unknown; women would have no need to establish a family with one man; adults would prey upon children; life would be sacrificed in the pursuit of pleasure. As with eating, rituals and taboos designed to keep sexual urges in check developed over generations. The proscriptions placed upon eating and sex were similar—what to eat, how to eat, and whom to eat with are parallel to customs on whom we can have sex with, how, and when we have sex.

Eating and sex are twinned. Orifices are seen as courseways to our inner self and inviolate except in designated circumstances and with circumscribed objects.[3] We have engrained images melding these behaviors: the epicure, devoted to sensual pleasures, is a fully fleshed individual doomed to a bad end; the ascetic, lean and wan, misses out on the fun in the denial of the flesh, but is well considered for his restrained behaviors. Eating is one of the first sensual pleasures we experience. How we approach eating is just as complicated as how we approach sex.

The shared diet and seasonal cycle of fasts and feasts create rituals and a sense of place. We remind ourselves that we belong, to a nation, to a tribe, when we plan a holiday meal. Friends and relatives are invited. The expected meal, such as the traditional New England Thanksgiving with turkey, oyster dressing, and cranberry relish, is prepared and shared with the assembled guests. We can be anywhere, from southern California to southern France, and we know, in partaking of this meal, that we are part of a larger community.

Examples of food rituals and eating behaviors could go on. Anthropologists, cultural historians, and nutritionists are far better prepared to expound on the intricacies of specific foodways and food signifiers. What we know in this context is that the need to eat has profound cultural resonance and the manifestations are subtle. Eating is a quotidian activity: it seems to occur without ritual or proscribed expectations, but in actuality it is a highly ritualized activity. We will see that when the expected doesn't occur, the deviant behavior may be shunned, disregarded, or just looked upon as odd.

How does eating alone fit into a culture where eating is primarily a group activity, and the group behavior a fixed part of the cultural expectations toward food and nourishment, physical and spiritual?

Eating alone is solitary, but it's not isolated. We are aware of the societal attitudes toward an activity before undertaking it. Impressed by societal values we form our actions and are observed by the community who will then reconfirm those values or question them. Eating alone is a separate behavior from eating with others. The societal signals are different and how solitary eaters eat is different. The cycle of signals is repeated as the community reconfirms its values by observing the behaviors of solo eaters.

When I spoke with friends, family, and colleagues about this topic, the overwhelming response was one of embarrassment, as if we were discussing their masturbation rituals. And who wants to admit they're having it, food or sex, alone? Some would rather go hungry than eat alone. Others approach their hunger as an empty fuel tank and pull into the nearest acceptable eatery and fill up. Many survive on take-out and share with those who cook a slightly skewed diet: either indulgence (ice cream for dinner) or denial (skip the meal).

All of us have indulged or denied ourselves certain eating behaviors and foods. For the most part, however, there is a sense of propriety we acknowledge and espouse. We know what is expected and follow through.

For the solitary eater there is no sense of proper eating behavior. There is no etiquette or societal expectation on how to eat alone. Some solo eaters may still behave as if they're being watched. Others find themselves freed from the responsibilities usually incurred when eating: responsibilities like a "balanced" meal, etiquette, a table, napkins.

More than the lack of dining companions separates eating alone from eating with others. Studies focusing on eating behaviors have demonstrated that when we eat alone we eat differently. We take less time to eat.[4] Obese subjects will eat more when eating alone; the non obese will eat less.[5] Older men and women living alone prepare fewer meals at home.[6] A survey of college students revealed that women were more likely to skip a meal if confronted with having to eat alone.[7]

The perception that those eating alone are odd is reinforced: people eating alone eat too fast, eat too much or too little, or are old. Where are the "normal" people—either at home or not eating.

He who eats alone, dies alone: an Italian proverb but understandable in almost any culture. Those participating in an activity that should be shared are obviously unwanted and unconnected. The solitary diner is either a social misfit or the victim of some tragedy. He or she all too easily reminds us of the precariousness of our own situation: but for the grace of God, there go I. The solitary diner is then subject to either pity or suspicion, both the product of the observer's projection. Pity can reach heights of sympathy and result in extending an invitation to the solitary eater; whether the invitation is wanted or accepted is another issue. Suspicion results not in sympathy but rather in fear, that the same situation (eating alone, being alone, being abandoned) could occur; and the solo diner is ignored.

Solitary diners provoke us. That they are alone and participating in an activity that should be shared hits a chord in us. We may want to relieve them of their perceived loneliness by having them join us or ignore them. In either case we are extending to them attention we rarely extend to those eating with others, or would be unthinkable in any other circumstance. For example, the unwanted attention directed toward men or women eating alone that borders on predatory. The "predator" feels comfortable in his or her actions: lacking dining companions, notably family or spouse, the solitary diner is signaling his or her availability. The "predator" further believes that the solitary diner is looking for, wants, companionship. If she or he doesn't, why is he or she eating in public? The solitary diner is on the defensive. The invitation could be wanted and accepted, but what if it isn't? The solitary diner then has to graciously decline an offer that was extended as a fait accompli. The onus is on the solitary diner: Why would anyone want to eat alone?

Many are cautious where they eat alone having been subjected to unwelcomed invitations or fearing an appearance of impropriety. Both men and women find their activities curtailed. Once, maybe still, women on out-of-town business trips were advised to stay in their hotel rooms and order room service: the idea being out of sight, out of mind. The solitary eater may then seek out venues that encourage anonymous eating and rapid turnover. There are times, however, when staying at home is best.

Eating in presents to the solitary eater comforting yet unsettling signals: the apotheosis of the family gathering is the home cooked meal. What can be more nourishing to the spirit than a lovingly prepared meal of favorite foods served at the kitchen table? Or the heights of culinary prowess demonstrated with fine wines in an entertaining and convivial atmosphere? The solitary eater is contending with a huge cultural signifier: preparing a meal at home is a cultural touchstone. The solitary eater, however, receives little encouragement to do so.

We learn to cook from example and from cookbooks. Some learn to reduce recipes to appropriate portions and to make room in the freezer for leftovers. Cookbooks such as "Meals for One," "Dinner Solo" are few, filled with simplistic recipes and a hollow cheeriness that barely masks a tone of disdain and pity. The solo diner is assumed to be a culinary tyro with infantile tastes and zero social skills. Compared to such abuse, a freezer filled with leftovers is a small inconvenience.

Other options for eating at home are take-out, the mainstay of many eating alone or not, and prepared foods. Prepared foods have been a welcomed convenience for the growing number of working women and their families.[8] There are also more single heads of households without families who depend upon what was thought to be the respite of mothers working outside the home. The prepared food industry has been sensitive to this difference and has marketed its products accordingly. For example, Lean Cuisine, unlike the television dinners of twenty years ago consumed en famille, is marketed specifically toward the solitary eater. Ads for entrees focus on a single serving, the quality, and the healthfulness of the meal. Mass-prepared foods, like frozen pizzas and french fries, are seen being consumed by hungry, eager families or large groups. Entrees are meals in themselves, and featured in commercials with only one person—usually a woman. For both the solitary eater and others, prepared foods create that just home cooked feeling.

Throughout this piece the term "eating with others" is contrasted with eating alone. It's an awkward term but necessary. We assume we eat in the company of family or friends. Those not following the set behavior are denoted not the majority. Eating alone then becomes a different activity from eating with others. What, where, and how the solo diner eats are unique to eating alone.

Very few families would gather for a meal of tuna eaten out of the can with a fork while standing in the kitchen. Neither would friends expecting to eat together bring their own books, magazines,

or newspapers to a restaurant. Yet this is how many eat when
they're alone. And given society's attitude on eating alone, it's not
surprising that eating alone is a furtive activity.

On the extreme of eating alone as a furtive activity, there are
those who eat alone because their eating behaviors are pathologi-
cal. Most bulimics and anorexics engage in their ritualized eating
in private. They are aware, especially the bulimics in binging and
purging, that the manner in which they eat is deviant. Eating for
the anorexic and bulimic is a matter of control or lack thereof:
control over familial expectations, gender expectations, and societal expectations. Psychotropic medications have assisted bulimics,
but this doesn't discount the dynamic situation that can give rise
to eating disorders. The bulimic, as everyone else, has internalized
society's attitude toward eating alone: it is a deviant, shameful
activity. Thus an activity as strange as binging could be done only
in private. Eating alone is then doubly shameful: for the out-of-
control binging and for doing it alone.

There are, however, those who are capable of eating by themselves in public and within the capacity of a normal appetite:

> I saw clearly for the first time that a woman traveling alone
> and behaving herself on a ship is an object of curiosity. . . . I
> developed a pattern of behavior which I still follow, on ships
> and trains and in hotels everywhere, and which impresses and
> undoubtedly irritates some people who see me, but always
> succeeds in keeping me aloof from skullduggery.
>
> There are many parts to it, but one of the most important
> is the way I eat; it not only surrounds me with a wall of awe,
> but makes my private life more interesting and keeps me
> from boredom.
>
> I discovered . . . I could be very firm with pursers and stew-
> ards and such. I could have a table assigned to me in any part
> of the dining room I wanted, and, best of all, I could have that
> table to myself. I needed no longer be put with officers or
> predatory passengers, just because I was under ninety and
> predominantly female. . . .
>
> And once seated, I could eat what I wanted and drink what
> I wanted. And if I felt like, I could invite another passen-
> ger. . . . But in general, I preferred to eat by myself, slowly,
> voluptuously, and with independence that heartened me against
> the coldness of my cabin and my thoughts.[9]

How did M. F. K. Fisher overcome the societal prejudice against eating alone, a woman eating alone at that, and frankly enjoy herself? It might have to do with her capacity to be alone.

According to D.W. Winnicott, "The capacity to be alone is a highly sophisticated phenomenon and has many contributory factors. It is closely related to emotional maturity."[10] Winnicott theorizes that we learn, as infants, to be alone in the presence of a care giver who in presenting a reliable support for the infant, allows the infant periodic moments of being alone. That is, the care giver while being with the infant, doesn't overtly interact with the infant. The infant, knowing it is in a supportive environment, can then in those moments "flounder to be in a state in which there is no orientation, to be able to exist for a time without being either a reactor to an external impingement or an active person with a direction of interest or movement. . . . In the course of time there arrives a sensation or an impulse. In this setting the sensation or impulse will feel real and be truly personal experience."[11]

Winnicott furthers goes on to state "The individual who has developed the capacity to be alone is constantly able to rediscover the personal impulse, and the personal impulse is not wasted because the state of being alone is something which (though paradoxically) always implies that someone else is there."[12] The adult who is able to be alone forgoes the actual presence of the care giver: the comfort and support the care giver offered in those first moments of being alone is internalized.

Are those of us who don't like eating alone the product of overinvolved care givers who never gave us those moments to feel a real and truly personal experience? I don't think so. Eating not only fulfills our physical hunger, but our human hungers as well—the need for love, security, and comfort. Our need for love and security is fulfilled in no small measure by what and how we eat. How we satisfy our hungers is directed by our cultural expectations. Eating has unambiguous expectations and behaviors associated with it: physical hungers, and so security and love, are best satiated with others.

Eating alone is a stigmatized behavior because it defies the expectations we have of eating. It will probably continue to be thought of as an unfortunate activity of the social outcast. Solo eaters will continue to feel uncomfortable and many will go hungry rather than be thought of as friendless.

There are those, however, who have discovered that their need for nourishment, security, and love may be satisfied outside the cultural expectations. They, like M. F. K. Fisher, have discovered that they can eat and drink what they want in whatever manner satisfies their hungers, and they can do so alone.

Notes

1. Ralph S. Hattox, *Coffee and Coffeehouses* (Seattle: University of Washington Press, 1985), pp. 126–27.

2. M. F. K. Fisher, *Serve it Forth* (San Francisco: North Point Press, 1989), p. 114.

3. Roger Abrahams, "Equal Opportunity Eating: A Structural Excursus on Things of the Mouth," *Ethnic and Regional Foodways in the United States,* Linda Keller Brown and Kay Mussell, editors (Knoxville: University of Tennessee Press), 1984, p. 19.

4. K. T. Strongman, and R. N. Hughes, "Eating Style and Body Weight," *New Zealand Psychologist,* 1980 Nov., Vol. 9(2) pp. 68–69, 84.

5. David S. Krantz, "A Naturalistic Study of Social Influences on Meal Size Among Moderately Obese and Nonobese Subjects," *Psychosomatic Medicine,* 1979 Feb., Vol. 41(1) pp. 19–27.

6. Maradee A. Davis, Suzanne Murphy, and John N. Neuhaus, "Living Arrangements and Eating Behaviors of Older Adults in the United States," *Journal of Gerontology,* 1988 May, Vol. 43(3) S96–98.

7. Bibb Latane, and Liane D. Bidwell, "Sex and Affiliation in College Cafeterias," *Personality and Social Psychology Bulletin,* 1977, Vol. 3(4) pp. 571–74.

8. Howard G. Schutz, and Katherine V. Diaz-Knauf, "The Role of the Mass Media in Influencing Eating," *Handbook of the Psychophysiology of Human Eating,* R. Shepherd editor (Chichester: Wiley, 1989), p. 141.

9. M. F. K. Fisher, *The Gastronomical Me* (San Francisco: North Point Press, 1989), p. 182.

10. D. W. Winnicott, "The Capacity to be Alone," *International Journal of Psycho-Analysis,* 1958, Vol. 39, pp. 416–20.

11. Ibid.

12. Ibid.

Chapter 8

Appetite

Alphonso Lingis

In the old days when people didn't travel very much, and those that did had wildly different experiences of places—Graham Greene hating every man, woman, child, meal, and hill of Mexico; André Gide finding the souks and casbahs of North Africa more beautiful and the people more cultured than those of Proust's Paris—there was travel literature. A genre akin to the novel, both in the high level of the writing that was cultivated in the genre and in the dimension of imagination and frank fiction one could put into travel books. Readers read them very much like novels, appreciating them for the descriptive virtuosity and narrative flair. They found the foreign lands and peoples described to have hardly anything in common with what they themselves saw and met when they went to those places.

Nowadays that so many people travel so much, this literary travel literature has given way to travel writing without the fiction. The consulates and the travel agents have wonderful brochures, the airlines have magazines, with dazzling photographs crowding one another off the page. For India the Taj Mahal, a beautiful young woman with a jewel in her nostril, and a table spread with curries, pomfret, koftas, mangos, crisp spiced breads and wafers; for Jamaica a colonial mansion, a stretch of beach viewed from the shade of coconut palms, a beautiful young woman garlanded with flowers, and a black man in white chef's hat holding a tray piled with lobster, rice light as snow, codfish and ackee, pineapples and sapodillas; for Cusco a street with colonial mansions built over Inca walls, a beautiful young woman in Indian embroideries and lace, and a table set with heavy brass candlesticks and crowded with coriander and mint soup, cebiche, lemons, beef hearts with peppers and corn-on-the-cob, quince and passionfruit.

Often we keep these brochures and airline magazines, as we are cordially invited to do; they give a better picture of what our trip was like than our own snapshots. We got some views of some of the most famous sights, the Taj Mahal, the colonial cathedral, Machu Picchu. We were greeted, at the airport, at the hotel, in restaurants, in night clubs by beautiful young women we feasted our eyes on, but did not make a project of trying to get one of them into our bed for the night before we left the country.

What we had in full abundance, what we really got into, explored, lingered over, discussed, learned about was the *food*. It's what will stay with us when we get back. Our friends will not ask us very often to describe the Taj Mahal or the viceroy's mansion in Cusco, and by the time we start thinking of the next trip, we ourselves no longer find ourselves picking up books on them. But when we go out we will think of exploring the Indian or Jamaican or Brazilian restaurants of Philadelphia or Austin or Cleveland, and our friends will ask us for help on the menu, and we will remember and learn more.

Pizarro was fascinated by the meals of the Inca Atahualpa. Nothing revealed his divinity more. The Inca ate alone. The table was set with dishes and utensils made of precious metals set with jewels. There were laid out before him the most exquisite dishes, thirty or forty of them. Fresh fish was brought by runners in relays from the sea to Cajamarca in forty-eight hours; ice was brought from the glaciers of the Andes above. The Inca came clad in dress made of vicuña wool, with bat-fur and hummingbird feather cloaks. These garments were worn but once. If in the course of the meal something fell or dripped on the Inca's garments, they were changed at once. The Inca was fed by hand by beautiful young women. When he spit out a fishbone or fruit-pit, he did so in the cupped hands of a serving-maiden.

Pizarro's men inquired what was done with the garments prepared anew for each meal, the uneaten food, what the Inca spit out into those cupped hands, and were told that all was kept in great chests, and were shown well-guarded warehouses full of these chests. Pizarro's chroniclers seemed a little unclear how to interpret this; they wrote that everything the Inca touched or that was brought to him was to such an extent held to be sacred, and also that the Inca was very afraid of sorcery, which requires hairs or fluids from the body of the one upon which evil spells are to be cast.

It's no hassle to travel anymore, but still the finest room in a resort hotel does not have the dozens of personal indulgences we have furnished our own homes with over the years. The air conditioned bus or even the private car is not like driving our own car back home over decent roads where people obey the traffic signals. However cordial the tour guides and hostesses were, they, whether Egyptian or French or even British, only make us understand the more poignantly how the really deep levels of friendship are only possible with people with whom one shared an enormous amount of everyday life together.

Actually going to a culture, as opposed to reading books and studying photographs of it, gives one a consistently inferior contact with that culture. The really telling views of the flying buttresses of Notre Dame cathedral or Machu Picchu or the Black Pagoda at Puri were taken from balconies in buildings we will not get access to, or from helicopters. The close-up views of the Emerald Buddha in Wat Phra Keo in Bangkok or the interior of Freud's study in London are views given only to the contracted photographer. We will not be able to wait weeks or months for the right season, the right light; we will not be able to clear everyone out of the Dolmabaché Palace and take the morning to arrange our network of photo floods that will show its opulence in sensual contours. So much of what is described in books will be off-limits: the harem in the Seraglio of Istanbul, the apartments of the Vatican, the palace of the king of Nepal, all the mosques of Kabul. The explanations we will get on the site from tour guides will be invariably anecdotal, insensitive to the real human or historical significance of an object or a place, and factually unreliable. We are not going to be led through the Royal Palace of Luang Prabang in Laos by a tragic princess whose childhood was spent there but by a tour guide who, like ourselves, responds more to a Rolex or a Sony TV than to an astrological instrument or medieval scroll.

Actually going to the Amazon to see the rain forest and some Amazonian tribal people is less interesting, less beautiful, less informative than watching a television documentary made by experts, biologists, and anthropologists. In fact, actually going to a culture—as opposed to reading books where everything is edited, composed, presented according to the techniques of literary art, and studying photographs of it, photographs of objects sprayed with dew or glycerin and back-lit or shot with polarizing or ultraviolet filters—is inevitably going to be a faked experience of that culture. The trance rituals we will see for ourselves in Bali will be faked; the macumba ceremonies in Salvador or Rio de Janeiro staged for tourists; the official or unofficial tour guides who alone speak English in Cusco or in Kuala Lumpur will tell us stories about their families and home villages they picked up from watching television programs or shorts the local movie house runs before showing the feature film made in Hollywood or Hong Kong; the English-speaking guru clad in saffron who comes to speak with us in the garden of our hotel in Katmandu hasn't done yoga or walked on pilgrimage to a sacred shrine or fasted for thirty years.

There was nothing second-rate, ersatz, faked about the meals. We could get "international cuisine" if we were a little worried about our stomach acidity and its workaday enzymes, or even get a hamburger from time to time. But everybody who travels eats real, wonderful, unforgettable French cuisine, Spanish paella, Moroccan couscous, Indonesian Reistafel, Brazilian feijoada. One eats, in the shadow of the Alhambra or the Taj Mahal or the Louvre, meals literally fit for kings, dishes using the very recipes of the royal courts, meals using ingredients that might well be fresher and of finer quality than they had back then without modern transport facilities.

One can eat, any day, in Yogyakarta or in Chiang Mai the meals even aristocrats had only for weddings or state occasions. At the No Hands Restaurant in Bangkok lovely maidens cut up the food for you and feed you—like the Inca Atahualpa—morsel by morsel; your idle hands can fondle their loins. Of all the local personnel we deal with in traveling, only the restaurant staff are impeccably accommodating, solicitous, treating us like royalty. We could wander around the planet as in our own dominion, stopping here and there at an inn to receive obeisance. When we tour palaces we begin to notice that the dining room at the Tour d'Argent or even at La Coupole really is as splendid as that in Versailles; that the dining room at the Great Wall Hotel in Beijing has a more sublime view than the imperial one in the Forbidden City; that the revolving top-floor restaurant in the Meridien Hotel is more grand than the dining hall of the Palace of the viceroy.

Wherever we go, Paris or Kyoto or Cuernavaca, we come back thinking that the one thing traveling gives us is a sense for the quality of life we did not have before. Sitting in the restaurant even of the train station, at a table covered with a real tablecloth, set with a vase of flowers and beautiful glasses and real silver, savoring each of a two-hour succession of dishes and wines, it seems to us that culture really is not to be measured by the pomp of its monuments, the grandiloquence of the literature and painting with which court artists celebrated military victories and marital alliances, or even by the loftiness and splendor of its sacred places. It might be important, for becoming cultivated, to see the Taj Mahal and the onion domes of the Kremlin, but the monuments of genius are in fact like freaks of nature; isn't it in the end a sort of freak of genetics that Fra Angelico and Raphael and Michelangelo and Dante were all born in Florence within a century, since in the following centuries Florence has produced less than Brooklyn? Conversely, one discovers in Rio de Janeiro, which has not produced a single writer or painter or composer anyone has ever heard of, a way of life refined and sensitive, hedonist and reflective that one comes to think is what high culture truly is. It is what one discovers, in those long hours in the dining rooms of old aristocratic cities. Saigon was a commercial port, not a cultural capital, and never had important pagodas, and HoChiMinh City today is dilapidated, polluted, and crowded with beggars, addicts, and thieves. Everybody goes to dine chez Madame Dai, the official tours tell you to make reservations. Madame Dai was a Sorbonne-trained lawyer and before the fall of Saigon President of the Senate. The second great love of my life always was cooking, she said as she greeted us in her home. In her living room, all the walls lined with bookshelves and art objects, she brought us the court dishes she prepared that afternoon, and joined us to talk in five languages late into the night. There we discovered the high culture of Vietnam.

Eating is biting, gnawing, masticating, ingesting, consuming, appropriating, devouring, absorbing, digesting, assimilating. At least that is what a certain kind of eating is, a certain time, place, and quality of eating: the royal dining, which traveling to other cultures achieves, the eating of the dominant class.

These same words are used everywhere when we speak of relating to culture: if one is cultivating oneself, if one is not just stagnating biliously in bigotry, one is, in turning the pages of books, watching public television, or strolling through museums, absorbing, assimilating, appropriating. And one is getting satisfactions and gratifications.

Somehow that does not sound very moral. Even though we have just agreed that the real daily high mass of high culture is celebrated in restaurants, where egoisms and affectations are forgotten in common needs being admitted, dining accompanied by that distinctive kind of language, of disinterested sharing, which culture developed about the dining table.

It's also appropriating the lives of other beings, animals and plants first violently killed, devouring them for the momentary satisfaction of one's own cravings. Whether in the restaurant or in the museum. The Japanese capitalist who bought for $82 million a vision Van Gogh obtained in an agonizing and irreversible descent into hell—whether he hangs the painting now in his own living room or on the wall of a museum he builds among the buildings of his corporation—is also appropriating the life of another being, which the system of domination this modern lord of industry has inherited violently tormented. That is also consuming the life of another for the momentary satisfaction of one's own appetite.

The answer to that, to the moral question, is: It's natural. Perhaps nowhere is the irrefutability of nature by morality so evident than in the inevitability of appetite. Annie Dillard speaks with unrelievable horror of the female wasp which was not able, due to a few days of uninterrupted rain, to find a suitable body of another animal to plant her eggs in, and now those eggs have hatched in her own body and are consuming it from within. The pages, in *Pilgrim at Tinker Creek*, where she forces herself to think of this are pure outcries of revulsion and revolt. All living things, however gentle, however enchantingly beautiful, however much marvel and adoration they evoke, are in reality segments of a global food chain, where nothing can live without eating, without devouring the lives of others, without being destined to feed the appetite of others.

Except us. Is not the great dogma being proclaimed in every one of those daily high masses of high culture that of a reverse Eucharist: Eat not of my body and drink not of my blood!

It is said that centuries of recurrent famine is what put bamboo shoots and seaweed, serpents and sea slugs in the Japanese cuisine. But we, in the measure that we rise in the ranks of the dominant classes, nibble at more and more. Gusanos de manguey, inch-long eel fry, ant's eggs were the hors d'oeuvres of the best restaurant I ate in in Mexico City, followed by steak cut from the bull killed that afternoon in the corrida. By bringing every plant, every fish, every serpent, every bird, every mammal to the table, we put ourselves at the summit of the great chain of being.

It is in this way that we posit our value, posit ourselves as values. More exactly, in philosophy's terminology, posit our dignity. Value is the measure of exchange; the value of something is determined by the other things taken to be equivalent to and interchangeable with it. In an economic system, something acquires more and more value in the measure that more and more things are required in exchange for it. Something acquires that transcendent state Kant calls dignity when all things may be or may have to be exchanged for it, but it is not exchanged for anything further. The members of a society exchange goods of necessity with one another, exchange goods and labor for protection, exchange labor and luxuries for temples and monuments, which are not exchanged for anything further; the society will sacrifice its wealth and the lives of its citizens to protect its temples and monuments.

In taking possession of jungle and tundra, the oceans and the polar ice caps, in unhesitatingly defying all the genii loci to make all substances resources for human needs and pleasures, the politico-economic institutions of humankind not only establish their sovereignty within the family of nations, but establish a cosmic sovereignty over all things. But in traveling from country to country, being served like the emperor by every alien culture in restaurants where any substance, any living plant or animal, is laid out for our consumption, each of us situates ourselves in the food chain at the top, making self the uneaten one, the unexchangeable value, the cosmic dignity.

⋘∞⋙∞⋘∞⋙

We had breakfast and lunch brought up as we spent the day in our honeymoon suite. Satin sheets and a pail full of roses. In the late afternoon we went down the beach and bathed and kissed and watched the tropical sunset, which were not overrated in those brochures. We had it practically to ourselves, the hotel owns a mile of this beach and the only Jamaicans we saw were in security-guard uniforms. The orchestra is playing good jazz, we're having the most expensive champagne on the list, the food melts in your mouth and we kiss, and from time to time transfer the melting food from one mouth to another. Around us there are four other tables where I bet diners are honeymooners, and two couples maybe on their twenty-fifth wedding anniversary the way they smile and glance at us. The waiter comes dressed in white, even white gloves, but his arms are so black and his pants are tight and his crotch is bulging. I caught him checking out my breasts when he leaned over and his lips trembling as he spooned out the steaming bouillabaisse and it's not that he's hungry for bouillabaisse. They pay him a month what they charge for this meal, but it's not my meal he wants to eat. Black men with round asses and that bouncy way they walk, looking at me lips trembling. They suck on cokes or coconut milk out of straws with their thick lips and look right at me, and not at my face either. They are not even whistling or calling out to me, no more than you would to a buffet being carried out to you. At home I walk downtown with the sidewalks full of blacks all the time, they at least look like they have other things on their minds, when they look at me they do it furtively and turn away if I catch their eye.

I have no idea where this dirt road is going, it looks like the road to perdition. There's enough light, not the full moon of honeymoon postcards, there's no moon at all, but there are stars. And eyes shining in the trees, bushes, shanties, eyes of black men with trembling lips, staring at me. What are they waiting for? The way I am stumbling on, anybody can hear my steps on the road. They are closing in, I am stumbling right into their arms black as tar; they don't hesitate a moment, their hands are on my breasts, between my thighs, under my ass. Big thick lips up against my mouth, tongue pushing in, he is nibbling on my upper lip now, now on the lower lip. I can feel the teeth against the soft tissue of my mouth, I poke my tongue up against his teeth, rub them, there are no melting morsels of food being transferred from him to me, he is folding into my flooding mouth the gamy taste of his saliva. I push him back, bend down over his mouth, I am turning inside out, spreading the inside of my mouth against his turned-back lips, his tongue.

How many tongues are licking at my sweaty belly, my streaming eyes, my pungent armpits. Other mouths, that's all I know, I can't see the faces, are nibbling, gnawing at my tits, sinking deep into my breasts stuffing themselves full of me. Other mouths nip-

ping at my neck, teeth biting at my flanks, gnawing at my hands.
My body heaves and twists as on a spit. Mouths sucking at my
fingers and at my toes, soaking them in digestive juices. How many
mouths at my cunt, teeth biting and pulling at my hairs, mouth
puckered over my clit, tongue working over my slit, tongue poking
inside making the juices flow. I am wet drenched soaked in juices
I cannot taste. They are never full, the more they bite into, the
more hungry they get, don't hold back, swallow me, devour me.
The more they suck me dry the more full I get, swelling up in all
these mouths, filling them, heaving full of so much violence in me,
so much blood. What they are sucking out of me is will, that's it,
that's why so full of fermentations and fluids I feel so drained, they
can do whatever they want with me, with my mouth, my teeth,
my tits, my toes, my ass, I have no idea what I want them for.
That's what they used to say in high school: hey chickie, what are
you saving it for? Not for you creep that's for sure, I would say.

Early this morning I finally gave away my cherry and don't
know what I was saving anything for, my clit, my ass, my armpits,
let them pass from mouth to mouth. There is a wet cavernous
mouth up against my pussy, with teeth and throat but it is up
against my cunt and its throat; there juices and tastes caught in an
eddy between currents, going nowhere, outpouring, throats not
swallowing but pouring out like champagne bottles not tilted over
glasses but pointed into one another.

One could get killed in these places, nothing but shanties,
beaten down kerosene cans and tarpaper and a few old boards, full
of roaches and rats, I was going to take off my watch and forgot,
it is glinting in the light, these dudes would knife you for a watch
and lick off the blood. I can see them sitting in doorways watching.
I'm like the fox blindly heading straight for the dogs. They would
probably do anything you asked, for a buck, just say I want a blow
job man, none of them are employed, half of them get their meals
by going over garbage cans. They want me because I taste good,
meat hard, no greasy fat in my belly, clean mouth, balls smelling
of spice and musk. Yeah sure man I got a cigarette, here you are,
need a match? What freaks them out is that I am just rambling
along like this, in the dark, alone, like I'm not scared of anything,
like I'm out looking for trouble. Don't want a cigarette, with that
meal and the champagne there's not room for the smoke.

Why did I sneak out as soon as she dozed off, what would I
have said I was going out to get if she asked? Funny how when you
jerk off you think of getting a blow job. Nobody knows how to

knead, tease, harden your cock like your own hand. Still you want another hand around it. You want a mouth with a tongue, you want to feel the teeth, when you cum it is into foamy saliva that overflows. You start to feel real in a place, not just a memory drifting through, when you leave something, not just your cash and your attitudes but something from your crotch. The other one is down on me, I am degrading myself, sinking into the dark, he thinks I want it, would do anything for it, pay for it even. He's going to take my wallet and watch, probably has already slipped them off and into his pocket. It's not like the white sahib leaving his babies all around the Raj; my jism is pouring into mouths, overflowing, dripping on the ground. It's not like a dog that is marking its slumming in the night by peeing on every post.

I would never find these mouths again, will not recognize them in the day tomorrow if I walked down this same road. Why do we make such an issue of it, fight, lie, kill rather than admit that my cock like every cock there is wants to get sucked, by a mouth, no matter what kind, in high school we talked of getting sucked by ponies, by dogs, and when you get sucked you feel not only the rubbing up and down your cock and the wet and the hot, but you feel the other mouth too, you feel how it feels, your own mouth opens and hollows out and salivates. It's like my cock itself is a throat, behind it the tube from my balls that is aching because it is empty, like that one's throat is aching because it is empty and is filling up not with food but with cock—that is, another aching throat. Bolting my ass now like a dog poking at a dog. You sit on your ass and feel nothing, you shake it some when jiving down the road, but it only comes alive when somebody's head is up against it, between the cheeks, licking the crack, kneading the cheeks, salivating, biting.

I heard that in Vietnam when you are sitting on the floor you can never point your feet at anybody, it is considered degrading, what would they think of putting your foot in somebody's face, sticking your toes in his or her mouth, getting your toes sucked like drumsticks. She would do it if I asked, if I worked up to it, doing it to her it would be like being a pasha being doted over by his harem girl. What's degenerate is going out and sticking your foot in anybody's mouth in the night, here take it, taste it, bite it, hungry mouth nibbling, not stopping, could go on all night, as though that was all she or he wanted, take your knife, chop it off, keep it for tomorrow. My ears can't hear anything, they are soaked with saliva, are being chewed, my eyes can't see anything, they are being licked, sucked. A mouth nibbling away at the side of my flank, I never knew what it was for anyhow. What was I keeping it for anyhow. Hot night smelling of seaweed, damp hot ground. Take this my meat and eat, take this my jism and drink and forget me.

Chapter 9

Untitled Artists' Projects by Janine Antoni, Ben Kinmont, Rirkrit Tiravanija

Laura Trippi

When Ron Scapp invited me to contribute to *Eating Culture*, he told me that he and the other editor, Brian Seitz, didn't want me to write about art, or about themes of eating in art, but on eating practices in the art world. The letter languished in my pending file and was sitting on the top of my desk the day before the deadline for my final reply. A slip of orange paper printed with a recipe for Thai curry arrived at the same time, quite by coincidence, waiting to be filed. On it was a post-it that said, in my own hand, "Rirkrit." At that moment, I realized the editors probably had no idea that there are artists orchestrating eating as their art.

For Janine Antoni, Ben Kinmont, and Rirkrit Tiravanija, eating and the practices and protocols connected with it are less the subject matter of their art than artistic material to be modeled. Treated as art, eating practices become a way of accessing the inmost individual—a zone of experience and understanding that is too corporeal to be "thinking" but too social to be conceived as pure perception. Their work also addresses the architecture, at once material, institutional, and interpersonal, of the spaces co-inhabited by objects and individuals in which we work and play. In the artistic practice of all three, the aesthetic accent shifts from isolated objects onto networks of embodied interactions that unfold in the built environment.

I have endeavored to present their work on its own terms, translating time- and space-based art works and projects into an editorial format. Documentary images of each artist's work appear together with excerpts of interviews conducted in cafes and at kitchen tables, as well as in the studio. In editing the interviews, I was struck by the convergence in Kinmont's and Tiravanija's work of, on the one hand, effects affiliated with Western art traditions of institutional critique and, on the other, techniques and textures of mindfulness associated with Buddhist thought. Antoni's inflection of process and body art could likewise be located close to this intersection, as yet largely unmarked, between Western and Eastern, abstrusely analytical and resolutely practical, traditions. Critical traditions in art making have emphasized the role of institutional structures in determining meaning in a given instance; Buddhist practices seek to sink thought into its basis in material conditions. In Buddhist thought, causality ascribed to the rational, individual will is relinquished, while meditative practices assist in sorting out from situations and releasing what might be called their *trans*individual potential.

Themes of bodily sensoria, language, and conversation, and the patterns of sociality can be seen, in the projects that follow, circling incessantly around the consumption and sharing of food. With this, I was reminded of the way that language figures as a foodlike substance for the French psychoanalysts Nicholas Abraham and Maria Torok. For them, language is an almost tangible material, filling mouths made empty by loss, by means of which society is constituted. With the acquisition of language, each speaker enters into a community of empty mouths. Similarly, for these artists, eating and the preparation and sharing of food are cultural occasions knitting speakers into a web of social intercourse. Eating practices serve for them as artistic material capable of working and reworking both the inner (corporeal) and the outer (societal) edges of that web—with potentially ethical effects.

⋘⋙⋘⋙⋘⋙

Ben Kinmont

Interviewed May 1 and June 1, 1994

Here was a show that was about art and life. There's been quite a history of artists bringing from life into the gallery, and I thought that was good, history is a nice precedent, but I wasn't so interested in that. I thought, let's instead have people go the other way, let's see if we can set up a situation of trust whereby people in the gallery will come to my home. So during the duration of that show, *Casual Ceremony*, which was about a month and a half, anybody who took a paper plate and called me and set up a mutually convenient time, could come over for breakfast. And four hundred and sixty-eight plates were taken and thirty-two people came by.

I thought it would end up that all my friends would come by and no strangers would come by. In fact almost none of my friends came by because I think they realized that they could come over anytime and have waffles with me. And those who came by, didn't

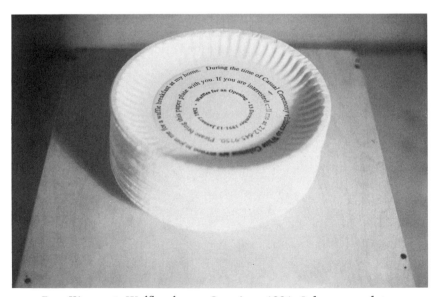

Ben Kinmont, Waffles for an Opening, *1991. Ink, paper plates.*
Installation view in Casual Ceremony *at White Columns,*
New York, New York, 1991.

know if it was going to be this heavy duty performance ceremony that they were going to be in. But it wasn't. It was just like, do you want maple syrup or do you want powdered sugar on your waffles?

Ninety percent of the time we would eventually talk about the project. All of them, as well as myself, were constantly thinking, well, is this art or isn't it? What's going to make this artful? I think that, ultimately, when they arrived there was the nervousness because they were strangers. And then there was the nervousness because they were going into a structure that they'd have no idea what was going to happen. There was a hesitancy at first. But when you start eating—when you're eating, you're eating and I'm eating and they're eating. And that was the other thing. They didn't know if I was going to serve *them* a waffle and watch them eat, or if I was going to eat with them. I said, of course I'm going to eat. I haven't had breakfast and I'm starving! It was part of my morning. It wasn't just, I'm going to make you breakfast, but that they were coming over to have breakfast *with* me.

◦◇◦◦◇◦◦◇◦

On Saturday mornings, my parents would sit Za-Zen and they would go to the Zendo, they started at 6:00 and wouldn't get home till noon or something. So we would be . . . famished! As kids. We finally realized, well, what we could do is go over there to the Zendo, which was only a ten-minute walk away, and we would go the Zendo and we had an agreement with the guys who ran the place and with my parents that if we meditated for ten to fifteen minutes beforehand, which was a hell of a long time for a kid, we got to eat. Because there's a ceremony on the Saturday Za-Zen where, at the end, it's a whole ceremony with these bowls within bowls and you have this little blanket around it and a spoon. So we would have to eat.

I always remember as a kid how heightened your senses were. For a kid to have been sitting still for that long and suddenly—the rice was not rice you'd ever had before. The squash was not. . . . It was very heightened, your senses were fully there and you were very attentive.

◦◇◦◦◇◦◦◇◦

I didn't want people to feel awkward, so I did no recording for that project. You're participating more than someone's keeping track of what's happening. That's a big difference.

After the breakfast, I signed the plate and the participant signed the plate as co-authorship of the piece. It's not like, you know, I don't like that reliquary—it's a nice way to make something meaningful. I appreciate that. And it's beautiful. You could do vitrines or beautiful installations with it. But I generally have made the decision not to do that.

To me the relics, or the leftover parts, are for purposes of . . . they're like academic mnemonic devices or something, these things to, like with a book, to find yourself inside of this development, this process, this choice that somebody made to kind of go through it.

It took me a long time to track down a plate. I got very lucky, and not only tracked down a plate, but there was one person who had come and taken a plate, had breakfast, but I had forgotten to sign their plate when they came. And this is like four years later and I had been always supposed to go sign this guy's plate. He had come and his wife had come and his plate I had signed—or his wife's plate I had signed and I hadn't signed his plate, something

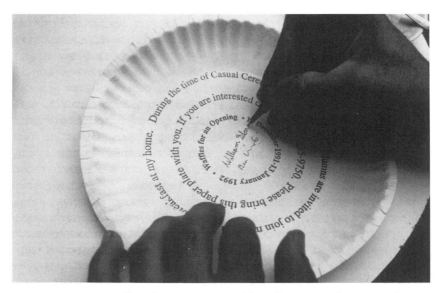

Ben Kinmont, Waffles for an Opening *(detail), 1991. Ink, paper plates. William Stone signing his plate with the artist, 1994.*

weird happened like this, so he'd always been wanting me to sign it. Finally, I actually signed it and I got photographs of him in the process of signing it.

The thing with the washing dishes project is that I wanted to do something that involved—people had been coming into my home, I wanted to get into other people's homes. I wanted to see what that would be, strangers homes! I thought, they were trusting enough to come to a stranger's home. I want to put myself a little bit in their shoes and see what it felt like. A lot of these projects have to do with distribution, and I wasn't sure, How am I going to distribute this idea? How am I going to create a structure and catalyst for this idea?

I liked washing dishes. I liked the idea of that because it was close to, like, seeing one's dirty laundry and it's something that people don't like to do normally. When you cook for someone, it's easy to become ceremonial and washing dishes is really functional.

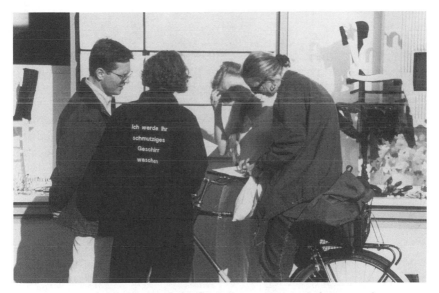

Ben Kinmont, Ich werde Ihr schmutziges Geschirr waschen
(I will wash your dirty dishes): *Munich, 1994. On Leopold Strasse.*
Artist with Annemarie Putterer, Eve Forschel, Barbara Schlegel.
Photo: Thomas Keller.

It *can* be ceremonial. I'm sure one could do that, but it's a little harder. But it connected with food, because you're seeing the leftovers of food, you're seeing the residue, you're seeing what people didn't want to eat, you're seeing what *type* of eaters they are, what do they use to eat with, where do they put their things that they eat with, do they wait a week to do their dishes? Did they do them before I came over and just left a couple things? All that kind of stuff. But I didn't know how I would distribute it, make this available.

So when Katerina asked me to do something about communication in public spaces, I said, well, I have this idea that I've been wanting to do. And I thought, I would love to do a piece about communication in public space, which then however led into the private space. I went in November to Munich, to pick out the neighborhoods where I'd be signing people up for the project. I wanted to be in demographically different neighborhoods and where different activities happened. So they're different spaces in terms of economics but also in terms of functions, what happens in those spaces.

There's little cards that will say their name and address and the time that I'm going to come over so that they have a reminder to be at their house when I'm coming over to do their dishes, also because it's the next week. Then I'll have a card with their address and the time I'm coming over. There's a separate page, which is a contract that, if they're willing to let me record and photograph and all that kind of stuff in their home, if they realize that that's what I'm doing, then they'll sign a waiver that that's ok. And there're two boxes, one to check if they would like to maintain anonymity and another if they want to be informed of all exhibitions and publications about the project. I had to have a German lawyer check all that out. I want it to be very clear what's going on. I don't want people to be upset about it. I'm really doing the dishes as a catalyst to get into their home and talk about these issues of art and life.

⊰◈⊱⊰◈⊱⊰◈⊱

I think it's a good thing for people to do their dishes. It's a good thing for people to take care of things. It slows people down. It is something that everybody can do. The whole idea of maintenance and not just the pursuit of a goal, like this will cause this will cause this eventual goal, it kind of slows it down a little.

Ben Kinmont, Ich werde Ihr schmutziges Geschirr waschen
[I will wash your dirty dishes]: *Munich, 1994. In Karl Jager's home.
Photo: Thomas Keller.*

In light of that too, it's really interesting dealing with these
kinds of projects with cleaning up, with eating, or making food, or
whatever, in the art world, because the art world wants an object,
the art world wants something that lasts, the art world wants
something that's grand. There're two things that are really interesting to me about this. One is the issue of how do you produce
something that is basic and ephemeral, but to maintain, to be paid
attention to and to be taken seriously and to develop a critical
discourse about it. And then the other one, which is a big issue
that I've thought a lot about, is the whole feminine thing. It's a
woman's activity. And what does it mean to be a *man* doing dishes
as art? What does it mean to be a man and doing food as art?
Between that and raising my son Ian a lot of the time, I've had a
whole different kind of outlook on why women don't have children
and how people deal with domestic activities. Because it's not like
this produce, produce, produce activity, it's not . . . it has its own
pace. You can't force it, you can't force a child at a certain pace,
you can't force eating, that's not the goal inherent in it, so as a
result it's very hard to put this into the machine of the art world.
    I think it's important for people to be able to ask me, Why are
you doing this? To say to me, why are you washing my dishes as

art? Why are you putting yourself out? Why are you giving away all these paintings you made? Why are you going to give me the money from the project that you're making, your profits? Very basic questions. Making artists more vulnerable and available.

❖❖❖

Nobody knew I was going to give them a gift at the end—the sponge, the signed sponge, which was then used to clean the sink and countertops after the dishes were done. So they were all surprised about that. They were all surprised that I was just doing the dishes. And then I think they were also surprised that I was, there's this German term that's like a ghost, a spirit—I just came in and took care of something and then disappeared, I was gone. There was something nice about there not being any. . . no fuss, no monument. I bought them boxes to put the sponges into. And it's all about that the sponge is—the symbol of the signature is the sign of authorship and the way that they co-authored the piece by being willing to invite me, and the sign of our interaction with one another. It was a sign of my appreciation. I think it's very interest-

Ben Kinmont, Ich werde Ihr schmutziges Geschirr waschen [I will wash your dirty dishes]: *Munich, 1994. In Barbara Schlegel's home.*

ing in a sense of practice to give something *back* to people when you're doing art. And it's very nice for me personally to do that. I feel better about it. Not knowing that I was giving them something, I had—three cakes that were made for me, homemade, freshly made cakes, I had dinner maybe four times. I would come in and they would say, oh, let's sit down and have some cake that I made for you, and we can talk while we're eating cake and then we can wash dishes.

The biggest personal, favorite thing of mine is, it is really fun and easy to talk about art while washing dishes. That was a great, great thing. Maybe it's because part of your body and hands, you're active. How can you be pretentious while washing dishes? I couldn't. Maybe that's why I chose it, because I couldn't be pretentious. So it was very easy to talk, even though these were complete strang ers. It was really easy to get into a good conversation with them.

❖❖❖

If everyone is washing their dishes, and I'm washing my dishes, why do I even have to bother going over there to do it, other than just helping someone out and the idea of the artist being a help? The reason is there's different levels of understanding and meaningfulness that we bring into our lives. There's raw experience and as it moves and you come to understand it and experience it more and more, you can come up with a comprehension of it, then we can shape it into something that's more meaningful. My goal I suppose is to make experience more meaningful. The great thing about a gallery and the separateness of a gallery is—there's all this distraction going on, it's difficult for us physically and psychologically to deal with. You go into a gallery and it's quiet, and you see something that you can focus on, that you can say, here's my moment to be quiet.

So the whole point of doing this in someone's home is that I'm doing something and they're going to look at washing their dishes differently perhaps. Even though I do it in a normal way, I don't want to make it theatrical. Through the normalcy it can perhaps also become more meaningful. It's really about life, it's about how do we have meaningful moments in our lives. The whole issue of art's separateness and parameters is that's just what we have to do in order to understand things. Even if we say, stream of consciousness, you're feeling everything, an all-sensory kind of thing you've gone into—you come out of it. There's still a moment

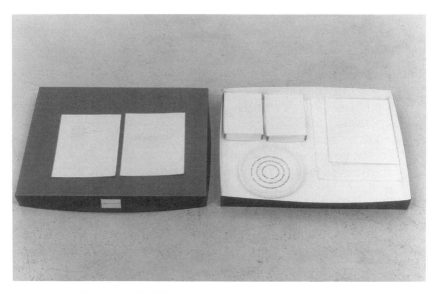

Ben Kinmont, Waffles for an Opening Archive, *1991–1992.*

when it occurs. That's why the archives are crucial. I'm trying to describe truthfully what happened. There's that and I'm also trying to allow someone else to experience what happened.

Janine Antoni

Interviewed May 12, 1992

And so I was covering his entire apartment with chocolate and lard, and finally I just had to leave or he was going to kill me. I got this old refrigerator and I made a heater with a hot plate, so I'm only now really moving in. . . . This is my brother and I pouring chocolate. And this is it as a cube, and it's six hundred pounds. We poured for two days straight to have the cooling process constant so it wouldn't crack. Then I gnawed on it for a month and half.

I had this idea that I wanted to make a traditional sculpture, that I wanted to carve. And I wanted to use an everyday activity that all of us could relate to, to take something that was so basic and turn it into a sculptural process. The logical step from there was to start with the idea that I wanted to sculpt with my mouth. The actual biting into the form is, you could say, prelinguistic. I was thinking about what babies do to understand something, that what they do is put it in their mouth. That's the basic way to know something. Often they destroy the object in the process. The act is intimate and destructive at the same time. So here I am, taking this

Janine Antoni, (above) Chocolate Gnaw, 1992. 600 lbs. chocolate
(before biting), marble pedestal. Collection Charles Saatchi. (Below),
Lard Gnaw, 1992. 600 lbs. lard (before biting), marble pedestal. Collection Charles Saatchi. Photo: Jenny L. Thompson.

minimalist cube and putting it in my mouth—it struck me as funny and seemed an accurate metaphor for my relationship to minimalism.

I asked myself, if I want to do a piece about eating, what material would be appropriate to sculpt out of? Chocolate seemed like a fantastic material because so many people have a charged relationship to chocolate. Lard also had a pretty consistent response. People were completely repulsed by the idea of my chewing on it. But fat is also the result of succumbing to the desire for chocolate.

I realized the moment I was going to spit out this material that people would have an association with bulimia. I knew I would be asked to account for this reference, so I read all the books I could on eating disorders. When the show opened, there was an article written about the work in *New York Magazine.* The readership was so wide that all of a sudden the media descended upon me. It was ridiculous—it was in *Food Arts Magazine,* it was in health magazines, it was in fashion magazines. It was used in so many different ways. Donahue even asked me to be on. Then I lived it again two years later when *Gnaw* showed in the Whitney Biennial. At the point that it first opened, I was a bit naive. It was my first one-person show. I had very little experience in the art world, and I was very excited by the fact that people outside the art world were interested. So I said, well this is a huge opportunity and I should engage people at whatever level they want. The fact that they're interested is wonderful.

If people wanted to talk about eating disorders, I felt pretty knowledgeable at that point, so I could engage them and I did. Little did I know that the piece would become a kind of illustration of the whole idea of eating disorders! My feeling about the work is that it was about *eating*. But the culture came back to me and said: "We have a disorder. That's what we're interested in." That reading of the work seems more about the culture's response to eating than my original intentions for the work. There's something very interesting about that. I think success for an artist often has to do with becoming a way of illustrating ideas that people are thinking about at the time and need a way to verbalize. In effect, though, I had produced this somehow. I wanted to introduce a dialog.

One way I came to look at it is that we're a culture that wants this fast fix. Bulimia seemed interesting as a metaphor for a society that ferociously gobbles everything up, and rather than digest it, they spit it up. In the end, though, the work has to do with the question of knowing an object or experiencing it.

Into the wall—they're negative imprints in the wall. The piece is called *Wean* and it mapped out an evolution that became an important model for all my work that followed. I was thinking about the stages of separation from the mother, about moving from some intimate contact with the body into the culture, to an object produced by the culture. It begins with my breast, my nipple, and then three latex nipples, and then the packaging that they come in. I was interested in the moment when the real nipple is replaced by the latex nipple. But I was also interested how we come back to the body through these kind of objects—how they locate the body in the culture and mediate our experience of our bodies. To me, the nipple, the lipstick, the soap are all the same kind of objects. They're the objects that we use to return to the body, to have an intimate interaction with our bodies.

How do you depict absence? If I take something that exists in the world like the wall and scoop these spaces out of them, then you can feel the absence. A lot of my early work dealt with architecture and exploring the body in the architecture. And also with architecture as the site for an artwork, this critique of the gallery space. With *Gnaw*, we could say the chocolate cube is equivalent to the wall. People make specific reference to minimalism, but to me the cube is an icon of architecture as well as of minimalism. To bite into the cube to me is the same gesture as my breast scooped out of the wall. In both works, you have an imprint or trace of the body left on a similar kind of object.

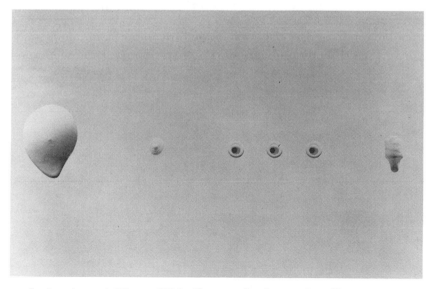

Janine Antoni, Wean, *1990. Sheet rock, plaster. Installation view.*

The cover of my invitation for *Gnaw* was lifted straight from the back of a the nipple package I used in *Wean*. This is the illustration of why it's a good nipple—because it's shaped like a breast. Can you imagine a breast shaped like that? The illustration is fairly abstract and many people didn't understand what the image was.

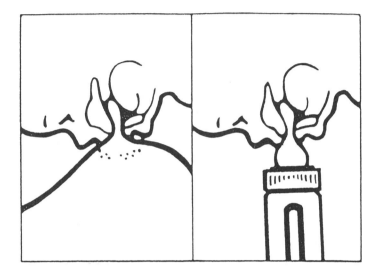

JANINE ANTONI

gnaw

February 22 - March 21

Opening - Saturday, February 22 6 - 8 pm

Janine Antoni, Gnaw exhibition invitation, 1994. Sandra Gering Gallery, New York, New York, 1994.

Some even thought it was a diagram for inserting tampons. There are a lot of these abstracted quasi-anatomical diagrams around— diagrams that aren't really anatomical at all but function as illustrations for using objects that relate intimately to our bodies.

My feeling is that we've lost a relationship to where things come from. What I try to do in all the work is to give a history of how the object made its way into the world. My feeling is that if you know that history, it changes your relationship to the object. I'm interested in the object's materiality, in how it is made, and to suggest a psychological dimension in the relationship with the object.

⋯◇⋯◇⋯◇⋯

Eureka was inspired by the story of Archimedes. While soaking in the tub, he realized that his body was displacing its exact capacity in water, and upon this revelation he jumped out of the tub and yelled Eureka! I like this story for two reasons. One is because

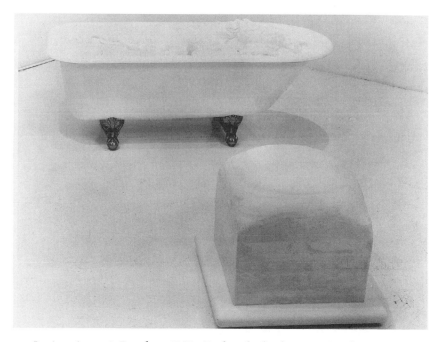

Janine Antoni, Eureka, *1993. Bath tub, lard, soap. Sandra Gering Gallery, New York, New York, 1994.*

Archimedes' body is the tool for the experiment, like my body is the tool making the work. But more important is the fact that he comes to this knowledge through his body. For *Eureka*, I submerged myself in a tub of lard, and, with the lard that was displaced, I made a cube of soap by mixing it with lye and water.

I put myself through these physical tasks to set up a situation where the viewer might empathize with the process. I want the viewer to imagine what it is like to do these things, to feel it through their body, to relate to the work in terms of body knowledge. They can consider their relationship to the object in terms of the process, as opposed to the normal way we approach these types of artworks by objectively decoding visual information. The decoding process is a form of analysis, and the problem is that it keeps you on the outside of the object. Analysis is a process of comparing the object in question to what is already known that is similar, which keeps you away from what is unique about that object. My work is an absurd attempt to enter the object, to be as intimate and obsessed as possible with the object. For me, lard is material of the body. By making soap out of this material, and using an amount equal to that of my body's capacity, metaphorically I would have entered the cube, and then I would be washing myself with myself. So that's what brought me to the idea of *Lick and Lather*—now I would work with my own image and literally wash myself with myself and feed myself with myself.

⊸◇⊷⊸◇⊷⊸◇⊷

I made a mold directly from my body so that there would be no sculpting except for the base. I used the mold to cast seven busts in chocolate and seven in soap. Washing and licking became the sculptural process through which I reshaped my own image. It was important to lick the chocolate busts as opposed to gnawing them, because it made it that much more obsessive. It was hard to remove anything just by licking! I liked the tension between the licking as a loving act and the fact that I was defacing myself. I took the soap busts into the tub and we washed together. It was like washing a baby. That also seemed like a caring act. The work really is an acting out of the complex relationship one has with one's physical appearance.

I intentionally work with clichés. Licking an image of myself in chocolate is a cliché of narcissism. The lipstick in *Gnaw* that was made from the lard I spit out is a cliché of women and beauty,

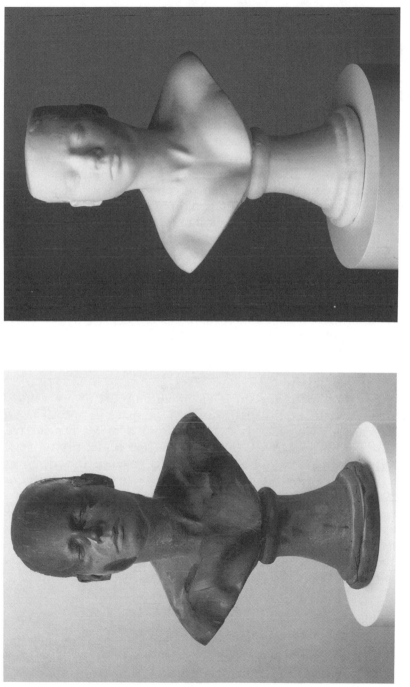

Janine Antoni, Lick and Lather, 1993–1994. One chocolate and one soap bust. Sandra Gering Gallery, New York, New York, 1994.

and the cube is a cliché of minimalism. What I want is for the viewer to walk in on my work and see something familiar. But hopefully as they spend time, it becomes less and less familiar. In terms of our feminism, or feminisms, it seems that we're at a point where certain black and white statements have been made. We hopefully have absorbed some of this and it is part of our conscious. But now we have to fine tune. There are gray areas, nuances, that need to be dealt with.

As we navigate through our everyday lives, we fall into these situations where intellectually we can make very clear decisions, but living through them it starts to get more complicated. In my work, I set up circumstances that directly deal with these areas, conditions that make me feel uncomfortable. It may sound strange, but to be in my studio alone licking my self-portrait is a difficult place to put myself in terms the contradictions these situations present.

I started with these basic features and then I was transforming the features slightly on each one. I was also thinking about the story of Pygmalion and Galatea. That reference is even more interesting than narcissism for me. All the work is a depiction of my relationship to that object. On the surface of the sculpture is a residue of my interaction with it. Pygmalion seems more correct as a reference. All the work is an acting out of the love/hate relationship with the object.

Sexuality and eroticism is an important part of my work. I feel it is time to explore desire from a woman's perspective. Art history has shown what is desirable from a man's perspective. Because I am a woman and my body is at the center of my work, it is easy for the work to be eroticized in a voyeuristic way, a way that goes against my intentions. One of my strategies for dealing with this problem is to make the work auto-erotic. In some ways it rejects the viewer. It's about a relationship I have with myself. And then not *showing*, not providing a picture of that relationship, again pushes the viewer out a bit. When things are working as planned, the work is calling you in and pushing you out at the same time. This is the tension I'm looking for.

⋞◇▷⋞◇▷⋞◇▷

I was casting as I was washing and licking. I would go back and forth from one to the other. That's basically how I work. I do a few winks of mascara and then I lick a little and then I wash a little. It's very fluid. I go from one obsessive task to the another.

I want to let the making take control of the form. I have a very articulated way in which I approach making an artwork. I start with an experience I want to give myself, rather than starting with something I want to communicate to the viewer. I feel as

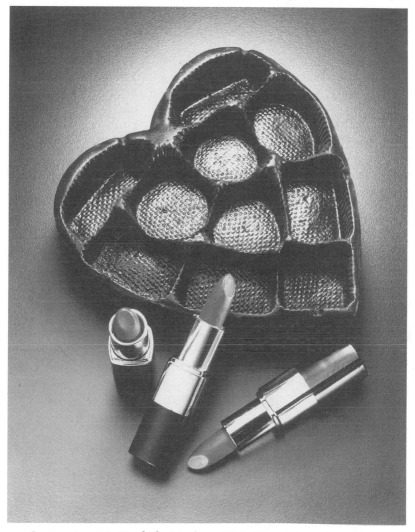

Janine Antoni, Lipslick Display, *1992. Heart-shaped packages for chocolate made from chewed chocolate removed from* Chocolate Gnaw, *lipsticks made with pigment, beeswax, and chewed lard removed from* Lard Gnaw. *Sandra Gering Gallery, New York, New York, 1994. Photo: John Bessler.*

though if I don't have an experience that's charged in some way, the viewers can't. I always have to stay very close to my experience. It is the only way it makes sense at all to me. I have to start at a very basic level. Once I've decided on the experience, I resist making for a very long time. And I think as rigorously as possible. I try to establish strict parameters for that experience, which I'm very aware set up a kind of meaning. Then when I begin to make, I try to suspend all that kind of thinking and I literally try to become obsessed with the process and fall in love with the object.

At that point, I feel that the object makes itself. And there is almost a point where I'm not sure whether I'm making the object or it's making me. That point is also where I'm reaching my own limits, whether it's psychological or physical limits. It always comes down to how far I will go for the object.

All the work means to be seductive. I try my best to pull you in. In *Gnaw*, I used an established form of seduction with the mirrored cosmetic display, which taps into conditioned desires. The lipstick and the heart-shaped packaging for chocolate candies in the display case were objects made from the material I spit out, all of it had been in my mouth, but they were conventionally desirable objects. For me, though, it was the hunk of chocolate and the collapsed lard that were beautiful. That's my aesthetic bias. The process of making the work is an actual enactment of that desire. Have you ever had the experience of being on the subway and sitting on a seat that is still warm from the person who sat there before? I want to give the viewer that experience. That is *my* way of accounting for the viewer. I want to get a little too close.

Rirkrit Tiravanija

Interviewed May 10 and May 14, 1994

It was good to disperse the activity. I'm always in there, but somehow to disperse it, even to whoever came up to get the food, even that exchange—saying, oh, yeah, you can tell them to do this. And people actually get themselves, go and tell people—get the chopsticks there, get your plates here. Subtle things like that. It works when people don't even consciously think it's anything. They just think, oh, it's the opening, obviously we're just eating the food and this is probably just part of that. It's not an immediate thing, like walking up to it, for some people, and saying, oh, yeah, I know

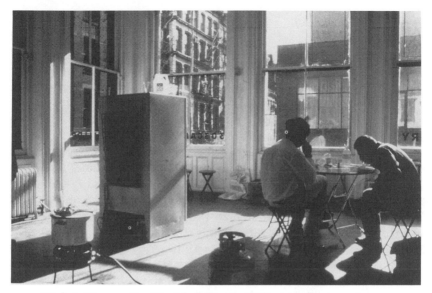

Rickrit Tiravanija, Untitled (Free), *1992. Installation view at 303 Gallery, New York, New York, 1992.*

what this is. It's perhaps even going home and falling asleep and waking up and realizing, What was that? I wcnt to this show, and I didn't see the show. . . ? It's more in the layers where it works. Some people won't even realize till later when they've read a review about it or they see it somewhere else.

So this occurs, people sit down with people they've never met and actually it's kind of more intimate. They have a discussion and develop a real relationship out of that experience. That was the sense of it, trying to make a situation that is—obviously it's not normal, but it could be quite simple. It wasn't anything different than what you would do anyway.

⬥⬦⬥⬦⬥

It was kind of a big shift in terms of scheme of things. I had been making works that were institutional critique. I still think this work is a critique, but in a different way. It developed out of certain specificity. Robert Longo made this show that was anti-image, this idea, no image, no text—I thought, well, I'll have to think about this. It was also a lot of things, it was my having to decide, What *is* important to myself and what is it that I have to do? What is really going on? What is it that has to change, or what is it that I have to change?

It was made for New York. It was in a space in the gallery where nobody wanted to be, and, being the way I work, it was fine. It was in the entryway where there was a window and a door. Everyone wanted to be inside the gallery. This was kind of the nonspace. It could be a prime space or it could be a really bad idea. For me, it really didn't make a difference. It ended up being, later I found, quite a prime spot because people would walk by and look at it day and night—it was in the window. People would say, yeah, I saw that. But of course, this was cooking, it was giving out smell through the space, it was a really strong yellow curry. But it was just for looks, and this related to the idea of displaying remnants from old pots and things like that, which die in the display case. Here, it was something that was active.

At the opening people would drink their cups and they would put it around, which I said, leave it. So certain things were already active within it. The reason I didn't serve it was because at that point it was just too early—I've always made dinner at home, always had lots of people over, made food for a lot of people. In that situation, I didn't really . . . it was on a pedestal. It was addressing certain traditions that were not quite over.

Rickrit Tiravanija, Beyond Good and Elvis, *1989. Installation view at Scott Hanson Gallery, New York, New York, 1989.*

I made that piece because I didn't want to do what everyone else was trying to do—"your first chance to be in a show on West Broadway." There were certain things I was playing with but it wasn't making a masterpiece. I decided I couldn't make something that would be just another thing to make. This was something else completely different. I think I felt there was more reason to making it than to making anything else. I thought it was a little bit of a subversion to smell up the space.

A lot of things turned at that point, in terms of thinking and realizing, This is what I do all the time and it is possible to make it with certain relationship to the context. I always try to do things that relate to the place or the situation it's in. It's not just food. Certain times it's particular kinds of food and within a relationship to certain things. Sometimes curry, but then sometimes—I did a piece in Hamburg, which was not Thai food at all but a very basic German soup, which developed out of a film that was playing in the installation.

⊰◈⊱⊰◈⊱⊰◈⊱

The setting for that piece was *Back Stage*, a show where they opened up the whole museum. It was the first show of the museum,

Rickrit Tiravanija, Fladder Soup, *1993. Installation view in* Back Stage *at Kunstverien in Hamburg, Germany, 1993.*

so they opened up all the spaces in the museum. I ended up in the loading dock. You walk into this loading dock and there was a typical German beerhall table, a long table with two long benches. There were shelves, one was a shelf with the soup being made and these pancakes, and the other was this storage shelf with boxes of instant things—instant soup and instant pancake mix. And then there's a monitor on the shelf that was playing the film. It was obvious it was a show, but it could very well just have been there. The film was made in Hamburg. It's a basic friendship story between a Chinese waiter and an Afghan man who ended up cooking in this Chinese kitchen in Hamburg. A discussion came up about soup. A soup got sent back and the African man, an assistant cook, said, Well, my wife makes good soup, she makes all these German soups. A dishwasher Pakistani man says, well, he's a good citizen, because he knows how to make this particular soup. Which was then the soup that was made for the piece. It was a key, this idea of being a foreigner and that making a good German soup would make you a good citizen or a good immigrant. It's like, you can be German. At a certain point you could maybe catch why the soup is being made. Out of my own relationship to the film, I felt this was the precise moment to what was going on.

So it doesn't always have to be Thai food. In a gallery or museum space, it's not a situation in which everything is handy, so you almost have to invent how to deal with it every time.

⊰◇⊱⊰◇⊱⊰◇⊱

One of the things I've come to realize doing this work is that it's really not so much about coming to see things, but to be in it. Which is not something I think a lot of people are really used to. You're still always looking for something, looking for it and looking for meaning, when actually you're in it and the meaning is made through *you*. I think it's a different way of experiencing art in that sense. It's not art as life, it's different.

This is something I'm always questioning. If you make life into art, then what would be more meaningful is just to have your life rather than to force it into something. So it's not just serving food. Food is kind of the frame and what happens within that frame is something else. It is an activity that is, on the one hand, it's quite a rupture to see food being served in a gallery, but on the other hand it is an activity that everyone does, it's something everyone can enter into after that initial point.

Rickrit Tiravanija, Untitled, *1994. Installation view in* Group Show *at Metro Pictures, New York, New York, 1994.*

I often use tables that are round, situations that are not quite closed—a round table is completely different from a rectangular table. I often think it's really architectural. It is kind of subtle architecture, and in relationship to the outside, the windows, where you sit. It makes a lot of difference in terms of how one deals with each other, and with the body. Those elements are always there, and they work in different situations in different ways.

I think there is always in Western cultural practice, that there is always some kind of investment in material and in objectness. It's never really let go. You still have to have a grasp on things, you can't just let it free float and understand it that way, or not understand it. You have to kind of ground everything.

I did the piece at Metro, which was these stools lined up in front of the window. That's the other thing, people generally would just sit on the stool and either look out the window or look in. The stools were there to be used in any situation, which means at some point somebody *could* carry it to the back and sit down, sit in front of a painting and look out that way. It is something that is about some kind of space and about social architecture. That kind of dynamic is something that I've tried to set up.

⋖◇⋗⋖◇⋗⋖◇⋗

Jerome's exhibition, being it was *Viennese Stories* and everything was kind of very invisible anyways, I went initially to feel out what was going on and the Secession has a coffee shop as part of the museum. Of course, a kind of obvious place. But the man who owns it has a restaurant and, total coincidence, in that restaurant he had two ladies cooking who were from Thailand.

That was a situation where, again, the idea was not to focus so much on myself but on something that was already there or somebody who was already there. There are certain levels—these two ladies having been there and working in a Viennese art cafe where they make Austrian food. One day a week, for dinner they would insert one Thai dish. This was something they already did, as their own. They were taught how to cook all these other meals and then they were given a free reign on one dish a week. They were really excellent cooks.

The thing about Thai cooking, it's not like you write things down and everything is measured, and you don't go and shop at the special place to get *the* particular mushroom so that it would taste this way. You just work with what you have and it's really just the

Rickrit Tiravanija, Untitled (Cooking with Tang and Timm), *1993.*
In Viennese Stories *at Vienna Secession, Vienna, Austria, 1993.*

spirit of it and the way it's done that comes through. So it's more than just tasting good, it's something else. They are very natural cooks, they just kind of throw things together. Which is the way I cook, I make recipes, but they're. . . . I mean, I often just say to people, look, we'll just cook together. That's the best way because you just kind of splash this in, splash that in.

So we cooked together and through that process, I got to know them and why they were there, why they were in Vienna, and how it came about. One of them has been there ten years and she's married to a lawyer. I couldn't figure out why she was working if she was married to a lawyer. It wasn't clear to me. But this is kind of, Vienna. It was a very strange coincidence that they were actually there. So this is, this happens.

I went before and met with the restaurant owner, and then went back and met them, and through that we had a discussion about what it would be, what we want to eat. What to make and how many people were going to be eating and basic things. We went shopping for food. After that, cooking together in the kitchen.

Irwin Wurm came around. It was his camera, so he recorded a lot of it. Then at some point he left and when we were shopping I pretty much shot it and I would hand it over to Michel, who was the owner of the restaurant, and he would shoot some things. Then when we cooked in the kitchen, we just set it down in one corner and let it run on its own. There were other people who were working around, other cooks and waiters who were around, and that was part of the interaction. They are very Thai, more Thai than I am, in their spirit and how they are and how they took people. It's such a foreign insertion into this Austrian situation.

In the end, the piece was just the videotape playing what we had recorded. It was sitting on top of the refrigerator in the cafe at the Succession. It was just sitting in the corner. It was like you might be any place and look up and see this thing that doesn't quite belong there. I try to make video function in a natural way. Otherwise it's too directed. I want it to be another layer rather than the central thing. And then you might just kind of slowly focus on it at some point or realize what it is that's happening in it.

⋖◈⋗⋖◈⋗⋖◈⋗

It may be there is never a defined work. When does the work actually occur? When does it actually become something or not? This is I think the idea that one is thinking about, kind of conscious about at a certain point. Is it just the sheet of paper that is the work? Or is it what I've just done, I've made that recipe? Or is it even the people who are just eating? So it's never. . . . I think it *is* that moment when you have to think, well, when is it art work? Or is it ever going to be? I think it occurs differently for different people with different experience. It might not occur at all—which I think is quite good! Or it might be constantly conscious. You bring yourself to it. I like that different level of things. Then maybe some people may try to bring themselves to a different level of thinking.

Chapter 10

Edible Architecture,
Cannibal Architecture

Allen S. Weiss

Beauty will be edible, or it will no longer be.
                              —*Salvador Dalí*

A miraculous gingerbread house in the middle of the forest,
ornamented with cakes and tarts and windows formed of barleysugar.
Two young children, Hansel and Gretel, abandoned by their parents,
lost in the woods, ravaged by hunger, come upon this hallucinatory
spectacle and partake of its delights. This wish fulfillment, this
extreme oral gratification, temporarily assuaging the terror of being
abandoned, in fact veils an evergreater and more primal fear: that of
being devoured. For the charming gingerbread house is but a lure, a
trap, inhabited by a wicked old woman who captures the children
and intends to eat them. The pleasure of eating dissimulates its
opposite, the threat of being devoured, for the confectionary house
hides its origin, the very oven that is to be the site of the childrens'
destiny. A single location, where the edible dissimulates the cannibal, is simultaneously utopic and dystopic, revealing the antithetical
sense of primal gustatory emotions. The architectural *heimlich*
(homey) conceals its *unheimlich* (uncanny) mystery, its *arcanum
arcanorum*, where the ultimate secret of life is revealed: death.[1] In
such intermingled pleasure and anxiety we have established the
antipodal limits of our subject. Yet, as we shall see, not all are as
lucky as these two children who escape from their gastronomic,
indeed gastrophobic or gastrophagic, fate.
        Edible architecture; cannibal architecture—the origins and
genesis of such monstrosities are a function of psychological

projection, where unconscious impulses organize the perceptual gestalt. Consider Leonardo da Vinci's fascination with the varied images that can be discovered in cloud formations or in a splotch of paint left by a sponge on a wall; human hands, animals, battle scenes, rocks, clouds, the sea, and so forth. Can we not discover in a distant landscape what appears to be a human head with gaping mouth, as objectified in scenes of hell painted by Bosch or Breughel, or in the double images of Salvador Dalí? The rhetorical trope of catachresis, producing monstrosities, creates such disquieting iconographic figures as "to enter the mouth of a cave" or "to be devoured by the earth," or "to descend into the bowels of the earth." Although the oneiric, infantile representations of the home tend toward the stable and the regular, as Gaston Bachelard reminded us, representations of the earth are often conducive of a dynamic, chaotic, labyrinthine imagination.[2] These images often skirt the limits of the horrific, the grotesque, the buffonic. For example, in the Bomarzo gardens, north of Rome, Orsini established a series of fantastic garden follies. We find there a gigantic, howling face, created by Pyrrho Ligorio. This *Ogre* (1551) is over ten feet tall, such that we may cautiously enter through the mouth into its shadowy interior to find the tongue formed by a picnic table, and the seats created by the teeth surrounding it. Here, the utopic and dystopic orders are reversed in relation to the gingerbread house: in Bomarzo, we are eaten, only to be invited to eat. Yet, as opposed to the marked symbolism of Grimm's fairy tale, the potentially dyspeptic, cannibalistic fantasy of Bomarzo in fact is highly theatrical and ultimately frivolous, as is the entirety of the space of the Italian renaissance garden. Indeed, the form of the mouth as theater also exists in the other arts. Consider, for example, Maurice Sendak's stage design for the film version of that other disquieting, balletic fairy tale, Tchaikovsky's *The Nutcracker*.[3] The stage curtain is composed of a gigantic head of the Nutcracker himself, closing vertically, it devours all those on stage. Or, in an equally astounding and disquieting theatrical representation, there exists a drawing by the famed geneticist turned psychotic artist Eugene Gabritschevsky, which depicts a stage setting where the proscenium is composed of an open, toothed, menacing mouth.[4] We find in his art the poetic manifestations of the Darwinian imagination gone berserk, where scientific genetic illustration is transformed into the most extreme iconography of the grotesque. How are we to understand these ravenous, often demonic, doubles of ourselves?

The major theoretical, polemical, statement on edible architecture and cannibal architecture was written by Salvador Dalí,
*"De la beauté terrifiante et comestible de l'architecture modern
style"* (On the terrifying and edible beauty of art nouveau architecture).[5] Dalí explained that Art Nouveau (Modern Style) architecture is the first to be based on the oneiric manifestations of desire.
This invention of a "hysterical sculpture" is derived from Art
Nouveau's fascination with organic, rather than mechanical forms.
The paradigm of Art Nouveau architecture is based on the fluid
"sculpting of reflections of crepescular clouds in water." These
forms manifest the "hard undulations of *sculpted water* with a
photographic concern for instantaneity." In fact, this notion explains the profound relations between Art Nouveau and the baroque, which can be summed up in Jean Rousset's observation that
a baroque facade is the aquatic reflection of a Renaissance facade.[6]
Dalí described these effects: "an immense and insane multicolored
and gleaming mosaic of pointillist iridescences from which emerge
the forms of pouring water, the forms of stagnant water, the forms
of glistening water, the forms of water grazed by the wind."[7]

These possibilities already existed, at least in the culinary creations of Carême, the greatest French chef of the nineteenth century,
who was able to create the waves of the sea, waterfalls, rivers, and
so forth by means of the subtle nuances of spun sugar.[8] Thus not
only do our arts and our dreams provide us with architecture in the
form of food. The history of gastronomy also exhibits creations where
food is presented in the form of architecture. Yet that which in
Dalí's architectural imagination approaches the perverse manifestations of the sublime would, in fact, reach the extreme of the picturesque in Carême's hands. The epitome of the influence of architecture
on gastronomy is undoubtedly to be found in Carême's pastry, where
he created a landscape architecture based on the organic forms of
nature that is truly, and not merely metaphorically, edible. Two of
his books, *Le Pâtissier Parisien* and *Le Pâtissier Pittoresque*, contain
numerous architectural drawings that are, in fact, projects for ex-
ceedingly elaborate desserts.[9] Carême, deemed the "Palladio of cooking," created gastronomic-architectural fantasies (sometimes over a
meter tall) that encompassed the entire range of subjects and nations: pavillions, rotundas, temples, ruins, towers, belvederes, for-
tresses, waterfalls, fountains, country homes, thatched cottages, mills,
hermitages; Italian, Turkish, Islamic, Russian, Polish, Venetian,
Chinese, Irish, Gallic, Egyptian. He even dreamed of a durability far
beyond that of the average dessert; by means of confectioning his

creations in a mixture of gum arabic, gum tragacanth, sugar, starch, and marble dust, his architectural desserts were able to last as long as six years. Consider, for example, his miniature trompe- l'oeil dessert representing a "grotto covered with moss," with the rocks constructed of small cakes glazed with different types of sugar (pink, carmelized, saffron) and coated with crystal sugar and chopped pistachios, then surrounded with meringue and vanilla cream, and crowned with a waterfall of silvered spun sugar.[10]

These fantasies could be seen as the frivolous doubles of Grimm's nightmarish gingerbread house, conceived in the same epoch. Today, such inventions are, alas, relegated to history. Contemporary gastronomic architecture is much more modest. For example at Lasserre, the renowned Parisian restaurant, each course arrives at the table accompanied by a small decorative spun sugar building. Or, most modest of all, are the sugar-coated praline pebbles of the great confectioner Auer in Nice, pebbles that can be distinguished from those on the nearby beach only by means of taste. It is rather in the cinema, with its desire for scopophilic excess and verisimilitude, that this tradition has been, at least briefly and ironically, resuscitated in Peter Greenaway's film, *The Belly of an Architect*, we witness a Roman feast in which the centerpiece consists of a culinary reproduction of one of the masterpieces of French revolutionary architecture: Etienne-Louis Boullée's *Cénataph à Newton*. This monument becomes an icon of the film and the architect's fate, a cinematic *vanitas* or memento mori. Like the oven in the gingerbread house, the mausoleum-cake reveals the intimate connection between food and death. It effectively symbolizes the morbid personality and impending demise of the architect himself. (And we might note that Carême's romantic miniature picturesque was in part a tangential reaction to Boullée's rationalist monumental sublime.)

Dalí understood the deepest psychological implications of such efforts, exemplified for him by the commonplace, yet delirious, comparison of Art Nouveau architecture with pastry. Such a homology affords us the unheard of possibility of eating the objects of our architectural desire. This return to a more primal, since edible, beauty evinces Dalí's realization that "erotic desire is the ruin of intellectualist aesthetics"—such that architecture is oneiric and symbolic before it is pragmatic.

Following the surrealist ontology and epistemology of transforming the forms of the world according to the lineaments of our desires, these gustatory passions were not lost on Dalí's own work.

His iconography, governed by the double imagery of his paranoic-critical method, abounds in mountains, monuments, and buildings in the form of melting cheese (e.g., *La Naissance des désirs liquides* [1932]; faces which are part of the landscape (e.g., *Apparition of a Face and a Fruit Dish a Beach* [1938]); and skulls transplanted in the scenery, transforming the landscape into a veritable *vanitas*, literally a *nature morte*, (e.g., *Tête de mort atmosphérique sodomisant un piano à queue* [1934]).

The connections between pleasure and nostalgia, mortality and destiny, history and monumentality are central to the pictorial genre of *vanitas*, of which the *still life* or *nature morte* is a subcategory often revealing the utmost gastronomic splendor. The pleasures of life, intense yet transitory, are represented by a network of symbols: tables overflowing with rare foods, adorned with intricate silverwork, fine crystal, brilliant floral bouquets.[11] Yet such sensual exhiliration is tempered by the threat of melancholy. The work of time the destroyer is everywhere apparent: the last grains of sand are about to drop in an hourglass; the fruit is just slightly too ripe and threatened by an insect; a bubble—perhaps reflecting the very image of the artist, our double—is about to burst.

Yet the threat to a portrayed figure can take a decidedly more culinary form. The tradition of the still life, in its most perverse manifestations, occasionally takes on a distinctly cannibalistic turn. Most astounding in this regard are Giuseppe Arcimboldo's composite portraits, such as *The Four Seasons* (1573), a strange variation on the classic iconography of the ages of man, where the heads are composed of flowers (spring), fruits and vegetables (summer and autumn), and leaves and branches (winter): his portrait of *The Cook* circa 1570), whose head is composed of animals on a platter, ready to be served; or *The Vegetable Gardener* (circa 1590), an image consisting of assorted vegetables in a bowl that, when turned upside down, reveals a man's head.[12] Other manifestations, by other artists, also exist, and that this passion should be displayed in pastry design is not surprising. Casanova recounted the story of a fabulous dinner he had created in Cologne. The finale was a cake on which were represented the portraits of all the sovereigns of Europe. Casanova's passion for royalty was symbolically manifested in this attempt at complete devoration. As Chantal Thomas explained. "A superb *potlach.* They risked indigestion, they gorged themselves with, they feasted upon kings. They stuffed their pockets with them. Upon their return they found bits of Louis XV or of Catherine stuck to the lining of their clothes, their fingers were sticky with them they distractedly nibbled on them."[13] Symbolic overcompensation or childish reaction? As we say of an adorable child: "I could eat him up!" Needless to say, as Kleinian psychoanalysis teaches us, the dynamics of love and hate are played out through the mechanics of devoration and expulsion, incorporation and expropriation.

This dialectic of "dead life" *(nature morte)* is played out in two related works by Marcel Duchamp: *Torture-morte* (1959), consisting of a plaster foot covered with flies; and *Sculpture-morte* (1959), a head à la Arcimboldo composed of marzipan vegetables and an insect, one of the very rare *trompe l'oeil* artworks that can actually be eaten. In these two works, the symbolism of *vanitas* is divided into its component parts: as the fly on *Sculpture-morte* (a perverse still life) symbolically warns us of our own destiny, the flies on *Torture-morte* (a morbid antiportrait) reveal the ultimate limit of our fate. Duchamp: "Men are mortal, pictures too."[14]

But the drama may be reversed architectural phantasmagoria can also be projected as a utopian, life-giving delicacy. In James Joyce's *Ulysses*, Leopold Bloom, who "ate with relish the inner organs of beasts and fowls" and whose famous breakfast consisted of fried kidneys, imagines at one point that a new era is at hand, where "ye shall ere long enter into the golden city which is to be, the new Bloomusalem in the Nova Hibernia of the future." The description that follows obeys classic dream logic, incorporating the residues of quotidian events, with their gastric and gastronomic homologues, into the dreamwork: "Thirty-two workmen wearing rosettes, from all the counties of Ireland, under the guidance of Derwan the builder, construct the new Bloomusalem. It is a colossal ediface with crystal roof, build in the shape of a huge pork kidney, containing forty thousand rooms."[15] Such an architectural design obeys the rare, surreal, organic laws foreshadowing the later work of Frederick Kiesler, whose model for the *Endless House* (1959) resembles Boschian plant husks or transected intestinal parts, who designed a house in the form of a tooth (1947). His *Grotto for Meditation* (1963) was conceived in the form of a fish.[16] An equally grotesque image is Victor Hugo's drawing, *L'intestin de Léviathan*, which illustrates the following passage from his *Les misérables* (Part 5): "PARIS! What are its intestines? The sewers . . . " Or quite differently, the surreal and the neoclassic occasionally combine in postmodern paradox: witness the project by Sacha Sosno of the École de Nice, consisting of a building in the form of a head, whose upper part is obliterated by a square block. Yet Sosno's perturbed neoclassicism does not quite reach the disquieting limits that his project announces and that is foreshadowed by the following thought of Victor Hugo: "The house, like man, can become a skeleton."[17]

Unlike the gingerbread house, here edible architecture and cannibal architecture find their common ground in the aesthetic sublimation of our most primal desires and fears. But what happens when the course of history transforms these passions and fears into prodigious instantiations of universal destiny? Dalí's exegesis of the desublimated oneiric beauty of liquid architecture also reveals what he terms "the apparition of the cannibal imperialism of the Modern Style." This enunciation of what we may term the *anxiety of architecture* was written in 1933: "cannibal imperialism" was already far more than just a psychoaesthetic metaphor. It was on the verge of becoming a historical nightmare, where the sheer terror and dread at the source of the aesthetic sublime came to the fore, placing us on the edge of, indeed within, the abyss. For the tale of the gingerbread house foreshadows its demonic, hyperbolic double: the ovens of Auschwitz.

Notes

1. On the problematic, see Anthony Vidler, "The Architecture of the Uncanny: The Unhomely Houses of the Romantic Sublime," *Assemblage* 3 (1987), 11–14 and passim.

2. Gaston Bachelard, *La terre et les rêveries du repos* (Paris: José Corti, 1948), passim.

3. This film version, created in 1986, was performed by the Pacific Northwest Ballet.

4. The drawing described here is to be found in the collection of the Galerie Alphonse Chave, in Vence, France. On his work, see Luc Debraine, "Eugène Gabritschevsky," *L'Art Brut*, Fascicule 16 (Lausanne: Collection de l'Art Brut, 1990). On the relations between physiognomy, psychopathology, and the grotesque, see Jean-Jacques Courtine, "Raw Bodies" in *Portraits from the Outside: Figurative Expression in Outsider Art*, pp. 37–42, passim.

5. Salvador Dalí, "De la beauté terrifiante et comestible de l'architecture modern style," *Minotaure* 3–4 (1933): 68–76.

6. Jean Rousset, *Le Miroir enchanté*, cited in Gérard Genette, *Figures I* (Paris: Seuil, 1966), p. 28.

7. Dalí, "De la beauté," p. 28.

8. Jean-Claude Bonnet, "Carême ou les derniers feux de la cuisine décorative," *Romantisme: Revue du Dix-Neuvième Siècle*, vol. 17–18 (Paris: Champion, 1977), p. 40.

9. Ibid., pp. 23–43.

10. Carême, *Le Pâtissier Parisien*, Fourth Part, p. 43; cited in Bonnet, ibid., p. 40.

11. See the recent catalogue of the exhibition *Les Vanités dans la peinture au XVIIe siècle* (Paris: Petit Palais, 1991).

12. See *The Arcimboldo Effect: Transformations of the Face from the 16th to the 20th Century*, ed. Pontus Hulten (New York: Abbeville, 1987).

13. Chantal Thomas, *Casanova: Un voyage libertin* (Paris: Denoël, 1985), p. 145.

14. Marcel Duchamp, *Dialogues with Marcel Duchamp by Pierre Cabanne*, trans. Ron Padgett (New York: Viking, 1971), p. 67. For a study of these works in the context of Duchamp's later production, see Dalia Judovitz, "(Non)sense and (Non)art in Duchamp," in *Nonsense, Art & Text* 37, (1990) 80–86, passim.

15. James Joyce, *Ulysses* [1914] (New York: Random House, 1961), p. 484.

16. See Lisa Phillips, *Frederick Kiesler* (New York: Whitney Museum and W. W. Norton, 1989).

17. Victor Hugo, *Les travailleurs de la mer* [1866], *Oeuvres complètes: Roman III* (Paris: Laffont, 1985) p. 51: cited in Vidler, "The Architecture of the Uncanny," p. 23.

Chapter 11

Food, Health, and Native-American Farming and Gathering

Gary Paul Nabhan

"It was this was, long time ago," the old Indian lady—a member of Arizona's Sand Papago tribe that calls itself the Hia O'odham—explained through a distant relative, who was translating: "The People were like a cultivated field producing after its kind, recognizing its kinship; the seeds remain to continue to produce. Today all the bad times have entered the People, and they [the O'odham] no longer recognize their way of life. The People separated from one another and became few in number. Today all the O'odham are vanishing."[1]

Candelaria Orosco sat in a small clapboard house in the depressed mining town of Ajo, Arizona, recalling the native foods that she had hunted, gathered, and farmed before the turn of the century. Her leg hurt her, for the sores on it were taking a long time to heal. Today this is a common diabetic affliction of her people, the O'odham, who now suffer from the highest incidence of diabetes of any ethnic population in the world.[2] Orosco was trying hard to describe the life of her kin, the Sand Papagos, as they had lived prior to such afflictions, when they had obtained their living from what outsiders consistently regard as a "hopeless desert." Around the time of Orosco's birth, a U.S. Indian agent had visited the O'odham and described their habitat in this way: "Place the same number of whites on a barren, sandy desert such as they live on, and tell them to subsist there; the probability is that in two years they would become extinct."[3]

Yet, when I spoke to Orosco, she invoked a litany of plant and animal names in her native language; these names refer to herbs and seeds and roots, birds and reptiles and mammals that once formed the bulk of her diet. Even when English rather than O'odham words are used for these nutritional resources, the names of the native food that once filled her larder still have an exotic ring to them. For meat, her family ate desert tortoises, pack rats, bighorn sheep, tomato hornworm larvae, desert cottontails, pronghorn antelope, Gambel's quail, mule deer, white-wing doves, Gila River fish, black-tailed jackrabbits, and occasional stray livestock. Although the unpredictability of desert rains kept her people from harvesting crops on a regular basis at too many places, they did successfully cultivate white tepary beans, Old Lady's Knees muskmelons, green-striped cushaw squash, sixty-day-flour corn, Spanish watermelons, white Sonora wheat, and Papago peas. Perhaps the variety of wild plant foods gathered by her family is more bewildering: broomrape stalks, screwbean mesquite pods, plantain seed, tansy mustard, amaranth, cholla cactus buds, honey mesquite, povertyweed, wolfberries, hog potato, lamb's-quarters, prickly pears, ironwood seed, wild chilies, chia, organ-pipe, senita, and sandfood.[4] When Orosco mentioned the latter plant—an underground parasite that attaches to the roots of wind-beaten shrubs on otherwise barren dunes—my facial expression must have given me away.

"What's that?" she asked in O'odham.

I stammered, "Sandfood . . . did you mean that you once heard from the old people that they knew how to find it, and they once told you how it tasted?" Few people alive today have ever seen this sandfood, let alone tasted it, for it is now endangered by habitat destruction.

"I said that *I* ate it. I wouldn't have told you that it had a good sweet taste if I hadn't eaten it myself. How could I explain to you what other people thought it tasted like or how to harvest it? Because it doesn't stick up above the ground like other plants, I had to learn to see where the little dried-up ones from the year before broke the surface. That's where I would dig."

As she described how to steam succulent plants in earthen pits, boil down cactus fruit into jam or syrup, roast meat over an open fire, and parch wild legume seeds to keep them for later use, Orosco spoke matter-of-factly of the work involved in desert subsistence. There were no smackings of romanticism about the halcyon days of her youth; nonetheless, it was clear that she felt some foods of value had been lost. Her concerns about the loss of gathering and farming traditions are much the same as those voiced by her fellow tribesman, the late Miguel Velasco, in an interview with Fillman Bell in 1979:

> We are from the sand, and known as Sand Indians, to find our way of life on the sand of the earth. That is why we go all over to seek our food to live as well. We cover a large portion of land in different harvest seasons to gather our food to store in time of winter season. Long time ago, this was our way of life. We did not buy food. We worked hard to gather foods. We never knew what coffee was until the White People came. We drank the desert fruit juices in harvest time. The desert food is meant for the Indians to eat. The reason so many Indians die young is because they don't eat their desert food. . . . They will not know how to survive if Anglos stopped selling their food. The old Indians lived well with their old way of life.[5]

Nonetheless, oral accounts such as these are often simply dismissed as "nostalgia for the old ways," even by eminent ethnobotanists such as Peter Raven, who used this phrase to introduce a critique of my book on Native American agricultural change, *Enduring Seeds.*[6] If we use a simple dictionary definition of "nostalgia"—a longing for experiences, things, or acquaintances belonging to the past—we may or may not include under its rubric some of the statements made by Indian elders. Consider, for instance, this commentary by Chona, recorded by Ruth Underhill in *Autobiography of a Papago Woman* during the early thirties:

> We always kept gruel in our house. It was in a big clay pot that my mother had made. She ground up seeds into flour. Not wheat flour—we had no wheat. But all the wild seeds, the good pigweed and the wild grasses. . . . Oh, how good that gruel was! I have never tasted anything like it. Wheat flour makes me sick. I think it has no strength. But when I am weak, when I am tired, my grandchildren make me a gruel out of the wild seeds. That is *food.*[7]

Chona was clearly referring to foodstuffs that had formed a greater proportion of her dietary intake in the past than they did at the time she spoke with Underhill. And yet these foods were not exclusively relegated to the past, because they retained their functional value when she was sick, providing her with nourishment that mainstream American foods could not. Moreover, in Chona's mind, the native desert seeds had remained as the quintessential foods, embodying her cultural definition of what food *should be*. Because she did not consider the value of her people's traditional diet to be obsolete. Chona's respect for that diet should not be relegated to the shelf of antiquarian trivia.

This point was again brought home to me by Candelaria Orosco. After we spent several hours looking at pressed herbs, museum collections of seeds, and historic photos of plants that I had presumed to be formerly part of her culture's daily subsistence, she brought out several of her own collections. She rolled out from under her bed two green-striped cushaw squashes that she had grown in her postage-stamp-sized garden. Then she reached under her stove and showed me caches of cholla cactus buds and some wild seeds she had gathered. These foodstuffs were not simply for "old times" sake"; they had been the fruits of her efforts toward self-reliance for more than ninety years.

Pessimists or self-described "realists" might still dismiss the relict consumption of native foods by Chona or Candelaria Orosco as nostalgic and trivial. Because these plants and animals now make up such a small portion of the diet of contemporary Indians, they are said to play no significant functional role in their nutrition or their culture. If a Navajo eats more Kentucky Fried Chicken than he does the mutton of Navajo Churro sheep, is it not true that, ecologically and nutritionally speaking, he is more like an urban Kentuckian than he is like his Dine ancestors?

The answer may be a qualified yes. I interpret many of the O'odham elders' statements as warnings to their descendents that they are indeed abandoning what it means to be culturally and ecologically O'odham. This concern is explicit in the following quote from the late great O'odham orator Venito Garcia:

> The way life is today, what will happen if the Anglos discontinued their money system? What will happen to our children? They will not want to eat the mountain turtle, because they have never eaten any. Maybe they will eat it if they get hungry enough. I think of all the desert plants we used to eat, the desert spinach we cooked with chile. . . . If we continue to practice eating our survival food, we may save our money we do receive sometimes. . . . The Chinese, they still practice their

old eating habits. They save all their money. The Anglos don't like this. They [the Chinese] like to eat their ant eggs [rice]. They even use their long sticks to eat with, picking the ant eggs up with their long sticks and pinning it to their mouths. This is their way of life.[8]

The argument stated so clearly by Garcia is that other cultures have persisted with culinary traditions in a way that is not dismissed as nostalgic conservatism. To be Chinese is to be one who eats rice with chopsticks, according to Garcia's view as an outsider; likewise, an outsider should be able to recognize the desert-dwelling O'odham by their consumption of cactus, amaranth greens, or mesquite. Although such dietary definitions are too restrictive for anthropologists to take seriously, traditional peoples often revealingly use culinary customs as primary indicators of a particular culture.

⊷◇⊷◇⊷◇⊶

A further connection is made by O'odham elders in relation to their culinary traditions, and that is their linkage with health and survival. The elders not only recall "survival foods" used during times of drought and political disruption, but they also remember the curative quality of the native foods that were a customary component of their diets. These presumed curative qualities are now being scientifically investigated, for, in a very real sense, native foods may indeed be the best medicine available to the O'odham. The O'odham metabolism evolved under the influence of native desert plant foods with peculiar characteristics that formerly protected the people from certain afflictions now common among them.

Through the thirties, native desert foods contributed a significant portion of Pima and Papago diets; mesquite, chia, tepary beans, cacti, and cucurbits were eaten as commonly as foods introduced by Europeans. At that time, the O'odham were generally regarded as lean, modest people who worked hard at obtaining a subsistence from one of the most unpredictable but biologically diverse deserts in the world. Then government work projects and World War II came along and, rather than tilling their own floodwater fields and small irrigated patches, the O'odham became cheap labor for extensive irrigated cotton farms in Anglo communities near their reservations. Others went off to the war and became accustomed to a cash economy and canned food.

When these people returned to their villages in the late forties, their fields were overgrown or eroded owing to lack of constant care, and off-reservation opportunities were still calling. Government advisers termed their ancient farming strategies risky and unproductive, and offered no assistance in renovating the fields that for centuries had remained fertile under periodic cultivation.[9] Instead, the tribal governments were encouraged either to develop their own large farms using the corporate model or to lease tribal lands to non-Indian farmers to do the same. Less than a tenth of the traditional farms of the O'odham survived these economic and social pressures. As the fifties came and went, subsistence farming ceased to be a way of life, while hunting and gathering remained activities for only a small percentage of the indigenes.

Before the war, diabetes had been no more common among the O'odham than it was among the population of the United States as a whole. And yet, twenty-five years later, the O'odham had a prevalence of diabetes fifteen times that of the typical American community. Young O'odham men in the early 1970s weighed an average of ten pounds more than their 1940 counterparts and were considered overweight verging on obesity. Since obesity is correlated with susceptibility to diabetes, pathologists at first concluded that the "escape" of the O'odham from their primitive, feast-or-famine cycle of subsistence had made calories more regularly available year-round; hence, they had gained weight and diabetes had set in.

The only flaw in this theory was that the modern wage-earning O'odham individual was not necessarily consuming any more calories than his or her traditional O'odham counterpart or, for that matter, than the average Arizona Anglo. The difference, I believe, was not in the number of calories consumed but in the kinds of cultivated and wild plants with which the O'odham had coevolved.

Recently, I sent a number of desert foods traditionally prepared by the O'odham to a team of Australian nutritionists, who analyzed the foods for any effects they might have on blood-sugar levels following meals.[10] High blood-sugar levels are of concern because they stress the pancreas. If stressed repeatedly, the pancreas essentially becomes poisoned. Insulin metabolism becomes permanently damaged, and the dangerous syndrome known as diabetes develops. Yet when a person is fed acorns, mesquite pods, and tepary or lima beans, the special dietary fiber in these foods reduces blood-sugar levels or at least prolongs the period over which sugar is absorbed into the blood. In short, these native foods may protect Indian diabetics from suffering high blood-sugar levels following a meal. Mesquite pods and acorns are among the ten percent most effective foods ever analyzed for their effects in controlling blood-sugar rises after a meal.[11]

Other recent studies suggest that many desert foods contain mucilaginous polysaccharide gums that are viscous enough to slow the digestion and absorption of sugary foods. These mucilages have probably evolved in many desert plants to slow water loss from the seeds, seedlings, and succulent tissues of mature plants. The O'odham metabolism may, in turn, have adapted to their qualities after centuries of dependence on them. Prickly pear fruit and pads, cholla cactus buds, plantain seeds, chia seeds, mesquite seeds, and tansy mustard seeds contain such gums. All were former seasonal staples of the O'odham; all are nearly absent from their diet today. Australian nutritionist Jennie Brand hypothesizes that these foods served to protect indigenous people from the diabetic syndrome to which they were genetically susceptible.[12]

For those on a traditional diet, diabetes was not likely to be expressed. But diabetes-prone Indians on a fast-food diet of fried potatoes, soft drinks or beer, sweets, and corn chips find their insulin metabolism going haywire. At the Phoenix Indian Hospital, Boyd Swinburn has recently compared the responses of twenty-two patients who changed from a reconstructed, traditional O'odham diet to a fast-food diet consisting of virtually the same number of calories. When they switched to what we nicknamed the "Circle-K diet," their insulin sensitivity to glucose worsened, as did their glucose tolerance. As Swinburn concluded, "The influence of westernization on the prevalence of type 2 diabetes may in part be due to changes in diet composition."[13] For the O'odham and other recently westernized indigenous peoples, a return to a diet similar to their traditional one is no nostalgic notion; it may, in fact, be a nutritional and survival imperative.

⊂⊚⊃⊂⊚⊃⊂⊚⊃

In desert villages where native food plants were formerly sown and gathered, the majority of the residents are now classified as unemployed or underemployed. Because their income levels are so low, they are eligible for government surplus commodity foods, nearly all of which have been shown to be nutritionally inferior to their native counterparts.[14] At the same time, the hyperabundance of these federally donated foodstuffs serves as a disincentive for local food production. As one O'odham woman lamented, "Why grow our different kinds of beans when someone delivers big bags of pinto beans to our house every month? The demise of local farming and gathering, indulgence in a welfare economy, and a worsening of health and self-esteem are linked. This syndrome is not restricted to the O'odham; by the year 2000 taxpayers will spend $2 billion annually on medical care for a quarter of a million diabetics of Mexican and Indian descent living in Arizona.[15]

Is it not ironic that, at the same time, more than a quarter-million agricultural acres in Arizona have been abandoned owing to excessive irrigation costs of producing water-consumptive, conventional crops? Native crops, some of which require a third to a fifth as much water as conventional crops to obtain the same economic yield, were not until recently even considered a feasible option.[16] The predominantly Anglo society to which the food industry caters is simply not accustomed to the tastes, textures, and preparation techniques associated with these pre-Columbian foods.

I am reminded of the words of ethnobotanist Melvin Gilmore, who began his work among Indian farmers and gatherers seventy years ago, before the tide of diabetes and agricultural desolation had swamped them:

> We shall make the best and most economical use of our land when our population shall become adjusted in habit to the natural conditions. The country cannot be wholly made over and adjusted to a people of foreign habits and tastes. There are large tracts of land in America whose bounty is wasted because the plants that can be grown on them are not acceptable to our people. This is not because the plants are not useful and desirable but because their value qualities are not known.... The adjustment of American consumption to American conditions of production will bring about greater improvement in conditions of life than any other material agency.[17]

If such a call for the return of the native seems to be an affliction of those of us preoccupied with the obscure scholarly pursuit of ethnobotany, perhaps it is pertinent to hear the same call echoed a few years ago by one of America's finest immigrant food writers, Angelo Pellegrini:

Since Walt Whitman sounded his barbaric yawp over the roof-tops of the world, the American landscape has undergone considerable change. The pastoral plains have been impoverished; many of the forests have been denuded; much of the subterranean treasure has been wastefully extracted. The builders of the nation, bold and reckless and impatient, have indeed used the body of America irreverently. . . . And yet, in an exhausted world, America remains a land of plenty. It is no exaggeration to say that its agricultural possibilities are relatively unlimited. An immediate and urgent problem for the American of today is how to use them toward humane living.[18]

I have written elsewhere:

We will have missed the point if we only select one of these profitable natives, create new hybrids with it, and grow them as monocultures just like any conventional cash crop. The Native American agricultural legacy is more than a few hardy, tasty cultigens waiting to be "cleaned up" genetically for consumers, and then commercialized as novelty foods. Our goal must be something beyond blue corn chips, tepary bean party dips, amaranth candy, sunflower seed snacks, and ornamental chiles. These nutritious crops deserve to be revived as mainstays of human diets, and not treated as passing curiosities. These cultivated foods are rich in taste and nutrition, yes, but they are also well adapted to the peculiarities of our land.[19]

And the peculiarities of the Native American metabolism may be well adapted to these plant foods. Would it not be less costly to subsidize the revival of native food production and consumption among the O'odham and other diabetes-prone Indians than to assume that an annual $2 billion for medical treatment that could have been prevented by nutrition education for Arizona's ethnic populations? Would it not be better to market native foods grown and gathered by native peoples than to appropriate from them the cream of the crop, only to patent, trademark, privatize, and price them out of the reach of most native peoples? This dilemma has already arisen with wild rice and blue corn: market prices for elite consumers have driven these native foods beyond a price thought reasonable by many Indian consumers.

And yet certain natives have responded by forming collectives to ensure that some portion of the supplies of these native foods does reach their own people. The Navajo Family Farm project in Leupp, Arizona, and the Ikwe Marketing Collective in White Earth, Minnesota, are but two examples of Native Americans funneling a greater abundance of traditional grains back into their own communities.[20]

Not all the seeds that formerly nourished Native Americans have vanished. Some may have fallen dormant from infrequent usage, but that does not mean that their production cannot be revived. And revival itself is not necessarily a nostalgic cop-out, a retreat from the supposed inexorable trend of dominant societies to make every place, every people, and every meal like all the others. The diminishment of diversity—cultural, culinary, or other—is not inexorable. Ultimately, such diversity may be the soundest means our species has to survive.

Notes

1. Candelaria Orosco interview in Fillman Bell, Keith Anderson, and Yvonne G. Stewart, *The Quitobaquito Cemetery and Its History* (Tuscon: Western Archaeological Center, National Park Service, 1980), p. 50.

2. W. C. Knowler, P. H. Bennett, R. F. Hamman, and M. Miller, "Diabetes Incidence and Prevalence in Pima Indians: A 19-fold Greater Incidence than in Rochester, Minnesota," *American Journal of Epidemiology* 108 (1978), p. 497.

3. E. A. Howard, an 1887 Indian agent at the Pima Agency, quoted in G. P. Nabhan, "Papago Indian Desert Agriculture and Water Control in the Sonoran Desert, 1697–1934," *Applied Geography* 6 (1986), pp. 43–59.

4. Gary Paul Nabhan, Wendy Hodgson, and Frances Fellows, "A Meager Living on Larva and Sand? Hia Ced O'odham, Food Resources and Habitat Diversity in Oral and Documentary Histories," *Journal of the Southwest* 31 (December, 1989), in press.

5. Miguel Velasco interview in Bell, Anderson, and Stewart, *Quitobaquito Cemetery*, p. 60.

6. Peter Raven, "Book Review: A Nostalgia for the Old Ways," *Natural History* (April-May, 1989); Gary Paul Nabhan, *Enduring Seeds: Native American Agriculture and Wild Plant Conservation* (San Fransicso: North Point Press, 1989).

7. Chona interview in Ruth Underhill, *Autobiography of a Papago Woman* (Menasha, Wisconsin: American Anthropological Association, 1936; reprint augmented ed., New York: Holt, Reinhart, and Winston, 1979).

8. Venito García interview in Bell, Anderson, Stewart, *Quitobaquito Cemetery*, p. 71.

9. For a discussion of outsiders' views of traditional O'odham Indian farming, see Nabhan, "Papago Indian Desert Agriculture," and Gary Paul Nabhan, "What Do You Do When the Rain Is Dying?" *The Desert Smells Like Rain: A Naturalist in Papago Indian Country* (San Francisco: North Point Press, 1982), p. 46.

10. Janette C. Brand, B. Janelle Snow, Gary P. Nabhan, and A. Stewart Truswell, "Plasma Glucose and Insulin Response to Traditional Pima Indian Meals," *American Journal of Clinical Nutrition* (1990 March); and Ron Cowen, "Seeds of Protection," *Science News* (1990 June).

11. Compare the values in Brand, Snow, Nabhan, and Truswell, "Plasma Glucose and Insulin Response," with those in the extensive survey by D. J. A. Jenkins, T. M. S. Wolever, and R. M. Taylor, "Glycemic index of foods: a physiological basis for carbohydrate exchange," *American Journal of Clinical Nutrition* 36 (1981), pp. 362–66.

12. Brand, Snow, Nabhan, and Truswell, "Plasma Glucose and Insulin Response." see also A. C. Frati-Munari, B. E. Gordillo, P. Alamiro, and C. R. Ariza, "Hypoglycemic Effect of *Opuntia streptacantha* Lemaire, in NIDDM," *Diabetes Care* II (1988), pp. 63–66; and Robert Becker, "Nutritive Value of Prosopis Pods," *Mesquite Utilization Symposium Proceedings* (Lubbock: Texas Tech University, 1982), p. M-1.

13. Boyd A. Swinburn and Vicki L. Boyce, "High-fat Diet Causes Deterioration in Glucose Tolerance, Insulin Secretion and Insulin Action," *Diabetes* (American Diabetes Association 49th Scientific Sessions) (May 1989).

14. Doris H. Calloway, R. D. Giaque, and F. M. Costa, "The Superior Mineral Content of Some American Indian Foods in Comparison to Federally Donated Counterpart Commodities," *Ecology of Food and Nutrition* 3 (1981), pp. 113–21.

15. Peter Alshire, "Experts Urge Diabetes Aid for Minorites," *Arizona Republic* 344 (April 28, 1989); "A Su Salud" Hispanic Diabetes Conference agenda (American Diabetes Association, Arizona Affiliate, Phoenix).

16. Gary Paul Nabhan, "Replenishing Desert Agriculture with Native Plants and Their Symbionts," in Wes Jackson, Wendell Berry, and Bruce Colman, eds., *Meeting the Expectations of the Land: Essays in Sustainable Agriculture and Stewardship* (San Francisco: North Point Press, 1984), pp. 172–83.

17. Melvin R. Gilmore, "Uses of Plants by the Indians of the Missouri River Region," *Bureau of American Ethnologlogy Annual Reports* 33 (1919), pp. 43–154.

18. Angelo Pellegrini, *The Unprejudiced Palate*, (San Francisco: North Point Press, 1984), p. 229.

19. Nabhan, *Enduring Seeds*, p. 193.

20. Seventh Generation Fund, *Rebuilding Native American Communities* (Star Route, Lee, Nevada: Seventh Generation Fund Annual Report, 1987–1988), p. 16; Winona La Duke, "Native Rice, Native Hands: The Ikwe Marketing Collective," *Cultural Survival Quarterly* 2 (1987), pp. 63–65.

Chapter 12

Eating the Other:
Desire and Resistance

bell hooks

*This is theory's acute dilemma that desire expresses it-
self most fully where only those absorbed in its delights
and torments are present, that it triumphs most completely over other human preoccupations in places sheltered from view. Thus it is paradoxically in hiding that
the secrets of desire come to light, that hegemonic impo-
sitions and their reversals, evasions, and subversions are
at their most honest and active, and that the identities
and disjunctures between felt passion and established
culture place themselves on most vivid display.*

—Joan Cocks
The Oppositional Imagination

Within current debates about race and difference, mass culture is the contemporary location that both publicly declares and
perpetuates the idea that there is pleasure to be found in the acknowledgment and enjoyment of racial difference. The commodification of Otherness has been so successful because it is offered
as a new delight, more intense, more satisfying than normal ways
of doing and feeling. Within commodity culture, ethnicity becomes
spice, seasoning that can liven up the dull dish that is mainstream
white culture. Cultural taboos around sexuality and desire are transgressed and made explicit as the media bombards folks with a
message of difference no longer based on the white supremacist
assumption that "blondes have more fun." The "real fun" is to be
had by bringing to the surface all those "nasty" unconscious fantasies and longings about contact with the Other embedded in the

secret (not so secret) deep structure of white supremacy. In many ways it is a contemporary revival of interest in the "primitive," with a distinctly postmodern slant. As Marianna Torgovnick argues in *Gone Primitive: Savage Intellects, Modern Lives:*

> What is clear now is that the West's fascination with the primitive has to do with its own crises in identity, with its own need to clearly demarcate subject and object even while flirting with other ways of experiencing the universe.

Certainly from the standpoint of white supremacist capitalist patriarchy, the hope is that desires for the "primitive" or fantasies about the Other can be continually exploited, and that such exploitation will occur in a manner that reinscribes and maintains the status quo. Whether or not desire for contact with the Other, for connection rooted in the longing for pleasure, can act as a critical intervention challenging and subverting racist domination, inviting and enabling critical resistance, is an unrealized political possibility. Exploring how desire for the Other is expressed, manipulated, and transformed by encounters with difference and the different is a critical terrain that can indicate whether these potentially revolutionary longings are ever fulfilled.

Contemporary working-class British slang playfully converges the discourse of desire, sexuality, and the Other, evoking the phrase getting "a bit of the Other" as a way to speak about sexual encounter. Fucking is the Other. Displacing the notion of Otherness from race, ethnicity, skin-color, the body emerges as a site of contestation where sexuality is the metaphoric Other that threatens to take over, consume, transform via the experience of pleasure. Desired and sought after, sexual pleasure alters the consenting subject, deconstructing notions of will, control, coercive domination. Commodity culture in the United States exploits conventional thinking about race, gender, and sexual desire by "working" both the idea that racial difference marks one as Other and the assumption that sexual agency expressed within the context of racialized sexual encounter is a conversion experience that alters one's place and participation in contemporary cultural politics. The seductive promise of this encounter is that it will counter the terrorizing force of the status quo that makes identity fixed, static, a condition of containment and death. And that it is this willingness to transgress racial boundaries within the realm of the sexual that eradicates the fear that one must always conform to the norm to remain "safe."

Difference can seduce precisely because the mainstream imposition of sameness is a provocation that terrorizes. And as Jean Baudrillard suggests in *Fatal Strategies:*

> Provocation—unlike seduction, which allows things to come into play and appear in secret, dual and ambiguous—does not leave you free to be; it calls on you to reveal yourself as you are. It is always blackmail by identity (and thus a symbolic murder, since you are never that, except precisely by being condemned to it).

To make one's self vulnerable to the seduction of difference, to seek an encounter with the Other, does not require that one relinquish forever one's mainstream positionality. When race and ethnicity become commodified as resources for pleasure, the culture of specific groups, as well as the bodies of individuals, can be seen as constituting an alternative playground where members of dominating races, genders, sexual practices affirm their power-over in intimate relation with the Other. While teaching at Yale, I walked one bright spring day in the downtown area of New Haven, which is close to campus and invariably brings one into contact with many of the poor black people who live nearby, and found myself walking behind a group of very blond, very white, jock type boys. (The downtown area was often talked about as an arena where racist domination of blacks by whites was contested on the sidewalks, as white people, usually male, often jocks, used their bodies to force black people off the sidewalk, to push our bodies aside, without ever looking at us or acknowledging our presence.) Seemingly unaware of my presence, these young men talked about their plans to fuck as many girls from other racial/ethnic groups as they could "catch" before graduation. They "ran" it down. Black girls were high on the list, Native American girls hard to find, Asian girls (all lumped into the same category), deemed easier to entice, were considered "prime targets." Talking about this overheard conversation with my students, I found that it was commonly accepted that one "shopped" for sexual partners in the same way one "shopped" for courses at Yale, and that race and ethnicity was a serious category on which selections were based.

To these young males and their buddies, fucking was a way to confront the Other, as well as a way to make themselves over, to leave behind white "innocence" and enter the world of "experience." As is often the case in this society, they were confident that nonwhite people had more life experience, were more worldly, sensual, and sexual because they were different. Getting a bit of the Other, in this case engaging in sexual encounters with non-white females, was considered a ritual of transcendence, a movement out into a world of difference that would transform, an acceptable rite of passage. The direct objective was not simply to sexually possess the Other; it was to be changed in some way by the encounter. "Naturally," the presence of the Other, the body of the Other, was seen as existing to serve the ends of white male desires. Writing about the way difference is recouped in the West in "The 'Primitive' Unconscious of Modern Art, or White Skin, Black Masks," Hal Foster reminds readers that Picasso regarded the tribal objects he had acquired as "witnesses" rather than as "models." Foster critiques this positioning of the Other, emphasizing that this recognition was "contingent upon instrumentality": "In this way, through affinity and use, the primitive is sent up into the service of the Western tradition (which is then seen to have partly produced it.)" A similar critique can be made of contemporary trends in interracial sexual desire and contact initiated by white males. They claim the body of the colored Other instrumentally, as unexplored terrain, a symbolic frontier that will be fertile ground for their reconstruction of the masculine norm, for asserting themselves as transgressive desiring subjects. They call upon the Other to be both witness and participant in this transformation.

For white boys to openly discuss their desire for colored girls (or boys) publicly announces their break with a white supremacist past that would have such desire articulated only as taboo, as secret, as shame. They see their willingness to openly name their desire for the Other as affirmation of cultural plurality (its impact on sexual preference and choice). Unlike racist white men who historically violated the bodies of black women/women of color to assert their position as colonizer/conqueror, these young men see themselves as nonracists, who choose to transgress racial boundaries within the sexual realm not to dominate the Other, but rather so that they can be acted upon, so that they can be changed utterly. Not at all attuned to those aspects of their sexual fantasies that irrevocably link them to collective white racist domination, they believe their desire for contact represents a progressive change in white attitudes toward nonwhites. They do not see themselves as perpetuating racism. To them the most potent indication of that change is the frank expression of longing, the open declaration of desire, the need to be intimate with dark Others. The point is to be changed by this convergence of pleasure and Otherness. One dares—acts—on the assumption that the exploration into the world of difference, into the body of the Other, will provide a greater, more intense pleasure than any that exists in the ordinary world of one's familiar racial group. And even though the conviction is that the familiar world will remain intact even as one ventures outside it, the hope is that they will reenter that world no longer the same.

The current wave of "imperialist nostalgia" (defined by Renato Rosaldo in *Culture and Truth* as nostalgia, often found under imperialism, where people mourn the passing of what they themselves have transformed" or as "a process of yearning for what one has destroyed that is a form of mystification") often obscures contemporary cultural strategies deployed not to mourn but to celebrate the sense of a continuum of "primitivism." In mass culture, imperialist nostalgia takes the form of reenacting and reritualizing in different ways the imperialist, colonizing journey as narrative fantasy of power and desire, of seduction by the Other. This longing is rooted in the atavistic belief that the spirit of the "primitive" resides in the bodies of dark Others whose cultures, traditions, and lifestyles may indeed be irrevocably changed by imperialism, colonization, and racist domination. The desire to make contact with those bodies deemed Other, with no apparent will to dominate, assuages the guilt of the past, even takes the form of a defiant gesture where one denies accountability and historical connection. Most importantly, it establishes a contemporary narrative where the suffering imposed by structures of domination on those designated Other is deflected by an emphasis on seduction and longing where the desire is not to make the Other over in one's image but to become the Other.

Whereas mournful imperialist nostalgia constitutes the betrayed and abandoned world of the Other as an accumulation of lack and loss, contemporary longing for the "primitive" is expressed by the projection onto the Other of a sense of plenty, bounty, a field of dreams. Commenting on this strategy in "Reading in Cultural Resistance." Hal Foster contends, "Difference is thus used productively; indeed, in a social order which seems to know no outside (and which must contrive its own transgressions to redefine its limits), difference is often fabricated in the interests of social control as well as of commodity innovation." Masses of young people dissatisfied by U.S. imperialism, unemployment, lack of economic opportunity, afflicted by the postmodern malaise of alienation, no sense of grounding, no redemptive identity, can be manipulated by cultural strategies that offer Otherness as appeasement, particularly through commodification. The contemporary crises of identity in the west, especially as experienced by white youth, are eased when the "primitive" is recouped via a focus on diversity and pluralism which suggests the Other can provide life-sustaining alternatives. Concurrently, diverse ethnic/racial groups can also embrace this sense of specialness, that histories and experience once seen as worthy only of disdain can be looked upon with awe.

Cultural appropriation of the Other assuages feelings of deprivation and lack that assault the psyches of radical white youth who choose to be disloyal to western civilization. Concurrently, marginalized groups, deemed Other, who have been ignored, rendered invisible, can be seduced by the emphasis on Otherness, by its commodification, because it offers the promise of recognition and reconciliation. When the dominant culture demands that the Other be offered as sign that progressive political change is talking place, that the American Dream can indeed be inclusive of difference, it invites a resurgence of essentialist cultural nationalism. the acknowledged Other must assume recognizable forms. Hence, it is not African American culture formed in resistance to contemporary situations that surfaces, but nostalgic evocation of a "glorious" past. And even though the focus is often on the ways that this past was "superior" to the present, this cultural narrative relies on stereotypes of the "primitive," even as it eschews the term, to evoke a world where black people were in harmony with nature and with one another. This narrative is linked to white Western conceptions of the dark Other, not to a radical questioning of those representations.

Should youth of any other color not know how to move closer to the Other, or how to get in touch with "primitive," consumer culture promises to show the way. It is within the commercial realm of advertising that the drama of Otherness finds expression. Encounters with Otherness are clearly marked as more exciting, more intense, and more threatening. The lure is the combination of pleasure and danger. In the cultural marketplace the Other is coded as having the capacity to be more alive, as holding the secret that will allow those who venture and dare to break with the cultural anhedonia (defined in Sam Keen's *The Passionate Life* as "the insensitivity to pleasure, the incapacity for experiencing happiness") and experience sensual and spiritual renewal. Before his untimely death, Michel Foucault, the quintessential transgressive thinker in the West, confessed that he had real difficulties experiencing pleasure.

> I think that pleasure is a very difficult behavior. It's not as simple as that to enjoy one's self. And I must say that's my dream. I would like and I hope I die of an overdose of pleasure of any kind. Because I think it's really difficult and I always have the feeling that I do not feel *the* pleasure, the complete total pleasure and, for me, it's related to death. Because I think that the kind of pleasure I would consider as the real pleasure, would be so deep, so intense, so overwhelming that I couldn't survive it. I would die.

Though speaking from the standpoint of his individual experience, Foucault voices a dilemma felt by many in the west. It is precisely that longing for *the* pleasure that has led the white west to sustain a romantic fantasy of the "primitive" and the concrete search for a real primitive paradise, whether that location be a country or a body, a dark continent or dark flesh, perceived as the perfect embodiment of that possibility.

Within this fantasy of Otherness, the longing for pleasure is projected as a force that can disrupt and subvert the will to dominate. It acts to both mediate and challenge. In Lorraine Hansberry's play *Les Blancs*, it is the desire to experience closeness and community that leads the white American journalist Charles to make contact and attempt to establish a friendship with Tshembe, the black revolutionary. Charles struggles to divest himself of white supremacist privilege, eschews the role of colonizer, and refuses racist exoticization of blacks. Yet he continues to assume that he alone can decide the nature of his relationship to a black person. Evoking the idea of a universal transcendent subject, he appeals to Tshembe by repudiating the role of oppressor, declaring, "I am a man who feels like talking." When Tshembe refuses to accept the familiar relationship offered him, refuses to satisfy Charles' longing for camaraderie and contact, he is accused of hating white men. Calling attention to situations where white people have oppressed other white people, Tshembe challenges Charles, declaring that "race is a device—no more, no less," that "it explains nothing at all." Pleased with this disavowal of the importance of race, Charles agrees, stating "race hasn't a thing to do with it." Tshembe then deconstructs the category "race" without minimizing or ignoring the impact of racism, telling him:

I believe in the recognition of devices as *devices*—but I also believe in the reality of those devices. In one century men choose to hide their conquests under religion, in another under race. So you and I may recognize the fraudulence of the device in both cases, but the fact remains that a man who has a sword run through him because he will not become a Moslem or a Christian—or who is lynched in Mississippi or Zatembe because he is black—is suffering the utter reality of that device of conquest. And it is pointless to pretend that it doesn't *exist*—merely because it is a lie.

Again and again Tshembe must make it clear to Charles that subject to subject contact between white and black which signals the absence of domination of an oppressor/opposed relationship must emerge through mutual choice and negotiation. That simply by expressing their desire for "intimate" contact with black people, white people do not eradicate the politics of racial domination as they are made manifest in personal interaction.

Mutual recognition of racism, its impact both on those who are dominated and those who dominate, is the only standpoint that makes possible an encounter between races that is not based on denial and fantasy. For it is the ever-present reality of racist domination, of white supremacy, that renders problematic the desire of white people to have contact with the Other. Often it is this reality that is most masked when representations of contact between white and nonwhite, white and black, appear in mass culture. One area where the politics of diversity and its concomitant insistence on inclusive representation have had serious impact is advertising. Now that sophisticated market surveys reveal the extent to which poor and materially underprivileged people of all races/ethnicities consume products, sometimes in a quantity disproportionate to income, it has become more evident that these markets can be appealed to with advertising. Market surveys revealed that black people buy more Pepsi than other soft drinks and suddenly we see more Pepsi commercials with black people in them.

The world of fashion has also come to understand that selling products is heightened by the exploitation of Otherness. The success of Benneton ads, which with their racially diverse images have become a model for various advertising strategies, epitomize this trend. Many ads that focus on Otherness make no explicit comments, or rely solely on visual messages, but the recent *Tweeds* catalogue provides an excellent example of the way contemporary culture exploits notions of Otherness with both visual images and text. The catalog cover shows a map of Egypt. Inserted into the heart of the country, so to speak, is a photo of a white male (an *Out of Africa* type) holding an Egyptian child in his arms. Behind them is not the scenery of Egypt as a modern city, but rather shadowy silhouettes resembling huts and palm trees. Inside, the copy quotes Gustave Flaubert's comments from *Flaubert in Egypt*. For seventy-five pages Egypt becomes a landscape of dreams, and its darker-skinned people background, scenery to highlight whiteness, and the longing of white to inhabit, if only for a time, the world of Other. The front page declares:

> We did not want our journal to be filled with snapshots of an antique land. Instead, we wanted to rediscover our clothing in the context of a different culture. Was it possible, we wondered, to express our style in an unaccustomed way, surrounded by Egyptian colors, Egyptian textures, even bathed in an ancient Egyptian light?

Is this not imperialist nostalgia at its best—potent expression of longing for the "primitive"? One desires "a bit of the Other" to enhance the blank landscape of whiteness. Nothing is said in the text about Egyptian people, yet their images are spread throughout its pages. Often their faces are blurred by the camera, a strategy that ensures that readers will not become more enthralled by the images of Otherness than those of whiteness. The point of this photographic attempt at defamiliarization is to distance us from whiteness, so that we will return to it more intently.

In most of the "snapshots," all carefully selected and posed, there is no mutual looking. One desires contact with the Other even as one wishes boundaries to remain intact. When bodies contact one another, touch, it almost always is a white hand doing the touching, white hands that rest on the bodies of colored people, unless the Other is a child. One snapshot of "intimate" contact shows two women with their arms linked, the way close friends might link arms. One is an Egyptian woman identified by a caption that reads "with her husband and baby, Ahmedio A'bass, 22, leads a gypsy's life"; the second woman is a white-skinned model. The linked hands suggest that these two women share something, have a basis of contact and indeed they do, they resemble one another, look more alike than different. The message again is that "primitivism," though more apparent in the Other, also resides in the white self. It is not the world of Egypt, of "gypsy" life, that is affirmed by this snapshot, but the ability of white people to roam the world, making contact. Wearing pants while standing next to her dark "sister" who wears a traditional skirt, the white woman appears to be crossdressing (an ongoing theme in *Tweeds*). Visually the image suggests that she and first world white women like her are liberated, have greater freedom to roam than darker women who live peripatetic lifestyles.

Significantly, the catalog that followed this one focused on Norway. There the people of Norway are not represented, only the scenery. Are we to assume that white folks from this country are as at "home" in Norway as they are here so there is no need for captions and explanations? In this visual text, whiteness is the unifying feature—not culture. Of course, for *Tweeds* to exploit Otherness to dramatize "whiteness" while in Egypt, it cannot include darker-skinned models since the play on contrasts that is meant to highlight "whiteness" could not happen nor could the exploitation that urges consumption of the Other whet the appetite in quite the same way; just as inclusion of darker-skinned models in the Norway issue might suggest that the West is not as unified by whiteness as this visual text suggests. Essentially speaking, both catalogs evoke a sense that white people are homogeneous and share "white bread culture."

Those progressive white intellectuals who are particularly critical of "essentialist" notions of identity when writing about mass culture, race, and gender have not focused their critiques on white identity and the way essentialism informs representations of whiteness. It is always the nonwhite, or in some cases the nonheterosexual Other, who is guilty of essentialism. Few white intellectuals call attention to the way in which the contemporary obsession with white consumption of the dark Other has served as a catalyst for the resurgence of essentialist based racial and ethnic nationalism. Black nationalism, with its emphasis on black separatism, is resurging as a response to the assumption that white cultural imperialism and white yearning to possess the Other are invading black life, appropriating and violating black culture. As a survival strategy, black nationalism surfaces most strongly when white cultural appropriation of black culture threatens to decontextualize and thereby erase knowledge of the specific historical and social context of black experience from which cultural productions and distinct black styles emerge. Yet most white intellectuals writing critically about black culture do not see these constructive dimensions of black nationalism and tend to see it instead as naive essentialism, rooted in notions of ethnic purity that resemble white racist assumptions.

In the essay *"Hip, and the Long Front of Color,"* white critic Andrew Ross interprets Langston Hughes's declaration ("You've taken my blues and gone—You sing 'em on Broadway—And you sing 'em in Hollywood Bowl—And you mixed 'em up with symphonies—And you fixed 'em—So they don't sound like me. Yep, you done taken my blues and gone") as a "complaint" that "celebrates . . . folk purism." Yet Hughes's declaration can be heard as a critical comment on appropriation (not a complaint). A distinction must be made between the longing for ongoing cultural recognition of the creative source of particular African American cultural productions that emerge from distinct black experience, and essentialist investments in notions of ethnic purity that undergird crude versions of black nationalism.

Currently, the commodification of difference promotes paradigms of consumption wherein whatever difference the Other inhabits is eradicated, via exchange, by a consumer cannibalism that not only displaces the Other but denies the significance of that Other's history through a process of decontextualization. Like the "primitivism" Hal Foster maintains "absorbs the primitive, in part via the concept of affinity" contemporary notions of "crossover" expand the parameters of cultural production to enable the voice of the nonwhite Other to be heard by a larger audience even as it denies the specificity of that voice, or as it recoups it for its own use.

This scenario is played out in the film *Heart Condition* when Mooney, a white racist cop, has a heart transplant and receives a heart from Stone, a black man he has been trying to destroy because Stone has seduced Chris, the white call girl whom Mooney loves. Transformed by his new "black heart," Mooney learns how to be more seductive, changes his attitudes toward race, and, in perfect Hollywood style, wins the girl in the end. Unabashedly dramatizing a process of "eating the Other" (in ancient religious practices among so called "primitive" people, the heart of a person may be ripped out and eaten so that one can embody that person's spirit or special characteristics), a film like *Heart Condition* addresses the fantasies of a white audience. At the end of the film, Mooney, reunited with Chris through marriage and surrounded by Stone's caring black kin, has become the "father" of Chris and Stone's biracial baby who is dark-skinned, the color of his father. Stone, whose ghost has haunted Mooney, is suddenly "history"—

gone. Interestingly, this mainstream film suggests that patriarchal struggle over "ownership" (i.e., sexual possession of white women's bodies) is the linchpin of racism. Once Mooney can accept and bond with Stone on the phallocentric basis of their mutual possession and "desire" for Chris, their homosocial bonding makes brotherhood possible and eradicates the racism that has kept them apart. Significantly, patriarchal bonding mediates and becomes the basis for the eradication of racism.

In part, this film offers a version of racial pluralism that challenges racism by suggesting that the white male's life will be richer, more pleasurable, if he accepts diversity. Yet it also offers a model of change that still leaves a white supremacist capitalist patriarchy intact, though no longer based on coercive domination of black people. It insists that white male desire must be sustained by the "labor" (in this case the heart) of a dark Other. The fantasy, of course, is that this labor will no longer be exacted via domination, but will be given willingly. Not surprisingly, most black folks talked about this film as "racist." The young desirable handsome intelligent black male (who we are told via his own self-portrait is "hung like a shetland pony") must die so that the aging white male can both restore his potency (he awakens from the transplant to find a replica of a huge black penis standing between his legs) and be more sensitive and loving. Torgovnick reminds readers in *Gone Primitive* that a central element in the Western fascination with primitivism is its focus on "overcoming alienation from the body, restoring the body, and hence the self, to a relation of full and easy harmony with nature or the cosmos." It is this conceptualization of the "primitive" and the black male as quintessential representative that is dramatized in *Heart Condition*. One weakness in Torgovnick's work is her refusal to recognize how deeply the idea of the "primitive" is entrenched in the psyches of everyday people, shaping contemporary racist stereotypes, perpetuating racism. When she suggests, "our own culture by and large rejects the association of blackness with rampant sexuality and irrationality, with decadence and corruption, with disease and death," one can only wonder what culture she is claiming as her own.

Films like *Heart Condition* make black culture and black life backdrop, scenery for narratives that essentially focus on white people. Nationalist black voices critique this cultural crossover, its decentering of black experience as it relates to black people, and its insistence that it is acceptable for whites to explore blackness as long as their ultimate agenda is appropriation. Politically "on the case" when they critique white cultural appropriation of black experience that reinscribes it within a "cool" narrative of white supremacy, these voices cannot be dismissed as naive. They are misguided when they suggest that white cultural imperialism is best critiqued and resisted by black separatism, or when they evoke outmoded notions of ethnic purity that deny the way in which black people exist in the West, are Western, and are at times positively influenced by aspects of white culture.

Steve Perry's essay *"The Politics of Crossover"* deconstructs notions of racial purity by outlining the diverse intercultural exchanges between black and white musicians. yet he seems unable to acknowledge that this reality does not alter the fact that white cultural imperialist appropriation of black culture maintains white supremacy and is a constant threat to black liberation. Even though Perry can admit that successful black crossover artists, such as Prince, carry the "crossover impulse" to the point where it "begins to be a denial of blackness," he is unable to see this as threatening to black people who are daily resisting racism, advocating ongoing decolonization, and in need of any effective black liberation struggle.

Underlying Perry's condescension, and at times contemptuous attitude toward all expressions of black nationalism, is a traditional leftist insistence on the primacy of class over race. This standpoint inhibits his capacity to understand the specific political needs of black people who are addressed, however inadequately, by essentialist-based black separatism. As Howard Winant clarifies in "Postmodern Racial Politics in the United States: Difference and inequality," one must understand race to understand class because "in the postmodern political framework of the contemporary United States, hegemony is determined by the articulation of race and class." And most importantly it is the "ability of the right to represent class issues in racial terms" that is "central to the current pattern of conservative hegemony." Certainly an essentialist-based black nationalism imbued with and perpetuating many racial stereotypes is an inadequate and ineffective response to the urgent demand that there be renewed and viable revolutionary black liberation struggle that would take radical politicization of black people, strategies of decolonization, critiques of capitalism, and ongoing resistance to racist domination as its central goals.

Resurgence of black nationalism as an expression of black people's desire to guard against white cultural appropriation indicates the extent to which the commodification of blackness (including the nationalist agenda) has been reinscribed and marketed with an atavistic narrative, a fantasy of Otherness that reduces protest to spectacle and stimulates even greater longing for the "primitive." Given this cultural context, black nationalism is more a gesture of powerlessness than a sign of critical resistance. Who can take seriously Public Enemy's insistence that the dominated and their allies "fight the power" when that declaration is in no way linked to a collective organized struggle. When young black people mouth 1960s' black nationalist rhetoric, don Kente cloth, gold medallions, dread their hair, and diss the white folks they hang out with, they expose the way meaningless commodification strips these signs of political integrity and meaning, denying the possibility that they can serve as a catalyst for concrete political action. As signs, their power to ignite critical consciousness is diffused when they are commodified. Communities of resistance are replaced by communities of consumption. As Stuart and Elizabeth Ewen emphasize in *Channels of Desire:*

> The politics of consumption must be understood as something more than what to buy, or even what to boycott. Consumption is a social relationship, the dominant relationship in our society—one that makes it harder and harder for people to hold together, to create continuity. At a time when for many of us the possibility of meaningful change seems to elude our grasp, it is a question of immense social and political proportions. To establish popular initiative, consumerism must be transcended—a difficult but central task facing all people who still seek a better way of life.

Work by black artists that is overtly political and radical is rarely linked to an oppositional political culture. When commodified it is easy for consumers to ignore political messages. And even though a product like rap articulates narratives of coming to critical political consciousness, it also exploits stereotypes and essentialist notions of blackness (like black people have natural rhythm and are more sexual). The television show *In Living Color* is introduced by lyrics that tell listeners "do what you wanna do." Positively, this show advocates transgression, yet it negatively promotes racist stereotypes, sexism and homophobia. Black youth culture comes to stand for the outer limits of "outness." The commercial nexus exploits the culture's desire (expressed by whites and blacks) to inscribe blackness as "primitive" sign, as wildness, and with it the suggestion that black people have secret access to intense pleasure, particularly pleasures of the body. It is the younger black male body that is seen as epitomizing this promise of wildness, of unlimited physical prowess and unbridled eroticism. It was this black body that was most "desired" for its labor in slavery, and it is this body that is most represented in contemporary popular culture as the body to be watched, imitated, desired, possessed. Rather than a sign of pleasure in daily life outside the realm of consumption, the young black male body is represented most graphically as the body in pain.

Regarded fetishisticly in the psychosexual racial imagination of youth culture, the real bodies of young black men are daily viciously assaulted by white racist violence, black on black violence, the violence of overwork, and the violence of addiction and disease. In her introduction to *The Body in Pain*, Elaine Scarry states that "there is ordinarily no language for pain," that "physical pain is difficult to express; and that this inexpressibility has political consequences." This is certainly true of black male pain. Black males are unable to fully articulate and acknowledge the pain in their lives. They do not have a public discourse or audience within racist society that enables them to give their pain a hearing. Sadly, black men often evoke racist rhetoric that identifies the black male as animal, speaking of themselves as "endangered species," as "primitive" in their bid to gain recognition of their suffering.

When young black men acquire a powerful public voice and presence via cultural production, as has happened with the explosion of rap music, it does not mean that they have a vehicle that will enable them to articulate that pain. Providing narratives that our mainly about power and pleasure, that advocate resistance to racism yet support phallocentrism, rap denies this pain. True, it was conditions of suffering and survival, of poverty, deprivation, and lack that characterized the marginal locations from which breakdancing and rap emerged. Described as "rituals" by participants in the poor urban nonwhite communities where they first took place, these practices offered individuals a means to gain public recognition and voice. Much of the psychic pain that black people experience daily in a white supremacist context is caused by dehumanizing oppressive forces, forces that render us invisible and deny us recognition.

Michael H. (commenting on style in Stuart Ewen's book *All Consuming Images*) also talks about this desire for attention, stating that breakdancing and rap are a way to say "listen to my story, about myself, life, and romance." Rap music provides a public voice for young black men who are usually silenced and overlooked. It emerged in the streets—outside the confines of a domesticity shaped and informed by poverty, outside enclosed spaces where young male body had to be contained and controlled.

In its earliest stages, rap was "a male thing." Young black and brown males could not breakdance and rap in cramped living spaces. Male creativity, expressed in rap and dancing, required wide-open spaces, symbolic frontiers where the body could do its thing, expand, grow, and move, surrounded by a watching crowd. Domestic space, equated with repression and containment, as well as with the "feminine" was resisted and rejected so that an assertive patriarchal paradigm of competitive masculinity and its concomitant emphasis on physical prowess could emerge. As a result, much rap music is riddled with sexism and misogyny. The public story of black male lives narrated by rap music speaks directly to and against white racist domination, but only indirectly hints at the enormity of black male pain. Constructing the black male body as site of pleasure and power, rap and the dances associated with it suggest vibrancy, intensity, and an unsurpassed joy in living. It may very well be that living on the edge, so close to the possibility of being "exterminated" (which is how many young black males feel) heightens one's ability to risk and make one's pleasure more intense. It is this charge, generated by the tension between pleasure and danger, death and desire, that Foucault evokes when he speaks of that *complete total pleasure* that is related to death. Though Foucault is speaking as an individual, his words resonate in a culture affected by anhedonia—the inability to feel pleasure. In the United States, where our senses are daily assaulted and bombarded to such an extent that an emotional numbness sets in, it may take being "on the edge" for individuals to feel intensely. Hence the overall tendency in the culture is to see young black men as both dangerous and desirable.

Certainly the relationship between the experience of Otherness, of pleasure and death, is explored in the film *The Cook, the Thief, His Wife and Her Lover.* It critiques white male imperialist domination even though this dimension of the movie was rarely mentioned when it was discussed in this country. Reviewers of the film did not talk about the representation of black characters, one would have assumed from such writing that the cast was all white and British. Yet black males are a part of the community of subordinates who are dominated by one controlling white man. After he has killed her lover, his blonde white wife speaks to the dark skinned cook, who clearly represents nonwhite immigrants, about the links between death and pleasure. It is he who explains to her the way blackness is viewed in the white imagination. The cook tells her that black foods are desired because they remind those who eat them of death, and that this is why they cost so much. When they are eaten (in the film, always and only by white people), the cook as native informant tells us that it is a way to flirt with death, to flaunt one's power. He says that to eat black food is a way to say "death, I am eating you" and thereby conquering fear and acknowledging power. White racism, imperialism, and sexist domination prevail by courageous consumption. It is by eating the Other (in this case, death) that one asserts power and privilege.

A similar confrontation may be taking place within popular culture in this society as young white people seek contact with dark Others. They may long to conquer their fear of darkness and death. On the reactionary right, white youth may be simply seeking to affirm "white power" when they flirt with having contact with the Other. Yet there are many white youths who desire to move beyond whiteness. Critical of white imperialism and "into" difference, they desire cultural spaces where boundaries can be transgressed, where new and alternative relations can be formed. These desires are dramatized by two contemporary films, John Waters' *Hairspray*, and the more recent film by Jim Jarmusch, *Mystery Train*. In *Hairspray*, the "cool" white people, working-class Traci and her middleclass boyfriend, transgress class and race boundaries to dance with black folks. She says to him as they stand in a rat-infested alley with winos walking about, "I wish I was dark-skinned." And he replies, "Traci, our souls are black even though our skin is white." Blackness—the culture, the music, the people—is once again associated with pleasure as well as death and decay. Yet their recognition of the particular pleasures and sorrows black folk experience does not lead to cultural appropriation but to an appreciation that extends into the realm of the political—Traci dares to support racial integration. In this film, the longing and desire whites express for contact with black culture is coupled with the recognition of the culture's value. One does not transgress boundaries to stay the same, to reassert white domination. *Hairspray* is nearly unique in its attempt to construct a fictive universe where white working class "undesirables" are in solidarity with black people. When Traci says she wants to be black, blackness becomes a metaphor for freedom, an end to boundaries. Blackness is vital not because it represents the "primitive" but because it invites engagement in a revolutionary ethos that dares to challenge and disrupt the status quo. Like white rappers M.C. Search and Prime Minister Pete Nice who state that they "want to bring forth some sort of positive message to black people, that there are white people out there who understand what this is all about, who understand we have to get past all the hatred," Traci shifts her positionality to stand in solidarity with black people. She is concerned about her freedom and sees her liberation linked to black liberation and an effort to end racist domination.

Expressing a similar solidarity with the agenda of "liberation," which includes freedom to transgress, Sandra Bernhard, in her new film *Without You I'm Nothing,* also associates blackness with this struggle. In the March issue of *Interview* she says that the movie has "this whole black theme, which is like a personal metaphor for being on the outside." This statement shows that Bernhard's sense of blackness is both problematic and complex. The film opens with her pretending she is black. Dressed in African clothing, she renders problematic the question of race and identity, for this representation suggests that racial identity can be socially constructed even as it implies that cultural appropriation falls short because it is always imitation, fake. Conversely, she contrasts her attempt to be a black woman in drag with the black female's attempt to imitate a white female look.

Bernhard's film suggests that alternative white culture derives its standpoint, its impetus' from black culture. Identifying herself with marginalized Others, Bernhard's Jewish heritage as well as her sexually ambiguous erotic practices are experiences that already place her outside the mainstream. Yet the film does not clarify the nature of her identification with black culture. Throughout the film, she places herself in a relationship of comparison and competition with black women, seemingly exposing white female envy of black women and their desire to "be" imitation black women; yet she also pokes fun a black females. The unidentified black woman who appears in the film, like a phantom, looking at herself in the mirror has no name and no voice. Yet her image is always contrasted with that of Bernhard. Is she the fantasy Other Bernhard desires to become? Is she the fantasy Other Bernhard desires? The last scene of the film seems to confirm that black womanhood is the yardstick Bernhard uses to measure herself. Though she playfully suggests in the film that the work of black women singers like Nina Simone and Diana Ross is derivative, "stolen" from her work, this inversion of reality ironically calls attention to the way white women have "borrowed" from black women without acknowledging the debt they owe. In many ways, the film critiques white cultural appropriation of "blackness" that leaves no trace. Indeed, Bernhard identifies that she had her artistic beginnings working in black clubs, among black people. Though acknowledging where she is coming from, the film shows Bernhard clearly defining an artistic performance space that only she as a white woman can inhabit. Black women have no public, paying audience for our funny imitations of white girls. Indeed, it is difficult to imagine any setting other than an all black space where black women could use comedy to critique and ridicule white womanhood in the way Bernhard mocks black womanhood.

Closing the scene shrouded in a cloak that resembles an American flag, Bernhard unveils her nearly nude body. The film ends with the figure of the black woman, who has heretofore only been in the background, foregrounded as the only remaining audience watching this seductive performance. As though she is seeking acknowledgment of her identity, her power, Bernhard stares at the black woman, who returns her look with a contemptuous gaze. As if this look of disinterest and dismissal is not enough to convey her indifference, she removes a tube of red lipstick from her purse and writes on the table "fuck Sandra Bernhard." Her message seems to be: "you may need black culture since without us you are nothing, but black women have no need of you." In the film, all the white women strip, flaunt their sexuality, and appear to be directing their attention to a black male gaze. It is this standpoint that the film suggests may lead them to ignore black women and only notice what black women think of them when we are "right up in their face."

Bernhard's film walks a critical tightrope. On the one hand it mocks white appropriation of black culture, white desire for black (as in the scene where Bernhard with a blonde white girl persona is seen being "boned" by a black man whom we later find is mainly concerned about his hair—i.e., his own image) even as the film works as spectacle largely because of the clever ways Bernhard "uses" black culture and standard racial stereotypes. Since so many of the representations of blackness in the film are stereotypes it does not really go against the Hollywood cinematic grain. And like the *Tweeds* catalog on Egypt, ultimately black people are reduced, as Bernhard declares in *Interview*, to "a personal metaphor." Blackness is the backdrop of Otherness she uses to insist on and clarify her status as Other, as cool, hip, and transgressive. Even though she lets her audiences know that as an entertainment "rookie" she had her start working in close association with black people, the point is to name where she begins to highlight how far she has come. When Bernhard "arrives," able to exploit Otherness in a big time way, she arrives alone, not in the company of black associates. They are scenery, backdrop, background. Yet the end of the film problematizes this leave-taking. Is Bernhard leaving black folks or has she been rejected and dismissed? Maybe it's mutual. Like her entertainment associate Madonna, Bernhard leaves her encounters with the Other richer than she was the onset. We have no idea how the Other leaves her.

⊸◈⊸◈⊸◈⊸

When I began thinking and doing research for this piece, I talked to folks from various locations about whether they thought the focus on race, Otherness, and difference in mass culture was challenging racism. There was overall agreement that the message that acknowledgment and exploration of racial difference can be pleasurable represents a breakthrough, a challenge to white supremacy, to various systems of domination. The overriding fear is that cultural, ethnic, and racial differences will be continually commodified and offered up as new dishes to enhance the white palate—that the Other will be eaten, consumed, and forgotten. After weeks of debating with one another about the distinction between cultural appropriation and cultural appreciation, students in my introductory course on black literature were convinced that something radical was happening, that these issues were "coming out in the open." Within a context where desire for contact with those who are different or deemed Other is not considered bad, politically incorrect, or wrong-minded, we can begin to conceptualize and identify ways that desire informs our political choices and affiliations. Acknowledging ways the desire for pleasure, and that includes erotic longings, informs our politics, our understanding of difference, we may know better how desire disrupts, subverts, and makes resistance possible. We cannot, however, accept these new images uncritically.

Chapter 13

Dining Out:
The Hyperreality of Appetite

Joanne Finkelstein

Introduction

Every anthropologist and cultural commentator has long recognized the centrality of food to a society. Styles of eating are
elaborate gestures that enunciate and perform a culture's speci-
ficities. Every group—whether it is a transitory congregation like a
youth gang or a dispersed network of persecuted minorities—evi-
dences signs of cultural membership through the manners attached
to food. The street kid, with a processed sausage in a bun, cooked
in a microwave at the corner store, and the religious zealot following the dietary habits written down a millennium before, are both
consciously describing a cultural location through their food habits. This illustrates the point made by the historian Norbert Elias
that "conduct while eating cannot be isolated. It is a segment—a
very characteristic one—of the totality of socially instilled forms of
conduct" (1939/78:68).

Dining out in westernized societies has become extremely
popular. By the close of the twentieth century, two out of every
three meals are expected to be purchased and consumed outside
the home (Hodgson 1982; Sargent 1985). The popularity of restaurants is usually accounted for by economic factors together with
the changing patterns of the family. Adults away from the home
for much of each day readily employ the services of the restaurant

to create a sense of family life. Indeed, some self-identified "family restaurants" trade on precisely this circumstance. As well, the restaurant can function as a site for gathering food knowledge; the diner can collect gastronomic experiences, follow trends in cuisine, become an epicure. This too can be traded on by the enterprising restaurateur who can so elaborately describe the food on the menu or have it so temptingly depicted in wall paintings and sculptured models that the diner's desire grows from an aesthetic appeal regardless of any nutritional qualities.

While social, economic, and aesthetic influences contribute to the popularity of the restaurant, entertainment also plays a part, a kind of subaltern function. From its modern beginnings, the restaurant has been associated with performative pleasures—namely, being seen in public, seeing who else was in public, being entertained by the restaurateur as well as other diners, and experimenting with new sensory pleasures. César Ritz, who opened the opulent dining room at the Savoy Hotel, London, in 1889, understood his bourgeois patrons to be most interested in the theatricality of the restaurant, especially the opportunities it offered as a three-dimensional advertisement, a diorama displaying cultural products and practices where the service of others could be commanded, where one was free to look at others, and display oneself, where one imbibed the ambience of the extravagant decor, occupying it as if it were one's own. Popular restaurants ever since have continued to provide these pleasures in artifice.

The modern restaurant has been instrumental in promulgating exhibitionist styles of public conduct. It has provided a domain for imitative public displays, a place where a diversity of styles in human exchange have been practiced and cultivated, and where the influences of social pretensions, guile, and the dictates of fashion have been strongly in evidence. In the restaurant, one is not only consuming food but one becomes the consumer par excellence: when we dine out we are simultaneously learning that all manner of our desires can be purchased, whether it be a need to be seen by others, a desire to display personal wealth, or to play the role of gastronome, bon vivant, ardent lover or fashion habitué. For this reason alone, the importance of the restaurant in the contouring of the bourgeois character cannot be overlooked. After all, dining out blends a lower order of being—namely, the nourishment of the human body—with a higher order of experience—namely, that of taking pleasure—and thereby elevates the banality of eating to the abstract, aesthetic, and symbolic.

Bourdieu (1984:196) has described how the act of eating is more than a process of bodily nourishment—it is an elaborate performance of gender, social class, and self-identity:

> The manner of presenting and consuming the food, the organisation of the meal and setting of places, strictly differentiated according to the sequence of the dishes and arranged to please the eye, the presentation of the dishes, considered as much in terms of shape and color (like works of art) as of their consumerable substance, the etiquette governing posture and gesture, ways of serving oneself and others, of using the different utensils, the seating plan, strictly but discreetly hierarchical, the censorship of bodily manifestations of the act or pleasure of eating (such as noise or haste), the very refinement of the things consumed, with quality more important than quantity—this whole commitment to stylisation tends to shift the emphasis from substance and function to form and manner, and so to deny the crudely material reality of the act of eating.

Hence, the immense popularity of the restaurant must be understood to involve much more than the immediate gratification of appetite, desire and whim. From its modern origins, the restaurant has been the setting for accidental experiments in human commerce. The styles of human exchange and social relations cultivated through the practice of dining out, and the nature of civility they express, vividly reflect bourgeois values: namely, the importance given to one's physical appearance, the concern with respectability and the other's good opinion of oneself. The restaurant marks the convergence of the personal and the social, the private and the public. It is a crucible in which cultural formations and the individual's private understanding of how sociality is effected can be found fermenting.

Eating as Entertainment

In a sense, the restaurant is a forerunner of the contemporary entertainment industry. Like other entertainment industries, dining out is much concerned with the marketing of certain states of mind, emotions, desires, and moods. The entertainment industries construct the practices and expressions through which individuals are encouraged to interpret their personal longings. Indeed, the ultimate accomplishment of these industries is the replacement of the consumer's sense of reality with that promoted by the manufacturer of the entertainment. This is precisely what the fashionability of dining out can accomplish.

The products of the culture industries are tastes and mannerisms that are acquired in the form of desired states of mind and experience. For example, if I desire the feeling of familiar contentment, or perhaps the excitement of romance and self-indulgence, I can select a restaurant that I believe will complement and even assist in the realization of these desires. If I want entertainment, then there are numerous restaurants which offer floorshows or unique cuisine or special service as palliatives to my desires. Many restaurants relieve the diner of the effort to be amusing; the floorshow and the service of the restaurant can substitute for sociality. The significance of this is that any efforts to realize or even define desires can be displayed on to the restaurant, and direct engagement in the shaping of sociality can thereby be reduced. In effect, with dining out, or with other forms of public entertainments, we are purchasing the ingredients for a desired state of being, and are spared much of the care of thinking about how these desires can best be developed and satisfied. The restaurant also invites overindulgence. The individual can eat and drink expansively, encouraging the consumption of foods and beverages irrespective of whether or not they are nutritionally inadequate, or even detrimental to the human body. Junk foods, and those rich in fats and sugars, are offered without reservation. Because one is dining out for pleasure, one can overlook the deficits of the diet and behave self-indulgently.

In the restaurant, we can find any number of acceptable and convincing images of how social life should be, including the desire for happy families—an image frequently advertised by the fast-food chain restaurants—or the desire for romance in an opulent setting, which is often the iconic representation, in advertisements and popular movies, of the fashionable bistro. As the restaurant offers the opportunity for individuals to act in ways largely removed from the actualities of the everyday, the practice of dining out becomes a passageway to a world without continuous form, a world that may be lavishly endowed with the fabulous, the desirable, the luxurious, and the exciting. In this way, dining out is appealing because it offers an actual means of realizing one's fantasies; it is as if the restaurant were a theater or a diorama in which individuals can appear as they desire without any of the risks that would be encountered were they to try to cross social barriers.

Dining out is also of immediate appeal because of the license it gives to pursue pleasure. In the restaurant, the individual need feel no sense of accountability or personal history, because the act of dining out is an occasion, taken among strangers, where one is free to assume whatever guise is desired, and to play out and absorb a plethora of fancies embedded in the ambience and character of the chosen restaurant. It is a striking feature of dining out that the restaurant, as an institution, offers all its patrons a sheltered anonymity within which there is ample opportunity to assume various roles and postures, whether it be a serious formal mien in a restaurant of imposing proportions, or a more frivolous attitude in a parodic cafe where a totally theatrical atmosphere is recreated. This aspect of dining out, which invites the enunciation and performance of private fantasies, is a feature of the restaurant's appeal, which dates from its modern origins.

Barthes (1982) has eloquently described this process with his analysis of the oriental restaurant. Europeans find Asian cuisine appealing because it allows them to experience the exoticism of the imaginary orient without actual contact with the culture. The Asian restaurant is popular because of the occidental's fear of contamination. In this way, dining out can be a flight to realms remote from the everyday; it can be a practice that invites the fanciful, fleeting, and disingenuous. To purchase entertainment that is safe, sanitized, and contained paradoxically amplifies the postmodern ethical confusion or incivility of the contemporary, unexamined life. Our pursuit of the new, exciting, and interesting through these mediated, circumscribed gestures allows us to contain the challenge of the exotic while simultaneously indulging in it.

Much of the attraction of dining out resides in what it offers, or appears to offer, for purchase. The restaurant, like other mass entertainments, functions to commodify private experiences—happiness and pleasure appear easily procurable, as if they were items to be selected from a menu or consumer guide. Many social commentators and theorists have claimed that the power of the manufactured image is unsurpassed in the Western world (see Marcuse 1964; Barthes 1972; Horkheimer and Adorno 1972; Williamson 1978, 1983; Baudrillard 1983). The restaurant has become a prime producer of seductive images that circulate through the various layers of social life. In the twentieth century, the era of mass consumerism, entrepreneurial links exist between the public domain and private interiorized pleasures. When these links are forged through desires that are themselves generated by fashions in ideas and tastes, then the ingredients for a postmodern condition of generalized ethnical confusion are at hand. For instance, when pleasure becomes de rigueur, when pleasure becomes a commodity pursued like other normatively defined activities, it comes under the surveillance of regulatory agencies (like the marketing of fashions in cuisine, specific styles of restaurants and dining out itself). It thereby is removed from a more immediate contested and interrogatory level of experience. The individual who succeeds in satisfying private pleasures in the public domain is vulnerable to being over socialized and overexposed to remote, structural influences. The restaurant, as a site for the satisfaction of these private pleasures, plays a part in defining, regulating, and structuring the individual's experience.

Indeed, the artifice of the restaurant provides an architecture for a kind of human commerce in which we are relieved of the task of defining exactly the nature of the desires we want to satisfy. Most diners would accept that dining out in restaurants has a certain amount of artifice and pretense attached to it. However, taking the next step, and seeing the artifice and pretense associated with the restaurant as the very ingredients that make dining out disappointing, is often resisted. Dining out is a highly mannered event. It requires that we employ a degree of reserve and aloofness that allows us to mix intimately with others without becoming immediately involved. One is able to ignore the other seductions, family celebrations, business deals, and so on, which are taking place at the very next table. Dining out emphasizes the necessity to blunt sensibilities, to function in some instances as an unresponsive audience to others. At the same time, we must be performers ourselves in order to best enjoy the restaurant experience. By being subtly instructed in these practices, our only responsibility is to perform according to the rules. In this way, the culture of dining out sequesters us from the rigors of spontaneous, interrogated, and contested sociality.

At first, this may seem relatively trivial and unproblematic. After all, how serious could it be that we dine out too much and think about it too little? Yet, the dangers of an over mannered life, where not enough time has been given to self-examination, produces a passivity that can leave us confused and victimized. Tolstoy's account of this in *The Death of Ivan Illich* demonstrates the danger of living according to social prescription: the mannered life is a refuge from critique and judgment, yet critique and judgment are nevertheless understood to be the basic elements of civility. So, if the pleasures of dining out derive largely from an acceptance of its overprescriptiveness, then it seems that a strong appeal of dining out is its provision of a formalized code of behavior which is advertised as pleasurable and urbane, but which in practice may be incipiently uncivilized.

Artifice and Consumerism

Consumer habits create an abiding attention to the visible and material details of human commerce. As individuals appropriate more of the objective, material culture into the repertoire of their private lives, a confusion arises as to what is adopted for its fashionability and what is genuinely enjoyed. For instance, the images that make dining out perennially attractive—namely, styles of cuisine and decor—become transposed into personal preferences and tastes. As a result, the individual begins to find pleasure in whatever practices are being offered. As a consequence, our everyday world comes to be lived at the surface in a dimension Eco (1986) has called the hyperreal, where the images of products and practices have gained the ascendancy over the even supplanted the actual.

In the consumer ethos of the modern age, the popular (perhaps, most advertised) view of the cultured individual appears to be that of the highest consumer of goods, the person who is the inveterate shopper, tourist and *mondaine*. Being civilized is represented as having the greatest choice and freedom in order to purchase and expose oneself to the abundance of the available material riches. To confuse the enduringly valuable with the temporarily fashionable and fleeting is an endemic problem of modernity (see Marcuse 1964; Heller 1976, 1982; Horkheimer and Adorno 1972). Two institutions that have blatantly promoted consumerism are the department store and the restaurant.

The history of the famous Parisian department store Bon Marché (Miller 1981) shows how the combination of entertainment and consumerism became widely accepted during the nineteenth century as being synonymous with urbanity, civility, and a sense of personal cultivation. Miller has described how the new department store was regarded as a "permanent fair" and "fantasy world" (p. 164) in which private, individual desires were translated into objects that could be purchased. In this way, the department store was like a "cultural primer," "it showed people how they should dress, how they should furnish their home, and how they should spend their leisure time" (p. 183).

The new era of consumerism promoted the idea that civility and urbanity were obtainable through the possession of certain objects. Purchasing an artifact, or accepting an advertised image, was not an immediate and direct passageway to another and presumably better world, but it was nonetheless a means for transforming what was desired into the readily identifiable and obtainable. The same opportunities were being made available in the modern restaurant. With the ethos of consumerism, a new state of mind was produced—that of a persistent sense of desire and interest in possession, regardless of whether the desired object had a tangible form, or was an idea, habit, or style of conduct. The department store was instrumental in the production and dissemination of such desires, the satisfaction of which were never meant to be effected.

When commodities of all kinds are invested with extraneous values and characteristics, then a confusion is created between the material and immaterial. The fashion industries encourage the belief that abstract qualities such as happiness, excitement, intimacy, emotionality, and so on, are available through the possession of material objects. Car bumper stickers proclaim *love is owning a Porsche*; McDonald's restaurants promise *fun and good times for the whole family*. The fashion system may be based on economics, but it is propelled by desire. Fundamental to it is the widespread belief in the power and irresistibility of the material: the assumption is that in the control of the material lies the opportunity for human perfection. Objects become valued for the status and prestige they confer: those dressed in the latest clothing fashions are assumed to be rich; those who dine at expensive bistros are thought to have superior tastes. Power and wealth tacitly invite goods and services to stand as evidence of an individual's claims of personal accomplishment. This conflation of the material with the immaterial, an essential feature of the bourgeois sensibility, constitutes one of the antinomies of modernity. And it is part of the attraction of dining out, especially for any analyst of modern social forms, a practice that vividly illustrates how this elision between appearances and actualities is continually and vigorously reconstituted.

The restaurant and department store are linked insofar as both house practices and promote images associated with the satisfactions of privately held desires. Walking about a department store, with its bountiful displays of the novel and entertaining, exposes the individual not only to what appears to be the ideal but also to the suggestion that these items and representations are readily within one's grasp. As with the department store, the restaurant has a dioramic effect that highlights what seems to be the popular, fashionable, and therefore desirable. In the restaurant, the items and details of its decor, service, menu, tableware, and so on, are employed to create a signature image in which customers expect to pursue their desires—be they feelings of success, luxury, extravagance, authority, or self-importance. In the restaurant, there is opportunity for momentarily possessing admired objects and for living out the style of conduct that they suggest. Importantly, it is not individual consumers who define what is valuable; rather, they are accepting what is offered. Thus, the codified patterns of conduct and the prefigured emotional responses embedded in public conduct make the pleasures of dining out much like the commodities on display in the department store. The individual chooses how to feel by choosing a specific restaurant.

Dining out conventionally and fashionably means that the individual is not provoked to reflection. Indeed, the opposite seems true—dining out is a formulaic practice that promotes the avoidance of reflection. It is an event dominated by social images and the constraints of fashions and customs. In this way, it is clear how the practice is antagonistic to the ideals of civility: it provides a well-formulated, orderly manner of acting, which subjugates the individual to what is popular. Through obedience to the patterns of conduct required by the form, one is absorbed into routines and habits. In turn, this can prevent recognition of the different and singular. It can also produce situations where anything novel or surprising is misread; one is just as likely to misconstrue the new as a failure of civility instead of a challenge to it.

To see dining out as a social practice that promulgates formalized social relations is to see how it can also be a sign of the incivility characteristic of contemporary manners. Norbert Elias (1978), in his study of the history of manners, argued that the civilizing process begins with the individual's talent for concealment, for being able to disguise the spontaneous and unruly. To acquire this sensibility, individuals need to exchange places imaginatively with the other; they must exercise reflection and invention in order to fabricate a plausible social mien, one in which concealment and the control of the spontaneous have been effected. This process exercises the imagination and prepares the way to a civilized future. However, Elias's argument is made without reference to a public reservoir of practices from which exemplary standards of conduct are daily broadcast. That is, Elias did not take into account the influences of the culture and entertainment industries and their capacity to promulgate styles of behavior and fashions in conduct that may preserve interests quite remote from those of the individual.

In the twentieth century, the culture industries with their consumerist ethic have independently produced a new layer of social knowledge that attempts to homogenize social life and gloss over the contestory processes of dissemblance—the very processes of self-reflection that Elias identified as necessary to a civilized society. Now, we more commonly live in a world where prescriptive social guises are available, and where the necessity to devise effective social roles is displaced from the individual onto the culture producers who are capable of offering repertoires of discourse and expressions of emotion in an era where such enunciations are seen as problematic (see Papson 1986). When simulations have replaced actualities, where events are cast in hyperbolic terms, when images obscure real events, when various beliefs are maintained in the face of challenging counterexamples, we have entered the world of Eco's hyperreality. In the world of the hyperreal, it seems possible to the modern individual that everything, including the constituents of a moral universe, can be procured from the marketplace. A practice, such as dining out, which is dominated by fashionability and public images, which in turn provide readily imitated formulaic social routines, is itself a practice that constructs the hyperreal.

The Hyperreality of Appetite

As social creatures, it is a truism to say that elements of the personal are in debt to structures of the public—although in the West, where individualism is enthusiastically promoted, that debt is not always fully acknowledged. At the turn of the twentieth century, Cooley (1902:36) criticized the belief in individualism; he maintained that "a separate individual is an abstraction unknown to experience, and so likewise is society when regarded as something apart from individuals." Such a view means that what is privately and emotionally valued by individuals is simultaneously an aspect of the everyday realm of public activities. More recently, Agnes Heller (1982:20) has made the same point, although in different terms. She has pointed out that individuals' consciousness of the general, of how they think society works, can be seen in the particular, in how they conduct the affairs of the everyday. Like Cooley, Heller shows that the individual's sense of the totality of reality, of understanding how society works, is implicitly expressed through the ordinary routines of the everyday. On this basis, an event such as dining out can be taken as an illustration of how historical and economic structures—that is, the largescale characteristics of a social epoch—enter human imagination and play a significant role in the manufacture of those nuances of behavior that are conventionally described as private, personal, and idiosyncratic.

If we take banal activities as summaries of broader cultural configurations, then the practices of the everyday can be seen as reproductions of an idealized, often imaginary, status quo. So, the customary elements of everyday life, which are widely regarded as normative, are also ideologically imbued proclamations of regnant views on human nature and the social order. By closely connecting the public event with the individual's private sensibilities, the idea is being reinforced that the structures of society generate specific kinds of internal, individualistic responses (Elias 1978:201). The significance of this for a habituated event like dining out is that the artificial and contrived performance required of the individual in the restaurant can no longer be treated as a trivial aspect of circumstances, but must be seen instead as inseparable from the imaginary universe individuals assume they inhabit, from which all manners of pleasures and events derive their shape and substance.

When we choose to dine out in restaurants because it fits our sense of fun or pleasure or convenience, we do not see ourselves as the believers of a received view. The firm cultural belief in individualism prevents us from seeing this. Instead, we assume that our preferences are reflective of our own private sensibilities. Even the mass popularity of an event such as dining out does not dissuade us from thinking our pleasures in the practice are highly personal, that they reflect our own good taste and developed sensibilities. Yet the role of the culture industries is aimed at shaping tastes in order to sustain mass consumption. Thus, to claim that a public event like dining out is pleasurable largely because it reflects or expresses private and idiosyncratic tastes is to overlook the existence and invasive effectiveness of the culture and entertainment industries.

The ethos of mass consumerism that emerged in the nineteenth century and has stridently continued into the late twentieth century has effectively stirred up and shaped new and previously unrealized personal appetites. Simmel (1903) recognized that people sought from the new entertainments and products of the material culture for a means for making life easier. The continuous production of new pleasures and pastimes meant that the individual's time and attention were fully absorbed by the material. Simmel well understood how a vast array of newly manufactured objects could be regarded as exciting, but he saw as well that such a fascination with the material diverted the individual from thinking about how society should be and what constituted proper social relations. Simmel saw that as the products of the objective culture became available to more people, a putative consensus appeared to exist: people came to act more alike and to enjoy similar interests. It was as if the more people came into contact with the material products of civilization, the narrower became the base of values and qualities upon which social life rested. The consequence of such a narrowing of interests was that the existence of alternative competing values became rare. In turn, this brought about a dilution of those intellectual pursuits—namely doubt, critique, and invention, which are the impetus of civility itself.

Incivility can be thought of as occurring where there is sociality without engagement, when individuals do not examine the purposes of their actions, but act from habit or in response to anonymous edicts, such as those dictated by fashion. The fashionability of an event predefines its meaning. Being in fashion means that the object or practice has already been valued, and this is itself an attraction. The individual does not have to examine cultural practices to ascertain their status: when they are fashionable, their meaning and value are perfectly clear. In this way, the fashionability of an event or practice can mask much of its character. This is precisely Eco's argument—that a life lived in hyperreality can be a negation of civility because individuals cannot separate the publicized views of an event from their reactions to it. The individual's inability to resist the appeal of habit and routine means that imagining and leading an examined life has been retarded. As the practice of dining out is thickly overlaid with advertising hyperbole and prescriptive representations, it can be a practice through which many people are induced into routinized habits of public performance to the detriment of the examined life. It can be an invitation to sacrifice the responsibilities attached to urbane social conduct in preference to a homogenization of the public domain.

Hirschman (1971) has suggested that a new feature of modern social life is individuals' failure to exercise effective judgment, especially so in regard to distinguishing their interests from those of the market. Bourdieu's (1984) study of tastes and cultural practices reaches similar conclusions. The popularity of pursuing one's personal desires in the public domain shows a willingness to accept fashions and regulations in public conduct as if they reflected personal sensibilities. It is a paradox that the individual does not recognize how the fashionability of a practice must make it, by definition, unable to satisfy private, idiosyncratic desires. Haug (1985) has made much the same point in his study of the commodification of aesthetics. He argues that when modern life requires that we procure relaxation and rehabilitation, and when a practice like dining out is used as such a restorative pleasure, then we are in jeopardy of having artificial market-induced pleasures determine our personal enjoyments. When we dine out in order to regenerate after a hard day at the office, or to repair a failing relationship, or to court romance, or in response to any number of other widely held conceptions, it can be argued that our sensory and critical faculties have been set aside as we accept patterns of conduct that are made to seem common and popular (and thereby, more legitimate and attractive) by market forces.

Haug (1985:50) has described our reading of pleasure and desire in the regulated choices on offer as an example of a failure of modern social relations. "Appearance always promises more, much more, than it can ever deliver. In this way the illusion deceives. The problem of modern social life, Haug (1985:19) has stated, is that the individual succumbs to the promises of appearance and then borrows back from these manufactured guises the language and sensations of the private. If we come to know luxury, extravagance, convenience, pleasure, relaxation, and romance through the restaurant, or some other popular and public entertainment, and we employ these representations to experience our own desires, then it means our sensibilities and feelings are being shaped by the regulatory codes of convention.

Conclusion

One of the functions of the entertainment and recreation industries is the manufacture of those feelings and experiences that individuals believe they should be having. It is taken as axiomatic that we should experience pleasure as an essential and normal part of a satisfying social life. So the artifice and fantasy found in the

restaurant, for example, are accepted as legitimate sources of pleasure because they help generate the emotions and experiences we
are supposed to be having in a world otherwise dominated by the
routines of a rationalized public domain. Yet what is thought of as
desirable is misunderstood as being materially calculable and procurable. Sontag (1966:26) identified this as a problem of modernity;
we are too ready to elide the appearance with the substance, the
manner of appearing as the manner of being. And when this happens, en masse, when our public conduct follows the patterns of
advertised trends, we have entered hyperreality. The problems of
experiencing pleasure of an enduring kind are greatly reduced. One
may dine out in search of pleasure but encounter more commonly
a tangle of rules that support its overprescribed, regimented, and
administered nature.

When we choose to dine out to pursue pleasure, not only are
we transforming bodily nourishment into a public event subject to
prescriptive rules, we are also agreeing tacitly to comply with certain codes of conduct and allow our experiences to be fashioned by
various structural imperatives. Dining out is not synonymous with
eating: it is not simply a biological or even an economic process.
Dining out becomes an event that brings the individual—figuratively
and literally—into the public arena and exposes him or her to the
scrutinizing eye of the other. It is an everyday event that expresses
views on human nature and the ethics of social relations. When,
what, and how we eat becomes a narrative retelling aspects of
biography and cultural knowledge. Our eating habits reflect a sense
of social competency and ease with interactional propinquity. They
summarize what we understand or misunderstand to be interesting, urbane, civilized, and pleasurable.

References

Barthes, Roland (1972). *Mythologies*. New York: Hill and Wang.

———— (1982). *Empire of Signs*. New York: Farrar, Straus and Giroux.

Baudrillard, Jean (1983). *Simulations*. New York: Semiotext(e).

Bourdieu, Pierre (1984). *Distinction: A Social Critique of the Judgment of
Taste*. Cambridge: Harvard University Press.

Cooley, Charles Horton (1902). *Human Relations and the Social Order*.
Chicago: University of Chicago Press.

Eco, Umberto (1986). *Faith in Fakes*. London: Secker and Warburg.

Elias, Norbert (1978). *The Civilizing Process*. New York: Urizen.

—— (1982). *Power and Civility*. New York: Patheon.

Finkelstein, Joanne (1989). *Dining Out. A Sociology of Modern Manners*. Cambridge: Polity.

Haug, Wolfgang Fritz (1985). *Critique of Commodity Aesthetics*. Cambridge: Polity.

Heller, Agnes (1976). *A Theory of Need in Marx*. London: Allison and Busby.

—— (1982). *A Theory of History*. London: Routledge & Kegan Paul.

Hirschman, Albert (1971). *The Passions and the Interests*. Princeton: Princeton University Press.

Hodgson, Moira (1982). "Ambiance of Eating: What Is Its Role?" *New York Times*, February 3, 17, 19.

Horkheimer, Max and Theodor Adorno (1972). *The Dialectic of Enlightenment*. New York: Herder and Herder.

Marcuse, Herbert (1964). *One-Dimensional Man*. Boston: Beacon Press.

Miller, Michael (1981). *The Bon Marché: Bourgeois Culture and the Department Store 1869–1920*. Princeton: Princeton University Press.

Papson, Stephen (1986). "From Symbolic Exchange to Bureaucratic Discourse: The Hallmark Greeting Card," *Theory, Culture and Society*, Vol. 3, No. 2.

Sargent, Sarah (1985). *The Foodmakers*. Ringwood: Penguin.

Simmel, Georg (1903). "The Metropolis and Mental Life." *On Individuality and Social Forms* (1971). Edited by D. Levine. Chicago: University of Chicago Press.

Sontag, Susan (1966). *Against Interpretation*. New York: Delta.

Williamson, Judith (1978). *Decoding Advertisements*. London: Marion Boyars.

—— (1983). *Consuming Passions*. London: Marion Boyars.

Chapter 14

Feeding the Audience:
Food, Feminism, and Performance Art

Deborah R. Geis

I am for art that is put on and taken off, like pants,
which develops holes, like socks, which is eaten, like a
piece of pie, or abandoned with great contempt, like a
piece of shit.

—Claes Oldenburg, Store Days

Fear of dining and dining conversation, acts of power
and manipulation. She wanted a little cake, something
she could carry with her. She could take little bites of
the cake, keeping it hidden. A small boy is eating, mean-
ing to expand. Fear of eating and eating conversation,
acts of power and false termination.

—Ellen Zweig, Fear of Dining and
Dining Conversation

One recent spring morning, in the midst of the commuter rush on the #6 train, I watched a man unwrap (slowly, lovingly) the various parts of his breakfast (Egg McMuffin, hash browns in styrofoam container, coffee with cream and sugar), and proceed—wholly oblivious to the crowd, the noise, the dirt of the subway car—to eat his food, slurping his coffee and spilling Egg McMuffin crumbs onto his business suit, absorbed in his meal to the point of being unaware that the eyes of every commuter in that subway car were upon him.

In my women's studies classes, when we talk about food, I ask the women in the room if they have ever felt self-conscious eating in public. Invariably, several of them recount stories of "first dates" during which they scanned the menu for something that would be easy to eat inconspicuously, picking a salad or chicken breast for fear that devouring a plate of spaghetti would expose an overeager appetite and would risk stains and spills and messiness; only later, still hungry and safely away from the judging eye across the table, would they open the refrigerator and stuff themselves with cold pizza, ice cream straight from the carton, anything deliciously gooey and sloppy.

It strikes me that in both of these cases, eating becomes the site of a public performance: an unselfconscious one for the man on the subway, and the opposite for the woman in the restaurant. Our boundaries between the public and the private are challenged at the moments when the primal act of feeding, having entered the realm of culture, becomes spec(tac)ular. Perhaps part of the appeal, for some, of watching county fair eating contests has been the opportunity to indulge vicariously, or voyeuristically, in a kind of obscene excess (similar to that which one can witness in "pornographic" films?); watching, or perhaps also engaging in, an orgy of public eating is simultaneously repulsive and gratifying in its temporary violation of cultural sanctions against appetite, sloppiness, and extreme consumption.

In postmodern American culture, the spectacle of consumption has extended to the preparation of food itself as a form of performance; one need only think of Benihana and sushi bar chefs, supermarket food demonstrators, and T.V. cooking shows as examples of the theatricalization of appetite—and, I would argue, the transference of gratification from the visceral to the visual. In the case of the "live" chefs and food demonstrators, one may be invited to partake of what has been prepared, but T.V. cooking shows offer the possibility of satisfying and denying the appetite at the same time. In perhaps the most vicarious forms of consumption, the spectacle itself is stripped of visible human agency: commercials and magazine covers or advertisements offer food that—like performers themselves, with makeup and coiffure and lighting assistance—has been "stylized," dressed up and staged like *Playboy* centerfolds for our visual projections of consumerist fantasies. Rosalind Coward goes so far as to call such photographs "food pornography," suggesting that their appeal to the forbidden, their relation to female servitude and objectification, and their repression of the processes of production resemble the aesthetic and ideological practices of the photos in soft-core mainstream centerfold pictures. As Jeremy MacClancy puts it, "Cropped close-ups may show a fat piece of gilded chicken, a larger-than-life cream tart with a hyper-real texture, or a slice of sponge cake, its dark chocolate filling threatening to ooze over the edge. Either way the message is not understated, but shouted: `Eat me! Eat me!' "[1]

All of this goes a long way toward explaining why, in the theater, the performance of eating or preparing food is a subject of fascination. Two contemporary playwrights for whom the "staging" of food figures repeatedly are Sam Shepard and Tina Howe. Shepard's plays feature everything from pouring milk into a bowl of Rice Krispies over a character's hand (*Forensic and the Navigators*) to frying bacon and boiling artichokes on stage (*Curse of the Starving Class*) to having characters carry in piles of corn and carrots (*Buried Child*) to making real toast in dozens of toasters that a character has stolen throughout the neighborhood and plugged in to impress his brother (*True West*).[2] Howe's work is concerned with more explicitly "female" images associating cooking and eating with problems of sexuality and creativity. While this exists mostly in narrative form in *Painting Churches, The Art of Dining* takes place in a restaurant where we see food being cooked and eaten, and the more recent *One Shoe Off* revolves around a dinner party gone haywire.[3] Both Shepard and Howe are aware of the spectacle inherent in the theatrical presentation of food and excess, as well as the pleasure of juxtaposing the corporeal/tangible (and "smellable") realm of real food with the fictionalized/vicarious/ untouchable realm of staged performance.

Part of the appeal of food in narrative drama, then, is simply the novelty of its "realness" when encountered in a medium that we are aware is *not* "real"; the audience of Shepard's *Curse of the Starving Class,* for instance, can smell the bacon actually cooking in a pan at the beginning of the play—a field of experience not available to them as film or television spectators. Performance art, though, goes one step further. Since performance art itself challenges the boundaries between the "lived" and the "performed," food in works of performance art—though usually still "framed" by the parameters of a designation as performance "piece," and still (again, usually) presented before "consumers," or spectators— is somewhat liberated from its role as a novel mode of disrupting the fictional/narrative milieu.[4] In its foregrounding of the gendered/ sexual desiring body, its conflations of and transgressions of private and public spaces, its connections with ritual, its paradoxical impermanence and corporeality, and its challenging of a consuming and consumerist audience, performance art becomes a site for theorizing the relationships between food and the spec(tac)ular—and our "eating culture," correspondingly, becomes terrain for better exploring the pleasures and possibilities of performance art.

⋘⋙⋘⋙⋘⋙

A fascinating precursor to contemporary performance art's interest in relationships between food and the body is the *lazzi* of the Commedia dell'Arte which flourished in Europe between 1550 and 1750. *Lazzi* were stock comic routines, often involving sexual, scatological, and violent slapstick, employed repeatedly in the *commedia* as a way of generating guaranteed laughter. It is possible to argue that despite their insertion into essentially narrative frameworks, the *lazzi*—in their emphasis on the body, their interplay with the audience, and their disruption of or disregard for the play's "plot"—were a version of popular performance art. One need only attend a performance of the Blue Man Group's *Tubes* to see the similarities. In Mel Gordon's collection of *lazzi* from this era, an entire section is devoted to routines involving food. As Gordon points out, many of the food *lazzi* drew upon involved an infantile fascination with seeking food, consuming enormous quantities of it or making a mess with it, and calling attention to the processes of excretion. I am particularly interested in the *lazzi* that involved the conflation of food and the body to the point that the body *becomes* food. In the "Lazzo of Being Brained," for instance, Arlecchino receives a blow on the head that is so strong that his "brains begin to spurt out." In response, "afraid that he will lose his intelligence, Arlecchino sits and feasts on his brains."[5] And the "Lazzo of Eating Oneself" proceeds as follows: "Famished, Arlecchino can find nothing to eat but himself. Starting with his feet and working up to his knees, thighs, and upper torso, Arlecchino devours himself."[6]

The transgressive (cannibalistic, masturbatory) quality of this act, as well as the absurd impossibility of the performer consuming himself (how would this be staged?) calls attention to the way that performance forces us to make leaps of the imagination: there is a beautifully Escherian (il)logic to what Arlecchino is doing. In a manner that calls to mind the performance pieces of Karen Finley, whose works will be discussed shortly, Arlecchino's action mirrors and parodies the spectators' appetite for "devouring" the performer's body. As with the *lazzi*, performance art has a predilection for taking such metaphors of consumption—always to some degree present in the theater—and pushing them toward a literalization, or embodiment, that (in the playful manner of much postmodern art) can be both serious and ludicrous at the same time.

The Futurists and Surrealists, too, staged playful events with food that could be considered early versions of performance art. In Russia in 1913 and 1914, Natalia Goncharova, Vladimir Larionov, Vladimir Mayakofsky, and the Burliuk brothers made a film, *Drama in Cabaret No. 13*, about their activity of walking in the streets with flowers and vegetables in their arms, radishes in their button-holes, and algebraic symbols painted on their faces.[7] In Italy, the food "events" of Marinetti and his followers have been well documented.[8] Salvador Dalí gave a lecture in London in 1936 with a loaf of French bread strapped to a helmet; in *The Secret Life of Salvador Dalí*, he describes his idea of making giant loaves of bread appear suddenly in conspicuous public places in Paris and other European cities. Dalí claims that the effect would be one of "collective hysteria," and the spectacle would thus become "the point of departure from which . . . one could subsequently try to ruin . . . systematically the logical meaning of all the mechanisms of the rational practical world."[9]

As performance art began to take on its own meanings distinct from visual art, several "environmental" artists in the early sixties through the mid-seventies began to experiment with creating interactive environments involving the preparation, serving, consumption, and sometimes decomposition of food. Daniel Spoerri *(Restaurant Spoerri)* in Dusseldorf and Les Levine *(Levine's Restaurant)* in New York set up actual restaurants; their "art" was the event of diners entering the space, discussing and consuming the food, and paying for it.[10] In a sense, Spoerri and Levine enacted a parody of the manner in which other, more traditional works of art are "consumed" by spectators who enter a gallery and "devour" the paintings; the impermanence of both the environment and the food in it called attention to the sense (also prevalent in Allan Kaprow's "Happenings," another performance art precursor that often involved food) that an artwork could be transitory and experiential, evolving only in its moments of reception.

Merret Oppenheim, one of the few woman French Surrealists, created a piece entitled *Spring Feast* for the Tenth Surrealist Exhibition of 1959. In it, a golden-faced woman (a real one in the private viewing of the piece) was stretched out on a long dinner table, her body covered with fruit, and surrounded by men (again, real ones at the private viewing) sitting at the table, poised to consume her.[11] In many ways, Oppenheim's creation anticipated the works of the women performance artists whose works emerged a decade or so later. Perhaps because of the obvious cultural connections between food and the female body as object for consumption, women performance artists in particular have used their work to call attention to, and sometimes to parody, these connections.[12] Sue-Ellen Case points out that doing so risks posing a "biologistic" model of female oppression that may, according to materialist feminists, simply participate in a mythologizing and universalizing of the female body at the expense of more socially and politically motivated critiques of such oppression. She cites Judy Chicago's "Dinner Party" as an example of "the formal influence of such biologistic thinking."[13] Although Case's point is well taken, I would argue that most of the women performance artists that I am about to describe, though sometimes essentialist in their tendency to privilege one female body (the performer's) as "representative" of "the female body," do incorporate a greater degree of materialist critique into the works than Case is willing to give them credit for having done.[14] Indeed, I think that by the specific strategies these artists use to communicate with (and sometimes to confront) their *audiences*, they question and politicize issues of representation; further, since food itself is a cultural commodity, its use moves their pieces beyond the biologistic and into the realm of *material* examinations of consumerism in its various forms (as mentioned above).[15]

Carolee Schneemann's *Meat Joy* (1964) celebrated—and to some degree eroticized—the associations between genital sexuality and meat as performers rolled nude on the floor in a display of orgiastic pleasure, covering themselves with shreds of paper, paint, sausages, fish, and chicken.[16] A series of photographs by Suzanne Lacy entitled *The Anatomy Lesson* (1973–76) included a sequence of Lacy consuming various parts of a chicken (*Wing, Arm, Breast Leg*) and another of her as a crazed, wild-eyed Julia Child explaining *Where the Meat Comes From* by wielding her knife at a lamb carcass.[17] In her early works, Linda Montano went from exhibiting chickens as "living sculptures" in galleries to dressing up as "Chicken Woman" (1971) and displaying herself in public places, thus mocking the connections between her own gender and her status as "food" or consumable object.[18] Schneemann, Lacy, and Montano, like several other women performance artists, take on the "biologistic" model by deconstructing what Carol Adams calls the "texts of meat." According to Adams, the "patriarchal nature of our meat-advocating cultural discourse" enforces social attitudes of reverence toward meat as a repository of signification, a "meaningful" food. Adams argues that this overwhelming sense of meat as an embodiment of "coherence" comes from "patriarchal attitudes including the idea that the end justifies the means, that the objectification of other beings is a necessary part of life, and that violence can and should be masked."[19] All of these cultural assumptions, in Adams's view, underly the "sexual politics of meat." Women performance artists who take on a critique of the sexual politics of meat may, on one level, be employing a "biologistic" model in Case's sense, given that their subject matter is the very material taken into their bodies; on the other hand, the "texts of meat" are also materialist texts about the gendering of consumption and consumerism. While such pieces as *Meat Joy* foregrounded ritual, others—like Montano's Chicken Woman, or Nina Sobell's video performance *Baby Chicky* (1981)—drew upon the ironies of the woman-meat image to create a more critical and materialist view. In *Baby Chicky*, the artist appeared nude with a raw chicken on her head and another cradled in her arms. Sobell's text reinforces the sense that little girls grow up prepared to become (and to see themselves as) pieces of meat:

> Once upon a time there was a little girl whose job it was to clean and season the Friday Night Chicken and put it in the oven. She stood on a stool so she could reach down into the sink to wash and shower the chicken with cool, clean water. When she held the chicken up it started to dance on the floor of the sink while the little girl sang. When they were finished playing and the chicken was sleepy she put it into the bedpan and into the oven. If the little girl was bad, or her mommy thought she was, she would pick up the little girl and say, "One, two, three, into the oven you go," and the little girl would say, "Hey, Ma, I might be bad but I ain't chicken."[20]

The domestic space of the kitchen is the realm of the private, a realm most often associated with the female (my landlord said to me yesterday, only half jokingly, "A woman's place is in the oven"). The public space of performance allows women artists to interrogate the boundaries between the private and the public as I mentioned at the beginning of this essay, entering the territory of public space through food can be a transgressive or defiant act, and some women performance artists have chosen to focus on—sometimes to literalize—the crossing of those boundaries. Nancy Barber, for instance, chose to "make visible" the domestic sphere by showing videos of people cooking in their homes on a local cable television channel.[21] As a reversal that brought the domestic into theatrical space, in Allison Knowles' "concert" piece *Make a Salad* (first performed by the Fluxus Group in Denmark in 1962, and repeated many times since then), an audience enters a concert hall, expecting a musical performance, but the "music" turns out to be the sounds and rhythms of the performers chopping carrots, tearing lettuce, and so forth, to make a huge salad for the audience to help consume.[22] In Barbara Smith's *Feed Me* (1973), the artist arranged a private room in a gallery where she sat nude, surrounded by items of comfort and nurturing such as soft pillows and a mattress and rug, food, incense, candles, wine, scented oils, and so forth; visitors were invited to enter the space individually to interact with her. As Jeanie Forte points out, although the piece was criticized for furthering audience voyeurism, the crucial distinction is that Smith was emphasizing her own pleasure (Forte points out that the piece was entitled "*Feed Me*," not "let me feed you," and therefore Smith did not simply make herself into a kind of "food" for the audience to consume).[23]

Performance artist Bonnie Sherk defied the boundaries of the public and the private even more overtly in a piece entitled *Public Lunch* (1971), which was the culmination of a series of performances in various locations entitled *Sitting Still*. Sherk arranged herself as an "exhibit" in the lions' house at the San Francisco Zoo so that she became, in effect, another "animal" on display for the spectators walking by. At feeding time, just when the lions were being thrown their raw, red hunks of meat, Sherk (dressed in formal wear) had an elegant catered lunch delivered to her, and ate it at a small, formally arranged table in her cage next to the lions' cage. The piece is interesting in several respects in addition to the clearly parodic (or "ethical") statement it makes about zoos and their purposes. Sherk comments, "It was about analogies and being an object on view."[24] By timing her meal to coincide with the lions', Sherk interrogates the differences between "civilized" and "primitive" rituals of eating, suggesting perhaps that the trappings of civilization (the silverware, tablecloth, etc.) are merely devices for deluding ourselves into thinking that our feeding does not serve the same primal purpose as it does for the lions tearing apart their raw meat in their cage. Sherk's performance—which could be interpreted as a feminist response to Kafka's story "A Hunger Artist"— challenges the voyeuristic desire of the passers-by (her audience) to *watch* her in the zoo, particularly while she is engaged in the act of eating.[25] Her position, moreover, calls Brechtian attention to her status as a woman who "performs" not only within the literal cage at the zoo (and one might think here, too, of the popularity of caged go-go dancers), but also within the metaphorical cage of patriarchal culture.

⊸◈⊸◈⊸◈⊸

By eating in public, Sherk makes herself part of a performative display. I began this essay by mentioning that self-consciousness about public eating can be, for women, symptomatic of a larger fear of their own hunger, their own appetites, and ultimately their own bodies. This, of course, is an issue that has frequently been addressed by feminist writers on women, eating, and body image, including Kim Chernin, Susie Orbach, and Susan Bordo.[26] Not surprisingly, several women performance artists have chosen to address the ways they have been implicated in the cultural obsession with idealized female body images and the subsequent effects on the way they approach food and eating. In Vanalyne Green's *Trick or Drink* (1984), Green used family photographs, children's books, and excerpts from her own diaries to create an autobiographical narrative that explored—in a performance that called for direct audience address and eye contact—her bulimia and weight obsessions as a teenager and its connections to other kinds of addiction in her life (her parents' alcoholism, her own later sexual addictions). The performance—unlike the testimony in, say, a twelve-step program—did not emphasize a confessional stance or a movement toward completion and catharsis. Rather, as Sue Ellen Case puts it, *Trick or Drink* was a representation or enactment of Green's "internal growth."[27]

A more dramatic physical performance of the effect of the aesthetic coding of women's bodies was Eleanor Antin's *Carving.* During the period from July 15 to August 21, 1972, Antin kept herself on a strict diet and had herself photographed, naked, from the same four angles every morning. The photographic series thus depicts Antin's body being "carved" thinner and thinner. The sculptor is, of course, the "hunger artist" Antin herself. Yet it is society's artistic/aesthetic "ideal" of the woman's body that sets the contours of the image that Antin's body-sculpture ostensibly aims for, but never quite achieves. In other words, by following the diet explicitly for the purpose of the performance/photographs, Antin foregrounds the purely aesthetic outcome of dieting—the sculpting of the body—and as a result provides an almost parodically clinical visual representation of what is "normally" a private, emotional, and psychological cultural obsession. This attitude is clear in Antin's textual commentary on the photographs, throughout which she refers to her body as "the material" and to the period of the dieting as the "carving" of a "work" according to the traditional Greek method of starting with a thick block and removing a layer at a time from all four sides of the block.

She concludes by saying that the sculpture always falls short of the artists's idealized image. She quotes Michelangelo: *non ho l'ottima artista alcun concetto che el marmo solo non in se circoscrive,* or "not even the greatest sculptor can make anything that isn't already inside the marble."[28] In *The Object of Performance,* Henry Sayre provides an interesting commentary:

> Antin's "ideal image" of herself is clearly problematized terrain, tied up, as it is, in dieting, in an image of woman inspired by the fashion and fitness industries, in a mystique of thinness that, if nothing else, would require Antin to be at least a foot taller than she is.... What her work underscores is her *difference* from the ideal, even as she subscribes (with tongue in cheek) to its codes. But the real message here is that, before submitting herself to carving, before dieting, Antin is not perceived to be "lifelike." She is a block of matter, awaiting animation by the sculptor's hand.[29]

While I agree with Sayre that Antin's unachieved "ideal image" is "problematized terrain," it seems to me that Sayre himself (in, for example, the comment that Antin would need to be taller) has assumed both the culturally sanctioned physical ideal and, to some degree, Antin's acceptance of it. I would be more inclined to bring Sayre's parenthetical "tongue in cheek" out of the parentheses, to suggest Antin's agency in her position as subject—as the artist—even while she ironically renders herself an object (i.e., both of sculpture and of the photographs). That is, I would read Antin's performance with, rather than against, its textual commentary. The work's resonance is less in Antin's psychological sense of her shortcomings as artist/sculpture than in her defiant act of making the so-called failure of her piece into the material of the performance itself.

In *Fear of Dining and Dining Conversation* (1981), a piece that its creator, Ellen Zweig, says should ideally be performed in a place where people are sitting at tables and eating (and possibly with dancers who also stop and occasionally peel potatoes), uses the verbal texts of food to confront the complications of women's appetites in a culture that attempts to suppress them. The piece is done with two voices; one of them recites a pastiche of food names, definitions of cooking terms, and calorie counts, while the other voice is a rhythmic prose poem about the fear of eating, punctuated with variations on the title phrase (see, for example, the epigraph to this essay). Some of the phrases of the first voice (e.g., "to blend a fragile mixture") take on wider metaphorical references when heard in counterpoint to the second voice's narrative of fear and denial ("she begins to mortify herself, by fasting and immoderate hikes").[30] The second voice, which seems to be inspired by the material in Kim Chernin's study on women and food, *The Obsession*, moves into an emphasis on starvation at the same time that the first voice speaks about Ellen West (a woman whose self-starvation is discussed by Chernin and others—and whose name, interestingly, resembles that of Ellen Zweig). The two voices come together at the end with the words, "No matter what you say./No matter what you say./There is no solace./There is no consolation."[31] Zweig's piece creates a sense of the ways that food has been inscripted, or entextualized, upon the bodies of its preparers and consumers. The litany of recipes and calorie counts, especially when heard in conjunction with the nightmarish repetitions of food-related compulsions and neuroses, suggests that the distinction between what one does to food and what the woman does to herself (or has done to her) has broken down; what is left are textual fragments (echoed in the emphasis throughout on blanching, reducing, boiling, chopping) that mark a history of repression and denial, embodied ultimately in the historical figure of West.[32] At the same time, perhaps Zweig's preference for having the piece performed in a room where people are eating together at tables suggests an impulse for breaking through the "fear of dining" by creating a sense of community.

Suzanne Lacy, whose works were mentioned once already in this essay in the context of meat-eating, places even greater emphasis on this notion of the community in her pieces' literal and metaphorical use of the "potluck." Food, says Lacy in an interview with Linda Montano, "serves as a bridge between private rituals and social issues."[33] In an early group piece for women, for example, Lacy says that everyone performed their images of food, and an enormous amount of anger emerged: among others, one participant "crammed food down her doll's mouth while someone else passed around Valentine chocolate candies filled with glass and nails." As a result, the group "discovered a close connection between food and insanity."[34] Lacy's later pieces, inspired by Judy Chicago's *Dinner Party*, sought to create healing ways for expressing women's relationships to food; she began by setting up a series of potlucks "probably because it's a metaphor for nurturing each other."[35] Lucy Lippard points out that the potluck allows Lacy to work through a prototypically feminist organizing structure (like that of a quilting party), and it also contains elements of ritual, as well as providing accessibility to a diverse group of women:

> Women who would never come to a meeting because they feel they "have nothing to contribute" will bring food to a potluck. Women traditionally allow the rest of the world to feed off their own bodies and lives, as epitomized by a Tlingit potlatch trough (owned by the Denver Museum of Natural History) in the form of a huge, disemboweled female body. Embraced by the healing framework of Lacy's art, women "make sacrifices" only to each other, and for the good of the female community.[36]

Although she does risk some degree of homogenization by attempting to use the "potluck" to bring together women of all ages, races, and classes (Lippard calls this taking them "in symbolic bites"), Lacy also is aware of the immense power inherent in transforming the private rituals of dining into the public space of shared food and the communal "performance" of consumption.[37] Even her slightly later "Whisper" pieces (*Whisper, the Waves, the Wind* [1984], *The Crystal Quilt* [1987]), which do not involve food but which still involve women sitting together at tables, draw upon this image of the dinner party. In all of these pieces, though there may of course be additional onlookers, it is crucial that Lacy blurs the boundaries between performers and spectators by having most of those present be participants; as a result, the spectators themselves perform rather than subjecting "othered" actors to their consuming gaze.

❧❦❧❦❧

The effect of Lacy's "potluck" performances is to nurture her spectators. For Karen Finley, a performance artist who challenges the consuming gaze in radically different ways, the effect is to confront them—to chew the audience up and spit it out. Finley's works test the boundaries between "acceptable" and "unacceptable" female behavior by staging private behavior in the public space of performance.[38] In Finley's pieces, food frequently becomes a device for underscoring the female body's appropriation as object of desire in a consumer culture. If, as Maria Nadotti puts it, the "language of seduction" is "an obligatory instrument in any practice of consumption," then Finley makes use of the ways products like "designer" food take advantage of sexualized forms of capitalist greed and longing.[39] Her works frequently fantasize a scatological sabotaging of this food, using the body to desecrate and decorate that which goes into the body. In *The Family that Never Was*, Finley says:

> Then I see what's in those dairy cases. It's that Frudgen Gladge [*sic*], that Haggen-Dazs, that Ben and Cherry Garcia ice cream bullshit that's ruining my culture. That $12.99-a-pint-cream. Then I open up all the cartons of ice cream and I piss in 'em, I jerk off in 'em, I fart in 'em. I go into little kids' butts and take their turds and put it into that chocolate-macadamia stuff. I stuff it back into the freezer and go back and stand at the great temple of our culture, the video rental counter.[40]

If the female body is an object of consumption, then in Finley's work, the literalizing (through performance) of this image becomes a way of expressing anger toward the patriarchy's efforts to reinforce this status; by claiming, exaggerating, and parodying the extremes of such sexual fantasies, Finley is able to enact a Brechtian/Artaudian confrontation of her audience members' roles as consumers of female flesh. Throughout *Quotes from a Hysterical Female*, for instance, the following passage's deliberate address to "the men" *within* the narrative mirrors Finley's implicit challenge to the men in the audience of her performance:

> The men are upchucking all over the place, and then it's time
> for our annual sushi party. Well, I open up a can of tuna and
> I put it into the folds of my vulva. Then I stand in front of the
> men, over the men, and then I say to the men, "SUSHI PARTY
> BOYS! EAT UP!" They are all out of their minds from the
> pills and the puking and they are chewing me, chewing me.
> Then they say this isn't like usual tuna, it's kinda juicy and
> soggy. Sushi, sushi, juicy sushi. And they are eating me up.
> I've got my party going.[41]

By taking the very material (her pussy) that is supposed to be the
source of titillation for her audience (both within the narrative and
in the theater), and literalizing and exaggerating its status as consumable object, Finley deprives the spectators of their opportunity
to "feed" upon her. As Nadotti says, she issues "an invitation to
voyeurism so hyperbolic that it deactivates itself in the very act of
its production."[42]

Food in Finley's work is frequently connected to violation: the
combinations of the domestic and the sexual are rendered comic
and shocking, but also all the more disturbing, by the ways that
Freudian connections between eating and the body—as in the passage cited above—are deconstructed so that the narrator enacts the
most primal fantasies of violation and consumption imaginable. In
The Constant State of Desire, incest taboos are imaged in terms of
transgressive eating, especially in the consecutive sequences of "First
Sexual Experience, Laundromat," in which the speaker describes
his mother, after he has fucked her in the ass, sucked his own cum
out of her asshole, and spit it back into her mouth, as saying, "Boy,
you got lazy ass cum. You can cum on my pancakes anytime," and
"Refrigerator," in which the little girl's father puts her in the fridge,
"opens up the vegetable bin ... [and] starts working on my little
hole."[43] The sequence concludes with the mother arriving home
and saying to the daughter, "Whatever happened to the vegetables
for the dinner for tonight? You've been playing with your food, girl?
I wanted to make your daddy's favorite."[44] Vivian Patraka has a
helpful reading of the way these incest passages, with their emphasis on the scatological, dramatize Finley's focus on the performance
of "damage":

> What is embedded in her language and her gestures is the
> resulting breakdown of distinctions, even among the organs
> and products of the body, and the confusion of taking in and

putting out, the traumatic shock to the directional signals of the girl child body, in its violation by an adult male. The scatological functions partly as protest, expressed in what comes out of the body, to what should never have been taken into it, and partly as a shitty enactment of the violation (of interior space, projected outward by Finley to invade the performative space). What issues forth, thus, in Finley's text is not the semiotic, it is history issuing from a female body. And it is the end, not the beginning, of seduction, desire constant because it is frozen, back in the ice-box of violation.[45]

As the title of Finley's piece (which is her "answer" both to Freud and to Betty Friedan's *The Feminine Mystique*) suggests, the "constant state" of desire is addressed on several levels; sexual desire and the desire to "consume" another being is conflated with the capitalist desire to acquire, to take, to feed off of others—and ultimately, the theater audience's concurrent desire to be titillated implicates them in the very fantasies of transgression, which they have paid to be shocked and disgusted by in Finley's performance itself (as Jeanie Forte points out, this is also what is implicitly appealed to or misleadingly "promised" in the title).[46] Finley makes this connection even more explicit in the "chocolate balls" sequence of *The Constant State of Desire*. The narrative of cutting off the testicles of Wall Street traders and making them into chocolate candies to sell in "gourmet chocolate shops"[47] creates a simultaneously castrating and scatological image as a parodic comeback to the male audience's desire to consume the female body: in response, Finley imaginatively appropriates and consumes the bodies of her spectators.

While the spoken texts of Finley's works invoke images of food, the visual counterparts body forth the metaphorical connections between eating and sexuality. In *The Constant State of Desire,* Finley at one point smashes uncooked colored Easter eggs in a plastic bag with stuffed animals, and applies the egg mixture to her nude body "using soaked animals as applicators"; at another point, she tosses candies to the audience.[48] One portion of *We Keep Our Victims Ready* involves Finley smearing melted chocolate on her bare torso; as she explains in an interview with Andrea Juno, the chocolate "ritual" (as she calls it), like the "chocolate balls" sequence of *The Constant State of Desire,* allows her to conflate eating, sexuality, and excretion—only the image is even more powerful as it is made visual:

I could use *real* shit, but we know that happens already . . . I use chocolate because it's a visual symbol that involves eating as well as basically being treated like shit . . . so it works on different levels. There are so many occasions where you go into a job or situation and you just have to *eat the shit*—there's no other way out.

Then I stick little candy hearts (symbolizing "love") all over my body—because after we've been treated like shit, then we're loved. And many times that's the only way people *get* love. Then I add the alfalfa sprouts (symbolizing sperm) because in a way it's all a big jack-off—we're all being jerked off . . . we're just something to jerk off onto, after the "love." Finally, I put tinsel on my body, because after going through all that, a woman still gets dressed up for dinner.[49]

In Finley's multiple-performer piece *The Theory of Total Blame* (1988), the family is gathered for Thanksgiving dinner; in Shepardian style, a tremendous, sickening quantity of food covers the table and spills from the refrigerator—but remains uneaten. As the mother prepares and serves the food (jello, meatloaf), she also renders it inedible as her children refuse it. Nadotti argues that in this piece, "as elsewhere in Finley's work, what is ordinarily considered consumable is . . . transformed into a threatening signifier of reciprocal aggression."[50] Excessive food is, as Coward suggests, one of the ritual elements of festive eating in its demonstration of "profusion and survival."[51] If the food seems to reproduce itself endlessly, though, for Finley this becomes part of its *un*consumability; once again, the exaggeration forces the spectators to reexamine their own literal and metaphorical hungers.

⊰◈⊱⊰◈⊱⊰◈⊱

In *Gender Trouble*, Judith Butler suggests that even what we would consider the "interior essence" of the gendered body is in itself a kind of fabrication, as "that very interiority is a function of a decidedly public and social discourse, the public regulation of fantasy through the surface politics of the body."[52] The "performance" of eating (in the sense of performance art, though I would argue, again, that any kind of public eating is always, to some degree, a performance), because it is so intimately connected with the gendering of the "eater," is one of the ways that this interiority is expressed through the body politic(s). Rosalind Coward's synecdochal image

of the mouth for women as a "site of drama" takes Butler's asser-
tion one step further. "When women attempt to lay claim to the
pleasures of the mouth," says Coward, "they are often constricted
by anxiety about transgressing the appropriate expression of female
desire."[53] Both Butler and Coward are suggesting that the sites of
possible transgressive activity are socially constricted by the rules
of public performance; since performance art provides a relatively
"safe" area in which to challenge these rules, expressions of appetite and desire can be exaggerated, parodied, resexualized or desexu-
alized, liberated, questioned, and deconstructed. There is always,
after all, an audience eager to be fed.

Notes

Epigraphs are from Claes Oldenburg, *Store Days* (1967), quoted in
Adrian Henri, *Total Art: Environments, Happenings and Performance* (New
York and Toronto: Oxford University Press, 1974), p. 27, and Ellen Zweig,
"Fear of Dining and Dining Conversation," *High Performance* 4 (Winter
1981–2): 56.

1. Rosalind Coward, *Female Desires: How They Are Sought, Bought
and Packaged* (New York: Grove, 1985), pp. 101–6; orig. publ. London:
Paladin Books, 1984; Jeremy MacClancy, *Consuming Culture* (London:
Chapmans, 1992), p. 141. For more on the male gaze and its role in
objectification, see John Berger, *Ways of Seeing* (Middlesex: Penguin/BBC,
1972), pp. 45–64; Laura Mulvey, "Visual Pleasure and Narrative Cinema,"
Screen 16 (Autumn 1975), pp. 8–10.

2. For further discussion of the role of food and other objects in
Shepard's work, see chap. 3, "Object, Objectivity and the Phenomenal
Body," in Stanton B. Garner Jr., *Bodied Spaces: Phenomenology and Per-
formance in Contemporary Drama* (Ithaca and London: Cornell University
Press, forthcoming).

3. For further discussion of the role of food in Howe's work, see Nancy
Backes, "Body Art: Hunger and Satiation in the Plays of Tina Howe," in
Lynda Hart, ed., *Making a Spectacle: Feminist Essays on Contemporary
Women's Theatre* (Ann Arbor: University of Michigan Press, 1989), pp. 41–60.

4. In the popular performance piece *Tony 'n' Tina's Wedding*, the
spectators participate in eating a catered wedding dinner (of Italian food)
as part of the simulated ceremony and reception. Just as the piece plays at
making the spectators into "performers" (as they are invited to participate
in the events of the "wedding" and as the actors improvise with them), the
actors join them as "consumers" in the communal act of eating. Thus,

although the piece is intended as a parody of the ritual events of weddings, it takes on its own ritual qualities in performance.

5. Mel Gordon, *Lazzi: The Comic Routines of the Commedia dell'Arte* (New York: Performing Arts Journal Publications, 1983), p. 23.

6. Ibid.

7. Adrian Henri, *Total Art: Environments, Happenings, and Performance* (New York and Toronto: Oxford University Press, 1974), p. 14.

8. For a description of these activities, see F. T. Marinetti, *The Futurist Cookbook*, ed. Lesley Chamberlain, trans. Suzanne Brill (San Francisco: Bedford Arts, 1989).

9. Quoted in Henri, *Total Art*, p. 24.

10. Ibid., p. 41. For a description of Spoerri's other works involving food, see also pp. 146, 156.

11. Ibid., p. 60.

12. For further discussion of the "consumable" female body, see Rosalind Coward, *Female Desires: How They are Sought, Bought and Packaged* (New York: Grove, 1985), and Carol J. Adams, *The Sexual Politics of Meat* (New York: Continuum, 1990).

13. Sue Ellen Case, *Feminism and Theatre* (New York: Methuen, 1988), pp. 55-56. Also see Judy Chicago, *Through the Flower: My Struggle as a Woman Artist* (New York: Doubleday, 1977).

14. I am inclined to agree with Jeanie Forte's argument that a feminist analysis can include a reading that joins the material body with the body as a cultural construct. The latter, when seen in terms of "the body in representation," provides a way of approaching feminist performance art in particular. Jeanie Forte, "Focus on the Body: Pain, Praxis, and Pleasure in Feminist Performance," in Janelle G. Reinelt and Joseph R. Roach, eds., *Critical Theory and Performance* (Ann Arbor: University of Michigan Press, 1992), p. 249.

15. For further discussion, see Fredric Jameson, *Postmodernism, or, The Cultural Logic of Late Capitalism* (Durham: Duke University Press, 1991). Pierre Bourdieu suggests that the body is a materialization of class taste. According to Bourdieu, not only are certain foods perceived in Western culture as masculine or feminine, but "male" and "female" ways of eating food (e.g., gulping vs. nibbling), involving respectively the back and the front of the mouth, can be compared to the ways men and women use their mouths for talking in social situations. See *Distinction: A Social Critique of the Judgement of Taste*, trans. Richard Nice (Cambridge: Harvard University Press, 1984), pp. 190–92.

16. See Johannes Birringer, "Imprints and Re-Visions: Carolee Schneemann's Visual Archeology," *Performing Arts Journal* 15 (May 1993): 44.

17. See Moira Roth, "Suzanne Lacy: Social Reformer and Witch," *TDR* 32 (Spring 1988): 56.

18. See Linda Montano, "Food and Art" (interviews), *High Performance* 4 (Winter 1981–82): 51.

19. Adams, *The Sexual Politics of Meat*, p. 14.

20. See Nina Sobell, *Baby Chicky* (in "Artists' Portfolio"), *High Performance* 4 (Winter 1981–82): 78.

21. Montano, "Food and Art," p. 47.

22. Ibid., p. 46.

23. Forte, "Focus on the Body," p. 257.

24. Montano, "Food and Art," p. 50.

25. One might think, for instance, about people watching chimps at the zoo: we see them pick their noses, defecate, etc.—all "private" acts that an audience is not, at least as far as other people are concerned, "supposed" to watch. Sherk's piece also reminds me of a recent tour I took of the CNN (Cable News Network) complex in Atlanta; the tour group is given a closed-circuit view of the "off-camera" Headline News anchor in the "cage" of the anchor booth/TV monitor so that an audience watches her scratching herself, yawning, and so forth (a real violation, I would argue, of her privacy).

26. See Kim Chernin, *The Hungry Self: Women, Eating and Identity* (New York: Harper/Perennial, 1985); Chernin, *The Obsession: Reflections on the Tyranny of Slenderness* (New York: Harper/Perennial, 1981); Susie Orbach, *Fat is a Feminist Issue* (New York: Berkley/Paddington, 1978); Susan Bordo, *Unbearable Weight: Feminism, Western Culture, and the Body* (Berkeley and Los Angeles: University of California Press, 1993).

27. Sue Ellen Case, *Feminism and Theatre*, p. 60.

28. Eleanor Antin, "Carving: A Traditional Sculpture" (in "Artists' Portfolio"), *High Performance* 4 (Winter 1981–82): 62.

29. Henry M. Sayre, *The Object of Performance: The American Avant-Garde Since 1970* (Chicago and London: University of Chicago Press, 1989), p. 78.

30. Ellen Zweig, *Fear of Dining and Dining Conversation*, *High Performance* 4 (Winter 1981–82): 57–58.

31. Ibid., p. 58. See also the discussion of Ellen West in Chernin, The Obsession, esp. pp. 162–79.

32. See also the section of Leeny Sack's performance piece *The Survivor and the Translator* (1980) in which the images of a female body and the chopping of a fish are conflated. In Lenora Champagne, ed., *Out from Under: Texts by Women Performance Artists* (New York: Theatre Communications Group, 1990), pp. 137-39.

33. Montano, "Food and Art," p. 49.

34. Ibid.

35. Ibid.

36. Lucy Lippard, "Lacy: Some of Her Own Medicine," *TDR* 32 (Spring 1988): 74.

37. Ibid.

38. See my discussion of Finley's work in chap. 7 of Deborah R. Geis, *Postmodern Theatric(k)s: Monologue in Contemporary American Drama* (Ann Arbor: University of Michigan Press, 1993), pp. 160-66.

39. Maria Nadotti, "Karen Finley's Poisoned Meatloaf," trans. Meg Shore, *Artforum* 27 (March 1989): 114.

40. Karen Finley, *The Family that Never Was,* in *Shock Treatment* (San Francisco: City Lights, 1990), p. 39.

41. Nadotti, "Karen Finley's Poisoned Meatloaf," p. 114.

42. Finley, *Quotes from a Hysterical Female,* in *Shock Treatment,* p. 48.

43. Karen Finley, *The Constant State of Desire,* TDR 32 (Spring 1988): 148. According to Rosalind Coward, "the boy child . . . never loses the possibility of restoring the mother's body as sexual object, and therefore the possibility of regarding sexual gratification as a form of nurturing." She points out, citing Melane Klein's work on infantile fantasies of devouring the mother, that the language of affection is also very much a language of sadism when it implies the devouring or consuming of the love object. Coward, *Female Desires,* p. 89.

44. Finley, *The Constant State of Desire,* p. 148.

45. Vivian Patraka, "Binary Terror and Feminist Performance: Reading Both Ways," *Discourse* 14 (spring 1992): 172.

46. Forte, "Focus on the Body," p. 257.

47. Finley, *The Constant State of Desire,* p. 142.

48. Ibid., p. 140.

49. Andrea Juno, interview with Karen Finley in *Re/Search #13: Angry Women*, eds. Andrea Juno and V. Vale (San Francisco: Re/Search Publications, 1991), p. 49.

50. Nadotti, "Karen Finley's Poisoned Meatloaf," p. 115.

51. Coward, *Female Desires*, p. 111.

52. Judith Butler, *Gender Trouble: Feminism and the Subversion of Identity* (New York and London: Routledge, 1990), p. 136.

53. Coward, *Female Desires*, p. 122.

Chapter 15

A Supper Party

Diana Fuss

This essay proceeds from the premise that stories of oral incorporation are rarely just about eating. Narratives of "eating culture" act out complex cultural fantasies of desire and inhibition, loss and plenitude, demand and refusal, wish and fulfillment. In the literature of food that calls attention to the cultural significance of eating, human subjects are defined by what lies outside them, by what can or cannot be introjected. Stories of "eating culture," in other words, are fundamentally dramas of *identification:* reflections on the human subject's insatiable desire for the Other.

In this essay I examine one such cultural narrative of wish and fulfillment, a short passage from Sigmund Freud's *The Interpretation of Dreams* (1900). It begins with a dream of an unfulfilled wish and concludes with Freud's virtuoso demonstration that even a forsaken wish can fulfill an unconscious desire. I speak, of course, of the dream of the abandoned supper party, a dream recounted to Freud by one of his cleverest patients, the witty butcher's wife:

> I wanted to give a supper-party, but I had nothing in the house but a little smoked salmon. I thought I would go out and buy something, but remembered then that it was Sunday afternoon and all the shops would be shut. Next I tried to ring up some caterers, but the telephone was out of order. So I had to abandon my wish to give a supper-party.[1]

237

Behind the dream of the abandoned supper party is a trio of characters composed of a stout butcher, his plump wife, and the wife's skinny friend. It is a rather ordinary story of weight reduction and food consumption, of gastronomic craving and fastidious self-denial, of sexual jealousy and unconscious desire. Each member of this hysterical triangle has a wish: the butcher wishes to lose weight and so begins a program of dieting and exercise, vowing to refuse all dinner invitations; the butcher's wife has a love for caviar but curiously begs her husband not to give her any; and the skinny friend, who begrudges herself salmon no less than the butcher's wife forswears caviar, wishes to grow stouter, inquiring of Freud's patient when she will host another dinner party. Jealous of her husband's admiration for her friend, the butcher's wife is consoled by the knowledge that her friend is thin and her husband prefers plump. With this last morsel of information, Freud is able to reconstruct the logic of the dream work. The dream of the abandoned supper party can now be understood as the fulfillment of the wife's unconscious wish *not* to help her friend grow fatter and thus attract her husband even more. The wife's wish is that her husband's wish should not be fulfilled.

But there is more: the "I" of the supper party dream is really "she"—the friend and not the wife. After all, Freud explains, it is smoked salmon, the friend's favorite dish, that figures in the dream, not the caviar favored by the butcher's wife. In her dream the butcher's wife has "put herself in her friend's place . . . identified herself with her friend" (149). The dream follows a hysterical thought process whereby the dreamer establishes an identification with her rival by "creating a symptom—the renounced wish" (150). Freud summarizes the hysterical identification in exact terms: "my patient put herself in her friend's place in the dream because her friend was taking my patient's place with her husband and because she (my patient) wanted to take her friend's place in her husband's high opinion" (150–51). Once again, an analysis of hysteria leads Freud back to the idea of feminine identification, an idea that has already achieved for Freud a certain definitional centrality. For Freud, hysteria *is* feminine identification, even (as the example of his own hysteria attests) where only men are concerned.

The dream of the butcher's wife is one of the primal scenes of psychoanalytic interpretation. Freud's commentators return to it again and again to learn the lesson Freud himself learns from the dream analysis, the lesson of interpretation. For Jacques Lacan, the dream of the supper party is preeminently an allegory of desire and its difficult structuration. In "The Direction of the Treatment and the Principles of Its Power," Lacan takes another look at the fish symbolism of the butcher's wife's dream and reads in the exchange of salmon for caviar (friend for wife) a formula for desire *as such:* "desire is the desire of the Other."[2] The witty hysteric both wants and does not want caviar. Her desire for caviar is "the desire of a woman who has everything, and who rejects precisely that" (261). The desire with which the butcher's wife identifies is her friend's desire, signified by the metaphoric dream substitution of a slice of smoked salmon for caviar. But why fish? In Lacan's interpretation, the hysteric's desire is always for the butcher's "pound of flesh" (265), his fleshy member, his sliding signifier. "To be the phallus, if only a somewhat thin one. Was not that the ultimate identification with the signifier of desire?" (262). For Lacan, the butcher with his wholesale meat is the most important figure in the hysterical triangle. Lacan is the first to ask: What does the butcher want? "Has he too, perhaps, not got a desire that is somewhat thwarted, when everything in him is satisfied?" The butcher, "the man of the slice of backside," has everything he ostensibly desires in his plump wife, and yet he is drawn to the thin woman like a fish to water. It is thus the husband's desire for the friend that becomes the point of identification for the wife: "the woman identifies herself with the man, and the slice of smoked salmon takes the place of the desire of the Other" (262). In contrast to Freud's analysis, the Lacanian reading situates the butcher at the end of the transferential circuit of desire and unveils a masculine identification structuring the unfulfilled wish fantasy.

Catherine Clément, in a clever piece called "No Caviar for the Butcher," takes Lacan's theory of a masculine identification to its logical *Freudian* conclusion. If the butcher's wife places herself in her husband's position, then she must desire the other woman as her husband does. Desire of the Other metonymically slides into desire *for* her: "in the dream the slice of smoked salmon stands in the place of the friend and hence it also stands for the desire for the friend, which goes unsatisfied." This drama of triangulated desire involves more than a case of heterosexual jealousy. The wife's identification with her husband's desire opens up a space for a forbidden homoerotic object choice. " 'How can another woman be loved?' (an essential question for any woman), becomes the butcher's wife's question, and . . . she in turn 'becomes' the question."[3] For Clément, the hysteric's "question" is weighted ultimately more in the direction of desire than identification. The hysteric asks not "How can

I be a woman?" but "How can another woman be loved?" The question of same sex desire between women, in Clément's reading, is indispensable to the interpretation of hysterical identification.

Cynthia Chase, in the most recent and most comprehensive rereading of the dream of the abandoned supper party, interprets the dream as a replay of primary narcissism and pre-Oedipal desire. The shift in focus from Freud to Lacan/Clément, "from *la belle bouchère*'s heterosexual desire and Oedipal identification with her friend, to her homosexual desire and pre-Oedipal identification with her husband,"[4] leads Chase to the conclusion that what we actually have in the story of the beautiful butcheress is an allegory of the infant's primary identification with the phallic mother: "*la belle bouchère* identifies with the *signifier* of her husband's desire, the phallus, and this is like the baby's identifying with the signifier of the mother's desire. As a story of the baby merges in with Lacan's story of *la belle bouchère*, it becomes a story of *la b.b.*" (WB, 1001). *La b.b.*'s identification with her husband's desire is thus a "recapitulation" (DI, 80) of her identification with the mother's phallic desire.

Chase offers maternal sexuality as the governing topos of Freud's story of identification and desire, locating identification *in* desire—desire not strictly *for* but *of* the mother. The Kristevan image of the desiring woman as phallic mother provides Chase with an alternative psychical model for lesbian desire, one that locates the wife's desire for her friend in a masculine identification with her husband that replays an earlier "primordial" relation to the pre-Oedipal phallic mother.

Chase is herself disturbed by the consequences of such a reading, a reading that posits identification with the phallus as the inevitable precondition of female subjectivity. As Chase usefully formulates the problem: "How could the notion of a necessary identification with the phallus or even the mere identification of the phallus as the signifier of desire form part of a feminist understanding of desire and meaning?" (DI, 66–67). How, indeed, can such a question even be posed without capitulating in advance to the presumption of a "*necessary* identification with the phallus?" Chase fully understands the risk involved in reclaiming the phallus for and as the mother's desire, but she takes it anyway, "for love of *la b.b.*" (DI, 67).[5] In many ways it is a risk worth taking: Chase's retelling of the story of *la b.b.* is by far the wittiest of them all, the most adventurous and even audacious in its reappropriation of the phallus for women. And yet, where lesbian desire is concerned, it is the same old story—a narrative of maternal care and female narcissism, of masculinization and pre-Oedipalization. How does Chase's project to uncover the "pre-Oedipal dimension" of both the story of the beautiful butcheress and the case of Dora (DI, 80) differ in any significant way from Freud's definition of lesbian desire as a woman's unresolved pre-Oedipal attachment to the phallic mother? How does the interpretation of *la belle bouchère* as *"la b.b.,"* and the coordinated reading of the wife's desire for her female friend as the replaying of a narcissistic relation to the maternal, advance us beyond Freud's understanding of lesbianism, in "Femininity," as two women "who play the parts of mother and baby with each other as often and as clearly as those of husband and wife?"[6] Is it possible to pose the question of desire between women outside the identity positions that, in fact, each of these readings offers—the twin poles of masculine identification and infantile pre-Oedipalization? In short, does the dream of the butcher's wife have any other stories to tell?

We might begin by returning to Freud and addressing one component of the story that all the commentaries overlook, the question of the butcher's identifications. Lacan asks what the butcher wants to *have*, not what he wants to *be*, and yet the two questions are fundamentally related. If it is true that the butcher's wife identifies with her husband's desire for the other woman, to what degree is the husband's desire for the friend itself motivated and structured by a prior identification? The husband, after all, has just one wish, the wish to lose weight, the wish to become as svelte and thin as his wife's skinny friend. Posing the matter slightly differently, why should we believe the claim of the jealous wife that her husband's close relation to her friend is based upon desire and not identification? Moreover, might the wife's own desire for her friend travel a slightly less circuitous route, one that does not necessarily bypass the husband but calls into question his strategic placement as both etiological starting point and teleological end-point of female sexual desire?

We perhaps need go no farther than Freud's own reading of the problem of sexual jealousy. Though none of the butcher's wife's interpreters reference Freud's later investigation of jealousy as a sign of both a repressed homosexual impulse and a simultaneous defense against it, the story of *la belle bouchère* provides a fitting illustration of Freud's interpretation of sexual rivalry as a manifestation of an insufficiently repressed homosexual desire.[7] In this instance, the wife's anxiety that "my husband is attracted to my woman friend" functions as a disguised declaration of the very opposite suspicion, "I am attracted to my woman friend." This narrative of identification and desire might easily be read as a story of relations "between women," with the butcher, at most, a convenient identificatory relay for a socially prohibited lesbian desire.

But even this retelling of the dream of the butcher's wife offers simply another narrative, another recasting of a tale that demonstrates a powerful resistance to interpretive mastery. Freud's compressed story of hysterical desire has produced a plethora of contradictory narratives on identification. The butcher's wife has been read, variously, as a feminine-identified heterosexual (Freud), a masculine-identified heterosexual (Lacan), a masculine-identified lesbian (Clément), a maternal-identified infant (Chase), and a feminine-identified lesbian (Fuss). If there is a story to be told in the dream of the abandoned supper party, it may well be the capacity of narrative to reproduce more narrative. What is finally at stake in these multiple condensations and displacements of a single abridged story of unfulfilled desire is a notion of interpretation *as* condensation and displacement. The critical desire for a readable and concise ending to the story of the butcher's wife—not only to the dream but to Freud's interpretation of the dream—paradoxically defers closure and keeps the story open to further rereading. By conflating and dislocating the meaning the butcher's wife has given to her own dream, psychoanalytic interpretation employs the very same techniques that organize the dream work.[8] In this regard, Freud's *Interpretation of Dreams* might be read as a dream of what interpretation can or might be—a prolongation of reading through the acts of condensation and displacement, metaphor and metonymy, identification and desire.

Notes

1. Freud, *The Interpretation of Dreams* (1900), *The Standard Edition of the Complete Psychological Works of Sigmund Freud*, trans. and ed. James Strachey, 24 vols. (London: Hogarth Press, 1953–74), 4:147.

2. Jacques Lacan, "The Direction of the Treatment and the Principles of Its Power," in *Écrits,* trans. Alan Sheridan (New York and London: W. W. Norton and Company, 1977), 264.

3. Catherine Clément, *The Lives and Legends of Jacques Lacan,* trans. Arthur Goldhammer (New York: Columbia University Press, 1983), 130.

4. Cynthia Chase, "The Witty Butcher's Wife: Freud, Lacan, and the Conversion of Resistance to Theory," *MLN* 102:5 (December 1987): 1000. This essay provides the groundwork for Chase's next discussion of the beautiful butcheress in "Desire and Identification in Lacan and Kristeva," in *Feminism and Psychoanalysis,* eds. Richard Feldstein and Judith Roof (Ithaca and London: Cornell University Press, 1989), 65–83. Hereafter all page numbers cited in the text after WB ("The Witty Butcher's Wife") or DI ("Desire and Identification").

5. In "The Witty Butcher's Wife," Chase swerves away from the Lacanian reading of the phallus as object of the woman's desire, arguing instead that it works quite the other way around: "what the woman wants— what the mother wants—counts as the phallus" (1003).

6. Freud, "Femininity," in *New Introductory Lectures on Psychoanalysis* (1933), *Standard Edition,* 22:130.

7. Freud, "Some Neurotic Mechanisms in Jealousy, Paranoia and Homosexuality" (1922), *Standard Edition,* 18: 221–32.

8. As Shoshana Felman demonstrates by her own powerful rereadings of Lacan, the emphasis in psychoanalytic interpretation is precisely on "the displacement operated by the interpreting." See *Jacques Lacan and the Adventure of Insight: Psychoanalysis in Contemporary Culture* (Cambridge, Mass.: Harvard University Press, 1987), 21.

Chapter 16

A Postcard History of the U.S. Restaurant

Jeff Weinstein

Postcards were once important. The period from 1900 to the beginning of World War I is called the "golden age" of the postcard by contemporary deltiolosists—those amateur and professional historians who have allowed picture postcards to become their collective obsession. During this commercially effulgent span, almost every class and race of literate person in almost every industrialized country, including Japan, took part in the craze to buy, send, and collect (often in specialized albums) cards that I think provided the greatest random profusion of reproduced images available at the time. Some have even conjectured that the billions of penny postcards sent enabled shaky public postal services to turn their first profits and thrive.

Is it a coincidence that these years also saw a profusion of urban restaurants? The postcard lover knows this is true because, all of a sudden, here they are, mammoth new feeding halls and forlorn cafers picturing themselves as significant enough to send to a friend: "I ate here" (and survived). This was better than word of mouth: it was word of eye, proof ahead of the pudding.

You could pick up a complimentary card by the cashier while selecting a stogie, if you liked, or fill out one from the pile on the table, and the restaurant would mail it anywhere in the world for free. Didn't know what to say? Here, it was printed for you: "Amid charming surroundings, the best meal I've ever had, so I'm sure (fill in name), that you'll enjoy it, too." Who could resist the piquant novelty of smallscale public manipulation?

Restaurant postcards were used as advertising even after World War II and continued to be widely sent until increased postal rates and routine acceptance of eating out made the now-corny idea much less appealing. Urban eating habits changed: after World War II, cooked food itself could be delivered faster than the mail. Recently, restaurants doing business in genre nostalgia (such as Mike's American Bar & Grill in Manhattan) tried to resurrect the idea of free postcard mailing, but few customers took the bait.

I've been scavenging among restaurant postcards for years. They provide, in lieu of any comprehensive, detailed, analytical history of American restaurant culture, an oblique picture of the phenomenon, eateries as they would themselves be seen. It doesn't matter if these images and captions are a species of lie. All history, I'm led to believe, is gleaned from self-interested representation, and constructed as another form of the same. Images so blatantly self-serving may additionally urge the sentimental observer to "see through" the hand-tinted tables and doctored decor and into what these restaurants may really have meant to those who built them, worked them, enjoyed them.

Churchill's

This is a scene at midnight, but what year? There's no postmark (the card's virgin). It's a divided card—half the blank side is to be used for the message and the other half for the address—and these were made in the U.S. only after 1907, when the post office finally understood that messages on penny cards wouldn't eat into revenues from two-cent letters. Similar cards show that Churchill's was an armory of a place on the corner of Broadway and 49th Street in New York City, one made to wine and dine the new middle-class hoardes who were filling fragrant department stores during the day and smoky theaters at night. New York City always drew evening crowds, but established tony restaurants of the previous century, such as Delmonico's and Louis Sherry's, served those who could afford them in a way that suggested Europhile elegance instead of gymnastic festivity.

Do these white-collar revelers look rich? No, more bloated and sated than rich. The noise level is high: conversations keen over others to be heard until a median din is reached. Are diners discussing the domestic farce they left an hour before? Their bumpy stock deals? The copious food? Anything, I expect, but the food.

I've seen these eaters somewhere else. Their confident, slouching postures are familiar to those of us who ate out in New York seventy-five years later. Look, for example, at the young men in the left foreground, the gent on the Thonet chair with his pants riding high enough above his shoes to show his gartered stockings, or his bow-tied companion staring somewhat arrogantly into the camera. Haven't we seen them someplace before—or since? Of course. They're yuppies, the world's first. This postcard has captured yuppies before their time.

"Kitchen," Blossom Health Inn

I like the way the captioner put quote marks around "kitchen." That's the way some folks think about restaurant kitchens even now: forbidden back rooms where animals are skinned and boiled by crude slavers "we" would never ask home for a drink. This kitchen card supports my generalization in an unusual way, because the three cooks in their whites, as well as the man seated, are black. (An unusual 1912 kitchen card from a large New York restaurant, Stanley's, shows the long line of kitchen help all sporting finger-twisted, Mediterranean mustaches.)

When African Americans are depicted on golden age postcards, they're usually cartoon pickanninies or Uncle Toms, advertising racism along with the Cream of Wheat. In postcard land as

"KITCHEN," BLOSSOM HEATH INN, LARCHMONT N. Y.

in historyland, only rarely are black persons depicted as "real." How long, I wonder, did it take these actual cooks to get from Larchmont, after the long last shift, back to their own unimagined homes?

I can't tell from the postcard if the Blossom Heath Inn was perchance black-owned or black-run, or even served blacks, but I doubt it. I do know that the card is postmarked "Fordham, N.Y.," dated August 7, sometime before 1907, and was sent to a Mr. George Gloe on Webster Avenue in the Bronx. The sender obviously treasured the droll ethnic possibilities restaurants provide, for this is what he wrote, as you can see, all over the dignified card (messages weren't allowed on the address side of early, undivided cards): "Gloe A La Mode and Davie pancakes for Dinner/Doyle pudding for Dissert/Soteldo [?] a la Carte and Hungarian Goulash for Supper/Extras Imported Sirloin of Peter/Where the Jew Makes the Ice Cream."

Old immigrant groups, you see, used restaurants as sites to mediate their hostility toward more recent or rivaling interlopers, learning to order and enjoy spaghetti and dago red while ordering the dagos around.

I'll wager my dinner that this card's mailer is white, likely male, and that his friend "Jerry," the name scrawled over the pristine uniform of one patient cook, isn't actually black. It goes without saying that George or Jerry or the unknown sender are probably dead, no longer able to read this.

Automat

"You see what you want and get it by dropping in your coin."
But how do you know what you want? Hunger can never be the same as desire, for any porridge will satisfy a stomach's lust, and what money can be made on that? Smart turn-of-the-century purveyors understand that desires are made, not born. The clever capitalist, then, will isolate and frame a single slice of pie behind thick, sparkling glass. Cut it off from the rest, from the smell of its oven origin. Make the pie visual, make it unattainable: make it

HORN & HARDART BAKING CO., PHILADELPHIA, PA.

Largest AUTOMATIC RESTAURANT in the World, 818-820 Chestnut St., Philada., Pa.
AUTOMAT 2ND, Juniper St., below Chestnut St., Philada., Pa.

THE AUTOMAT — DRAWING COFFEE

VISIT THE AUTOMAT RESTAURANTS
You see what you want and get it by dropping in your coin
YOU ABSOLUTELY HELP YOURSELF

desirable. Make it uniform, make it cheap: make it democratic. Make the pie both the object of longing, and that acute desire's own spur, its goad. Create the modern, reflexive appetite.

I peer into the window and spy the pie snared in the mirrored reflection of my own questing face. Pie: in my eye. Fingers search blindly for the buffalo nickel, drop it into the ornate slot, hear metal roll through metal, and, to my delight, clink, I've won a sure thing! The window-door springs open and exactly what I wish becomes mine, mine on a tray. My shot silk skirt rustles as I carry it away. At some moment, though I've never actually seen it, the dark hole becomes inhabited again with the same piece of advertising pie, beige and red, as if it had never been, and will never be, eaten.

We should note that the kitchen, with its crusted pans, cracked hands, sweat and steam, has entirely dematerialized. The sullen, hatless waiter with his tray, a real man still visible at the end of the line, is himself about to become a ghost, the spirit of labor past.

Lobster King Harry Hackney's Lobster Waitresses

Here we have the spirit of labor's future, female department. I've thought long and hard trying to crack this card, how it demeans work, how it objectifies women, how it confuses and

Lobster King Harry Hackney with his Lobster Waitresses who won the Prize in Atlantic City's Famous Beauty Pageant Parade on the Atlantic City Boardwalk

conflates signifryer and signifried. But I have to admit, all I can
come up with are short narratives about the petty jealousies concerning which happy few of Hackney's two hundred waitresses get
to wear the claws; or fantasies about how the red lobster-women
turn on Harry right after this photo is taken and pull him apart
piece by piece, or drown him in his own Famous Lobster Pool,
because, as Hackney himself says of his holding tank on another of
his many cards, "Never Eat a Lobster Until It Has Been Purified."

"Owl Bar," Mexicali

It's lucky there are bartenders keeping these men and women
apart.

INTERIOR DE LA CANTINA "OWL BAR", MEXICALI—BAJA CAL., MEX.

X-86   INTERIOR—A. B. W. CLUB—"OWL" BAR—MEXICALI, LOWER CALIF., MEXICO   109758

The Longest Lunch Counter in the World

(These diners) Have just had an Elegant Meal at the famous
Home Dairy Restaurant, the largest and best appointed restaurant
in the United States. The State Cafe, the Most Sanitary Restaurant
in the City. The Best Ventilated Restaurant in Chicago. Alabama's
Most Distinctive Restaurant (Home of the Glorified Curleyene

Potatoe). The Most Unique Dining Room in California. Two hundred Waitresses, All With Two hundred Smiles. World's Largest Seafood Restaurant, Seating Capacity Three Thousand Two Hundred. Your order of Oysters à la Rockefeller since 1889 when this dish was concocted by Jules Alciatore at the Restaurant Antoine is number: 1277165 (the recipe is a sacred family secret). The food is world famous, as MILLIONS of patrons can testify. The charm of the old world in a new world setting, and where HOLLYWOOD begins. The late O. O. McIntyre, columnist, says: the Best Fried Chicken Dinner I ever Ate was at King's Tropical Inn.

Who knows what would have happened to Mr. McIntyre if he had found his most unique best ventilated chicken at this L.A. Woolworth's? Would he have expired on the spot, head slumped on his plate, pen poised in his hand, crust-flecked lips frozen in a grin of poultriotic ecstasy? This swivel-stool chorus line would be enough to send any artistic press agent to hyperbole heaven, where lunch counters stretch to kingdom come.

Too bad the Renaissance linearity of Woolworth's burgers and Cokes would soon be replaced by the medieval arch, its hamburger seating confined to station wagons and Levittowns. But be certain that nothing else has changed, because "our" claim to most and best—to Billions Served, Billions Spent—remains fresh as the morning's grease on the griddle.

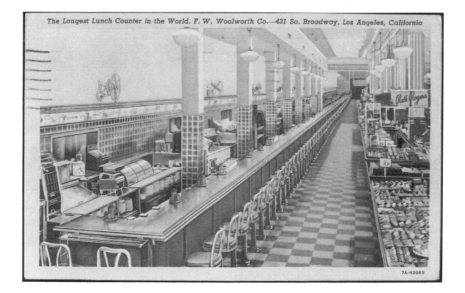

The Longest Lunch Counter in the World. F. W. Woolworth Co.—431 So. Broadway, Los Angeles, California

Willard's

The back of this card has blank areas at the top for the date and a salutation. Then, in printed type, "Just had one of Willard's Chicken Dinners and below I have checked the description that expresses my opinion of it.

Exceptionally Good

Good

Fair."

It's filled in with a pencil: "Sept. 9, 1935. Dear Bertha." (Bertha lives in Westerly, Rhode Island.) The sender checked Exceptionally Good: it seems almost rude not to, the card being free and all. And then she added, in the lines below: "Oh boy am I full, I mean stomach full. Mrs. B."

What other kind of full did she have in mind?

The cinematic flatness of nascent Los Angeles is a dramatic background for this cast of fully articulated automobiles. Most restaurants there can't do without them. Of course, cars have their own feeding places (gas stations), but anyone studying just the volumes involved might come to the conclusion that cars are the pigs at any L.A. restaurant's far-famed trough.

The little house on the corner converted to a blinking-neon eatery is a Lost Angeles rags-to-riches archetype: that's where

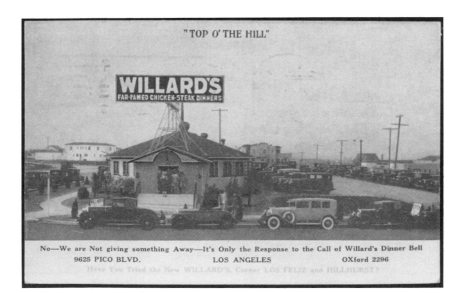

"TOP O' THE HILL"

WILLARD'S
FAR-FAMED CHICKEN-STEAK DINNERS

No—We are Not giving something Away—It's Only the Response to the Call of Willard's Dinner Bell
9625 PICO BLVD.   LOS ANGELES   OXford 2296
Have You Tried the New WILLARD'S, Corner LOS FELIZ and HILLHURST?

Mildred Pierce—and by extension, Joan Crawford—made her pile, and her mistakes. Willard's seems too small to feed all these cars, but, according to another Willard's postcard, it has a spatial secret: "This is the house that serves the farm-fresh chickens whose feet never touch the ground." That explains it: the customers sit, the chickens float.

Eaton's

"This is a picture of the dinner I have just had at Eaton's in Los Angeles, California."

It's really the dinner I'm about to have; some of the dinner I have just had is caught between my teeth. This postcard conceit works only if we understand that all Eaton's dinners are alike—chicken dinners yet again, 'cause we can't seem to break with fowl. Eaton's is Willard's is Mildred's.

In real life, Eaton's card glows with the same muted, evocative colors found in early technicolor movies, photographed objects drenched with the erotic gravy that makes California dreams so luscious and popular. What precious metals and stones can match the gold of this butter, the emerald of these peas, the ivory of the potatoes and gravy, and the sapphire of the water glass? "This is

This is a picture of the dinner I have just had at Eaton's in Los Angeles, California

where we had dinner one Sunday afternoon. A very nice place to go, plenty of chicken."

That's triple-layered silver plate, gleaming no matter how many hands grasp it, aside virtually unbreakable restaurant ware. I'll eat the salad first, 'cause we're in California, where this revenge on Paris was invented. Then I'll split the beaten biscuits and press the just-melting farm-fresh butter into 'em. No, don't take the salad yet, I'm not finished. The aroma of that lard-fried crust is driving me crazy, so, if you'll pardon me, I'll pick up the leg with my fingers. Mmm. It's crispy, spicy, doesn't need salt, and no tepid chicken water hides inside pockets of pasty undercooked batter. I've always loved the way peas are trapped by quicksand mashed.

After sixty, no seventy years, I can devour this chicken dinner just by looking at it. It's got to be the perfect all-American meal, don't you agree?

Mike's Ship-a-Hoy

"When in New York be sure to visit the ship that never goes to sea."

And be sure to order the halibut or trout that came to us God knows how. The back of the card claims that it's "A fact! Fish caught at 5 a.m. served here the same day." Could this be? Is our

WHEN IN NEW YORK BE SURE TO VISIT THE SHIP THAT NEVER GOES TO SEA

MIKE'S SHIP-A-HOY N.Y.

MIKE'S SHIP-A-HOY YACHT BAR "WHERE COLUMBUS MEETS BROADWAY AT 66th STREET, N. Y. C.

urban stomach's past so untainted by mistrust? After all, not so long ago milk was doubled with dirty water and flour was cut talc. Sores spurted into future steak as diseased steers were blindly slaughtered.

On the other hand, sturgeon the size of bulldogs frolicked in the crystalline colonial Hudson, while farmers' pigs feasted on as many plump oysters as could be plucked from New York harbor's pristine sand.

No, yo ho ho, let's sit leeward and have a highball, then we'll ask the captain to steer us to his Submarine Room to dine (a perfect replica as a giveaway menu makes clear), or to one of those little dinghies, perhaps the "Nellie," as soon as those sailors—at least I think they're real sailors—finish their beers. (What on earth would drive a sailor to eat here?) No, dear, please don't cry, I know you miss him, I miss him too, but so many brave boys save their lives in the Pacific for our liberty, our happiness, happiness just like this!

I don't know why we torture ourselves by coming back to this place again and again. . . .

Union Pacific Dining Room

It makes no difference that these folks are actors, actually extras, cheap to hire because of the Hollywood glut. Everyone in a restaurant acts, acts as if someone is watching her or him—and we are certain of this because we're the ones watching! It's even more theatrical in

a Union Pacific dining car, because the field of vision is so framed, so blocked. We can't help but recall the train movies we've seen in which cocktails are served as whole farms roll by outside, farmhands picking the very lemons whose peel oils our martinis.

This now defunct dining car is filled with questions. Do steak and eggs taste better when they're moving, clataclat, clataclat? When coffee is poured from its silver pot, does it veer a bit before it hits the cup? Do migrant farmworkers ever take this train—and what do they order if they do? Let's ask the waiter, maybe he'll know.

I forgot, he's just an extra. I'll bet his parts are few and far between.

Mess Room, Auburn State Prison

Yes, I know, a prison mess is not a restaurant, but what mess rooms and restaurants do and don't have in common may be instructive. If you compare this postcard to the first one I chose, the scene at Churchill's, you'll see tables, pillars, dishes, mugs, bottles, and food pictured on both, but everything else is so different that the disparity takes on philosophical weight.

The space at Churchill's is round, actually a maze of curving peripatetic paths. This curvaceousness is rhymed by the bentwood chairs, the men's cheeks, the women's hats. One can easily fancy

the sound of the room to be round. The mess hall space is rectilin-
ear, a Cartesian grid.

The only roundness in this room—the dishes and the seats
directly under them—happens to be circular, to be flat. The room
is appallingly quiet, and not just because no one is there: prisoners
then were not allowed to speak at meals. The dull rub of wooden
plates are the only echoes the silent scene allows.

Both rooms imply an infinity, but one is social, and the other
isolate.

It's difficult to see the food at Churchill's because of the customers. The food in prison, however, sits heaped on plates, waiting.
On the card, these piles are tinted brown. They look exactly like
what they will become. We can extrapolate to the invisible eaters
themselves. They too are what they will become. They can never
change.

The post-card image of Churchill's speaks to everything that
was and is joyful about being alive. In this world, one may choose
one's seat, one's food, one's company. One may, at least superficially,
choose to invigorate public life. Auburn State Prison subtracts all
choice from eating, from its world, and the difference is deadly.

Still, I wish I knew whose idea was it to make this prison
card, and whose to send it. I am hard pressed even to guess what
anyone receiving it could possibly think.

Chapter 17

Soul Food: Where the Chitterling Hits the (Primal) Pan

Doris Witt

"Yessuh," he said, handing over the yams, "I can see you
one of these old-fashioned yam eaters."
"They're my birthmark," I said. "I yam what I am."

—*Ralph Ellison*
Invisible Man, *1952*

Readers of Tom Wolfe's *Radical Chic and Mau-Mauing the Flak Catchers* (1970) will perhaps recall that the March 1970 issue of *Vogue* magazine carried a column by Gene Baro on "Soul Food." Published four years after chants of "black and white together" had given way to demands for "Black Power," two years after the Black Panthers unveiled the slogan "Off the Pigs" at Huey Newton's trial. It begins, not surprisingly, with a nostalgic, quasireligious fantasy of interracial gastronomy:

> The cult of Soul Food is a form of black self-awareness and, to a lesser degree, of white sympathy for the Black drive to self-reliance. It is as if those who ate the beans and greens of necessity in the cabin doorways were brought into communion with those who, not having to, eat those foods voluntarily now as a sacrament. The present struggle is emphasized in the act of breaking traditional bread. [Baro 80; Wolfe 31]

This short-lived outbreak of *"nostalgie de la boue,* or romanticizing of primitive souls," as Wolfe puts it, is not without intrinsic interest as an episode in the ongoing narrative comprising white patronage of (white productions of) black culture (Wolfe 33). Often functioning, according to *Gone Primitive* author Marianna Torgovnick, as a surrogate mode of articulating the West's fears and obsessions about itself, fascination with the primitive might also be interpreted following Stuart Hall's model for racism. Hall has argued that racism is best understood not as a "simple process, structured around fixed 'selves'," in which blacks are positioned "as the inferior species," but instead as a far more intricate dynamic of attraction and aversion, of "inexpressible envy and desire" (28). Imbricated not only in the production of the psyche but also in the relations of production, the food practices of radical chic offer an ideal site to investigate the complicated processes of "othering" and identification, which have helped constitute certain strains of both white racism and white radicalism in America.[1]

But while acknowledging that too often the status of "whiteness" has been assumed rather than interrogated, it is important to recognize that within African American culture one readily encounters a multiplicity of competing discourses about what had come by the early 1960s to be called "soul food." These discourses span a historically far-ranging social, political and perspectival complexity that have been obscured because discussions of soul tend to rely on simplistic, a historical dichotomies of master versus slave, white versus black, and especially black bourgeoisie versus ghettoite.

With this concern in mind, I want to take a closer look at the ideological contestation over the emergence of soul food after World War II. My aim is to foreground some of the subtleties that are lost when soul is either uncritically embraced as the essence of blackness or else dismissed as an inauthentic, blackface product of white radical chic or black bourgeois "slumming." In the process I also hope to make some sense of soul food's complicity with certain pivotal, powerful, and enduring stereotypes of blackness. We need to understand, in other words, not just why soul food is more complicated than we have thought, but also why it has been so easy to think that it is less complicated than it is.

Soul food is generally subsumed under the 1960s rubric "soul," a term often defined (generally by African Americans) as "indefinable" and discussed with reference primarily to men and music. These obfuscations and elisions deserve scrutiny.[2] At the same time, the emergence of soul food should be construed not just synchronically but also diachronically, as part of an ongoing debate among African-Americans over the appropriate food practices of blackness. This debate became particularly fraught in the wake of a resurgent struggle for the rights of American citizenship after World War II.

During this period numerous individuals and organizations were attempting to formulate, enact, or critique a paradigmatic black identity based upon what I will term, borrowing from critical legal theory, the "juridical fiction" of the Western humanistic subject: rational, autonomous, self-interested, heterosexual, white, male.[3] It was in this sociopolitical context that proponents of soul food such as LeRoi Jones (prior to his reincarnation as Black Arts guru Amiri Baraka) began valorizing it as an expression of pride in the cultural forms created out of and articulated through a history of black oppression. In this same context, detractors such as Nation of Islam leader Elijah Muhammad and, subsequently, comedian/activist/natural foods enthusiast Dick Gregory condemned the "slave diet" (Muhammad's locution) as an "unclean" and "unhealthy" practice of racial genocide.

Yet it is intriguing that aficionados and abstainers alike often betrayed a profound and seemingly unconscious ambivalence toward the cuisine they associated with black slavery, black poverty, and black Christianity. This ambivalence is surely not unrelated to Hall's model for racism. It might be more accurately interpreted, however, as a dynamic of *intraracial* identification and othering, a dynamic that can likewise give way to what Hall calls a "surreptitious return of desire" (29).

My discussion will foreground this dynamic to probe the dialectic between soul food and selfhood. It will try to understand the passionate intensity of the debate by asking whether or to what extent certain key ontologies of blackness—particularly those in which blackness is stigmatized as "filthy," "polluted," or "dangerous"—have been thought to reside not in black bodies but instead in foods said to nourish those bodies. My goal in posing this question is not to embark on the surely futile task of trying to provide an answer. Instead I will use it as a modus operandi, a way of thinking about why a reference to chitterlings, to use the obvious titular example, can elicit the sort of response usually reserved for the word "nigger."

The challenge as I see it is not just to posit a structuralist, metonymic relationship leading from soul food to chitterlings to blackness to filth. It is also to understand how and why the metonymy was operating as it did for specific persons at a specific historical moment. My working hypothesis will be that the debate over soul food was constituted by, and in turn helped constitute, many of the contradictions inherent in postwar attempts to revalue or reconstruct blackness, especially Black Power era efforts to control, to contain, and, borrowing from Julia Kristeva, to "abject" the often fungible category of the "feminine." The intraracial debate over soul food was so fraught, in other words, neither because it was about blackness and filth, nor about black poverty and filth. The debate was fraught, I want to claim, because it was about black femaleness and filth, particularly about fear of the enslaved, enslaving black feminine within the self.

It is important to examine this "black matriarchal panic" by locating it in relation to contemporaneous and contemporary efforts to blame poverty on the impoverished and to demonize homosexuality and female (reproductive) autonomy.[4] Even as I write, almost a third of a century after the rise of Black Power, the emasculating matriarch of the 1960s and 1970s is merging with the welfare queen of the 1980s to create yet another variation on the stereotype of the unruly, voracious black female: the "quota" queen.[5] Soul food can help us understand the deeply-embedded psychic sources of this fear of a poor, black, queer, female planet.

"Relishing Hog Bowels"

Today, as 200 years ago, the true "stone soul" dish is chitterlings, pronounced "chitlins."

—"Eating Like Soul Brothers"
Time Magazine, January 1969

What constitutes through division the "inner" and "outer" worlds of the subject is a border and boundary tenuously maintained for the purposes of social regulation and control. The boundary between the inner and outer is confounded by those excremental passages in which the inner effectively becomes outer, and this excreting function becomes, as it were, the model by which other forms of identity-differentiation are accomplished. In effect, this is the mode by which Others become shit.

—Judith Butler
Gender Trouble, 1990

Chicken ain't nothing but a bird
White man ain't nothing but a turd
Nigger ain't shit

—Melvin Van Peebles
Sweet Sweetback's Baadasssss Song, 1971

Soul food circulated relatively unheeded among a variety of discursive contexts until the mid-1960s. But in the wake of the rise of Black Power in 1966 it became a site of interracial struggle over the regulation of (a seemingly unregulated explosion of) blackness. Purveyors of soul food attempted to negotiate or contain, via their representations of black culinary practices, the volatile racial and sexual politics of the late 1960s.[6] And for reasons that should become increasingly clearer as we progress, the food fetishes of choice were not the "beans and greens of necessity" but instead the entrails and extremities of hogs—intestines in particular. For my purposes here it would be pointless to try to identify an ordinary moment when chitterlings became racially encoded as a site of dietary dissension among African Americans. Instead I will take as my focal point Part I of Ralph Ellison. *Invisible Man* (1952) is surely the most famous post-WWII literary expression of the contradictory quest for a paradigm of black male identity. It also provides a valuable site for exploring the triangulated relationship among blackness, food, and filth prior to the valorization of "soul."

The narrator of *Invisible Man* has been educated at a black college in the south. The college is led by Dr. Bledsoe, who is generally understood to have been modeled after Booker T. Washington, founder and president of Tuskegee. Cynical yet naive, the narrator has grown to despise Dr. Bledsoe as a fraudulent "race man" who secretly thinks "white is right," a "Tom" who teaches the students to aspire to be accepted by whites while simultaneously staying in a subordinate place as blacks. After leaving the college and going north to New York, The Invisible Man vacillates between embracing his racial identity, including the foods eaten by poor southern blacks, and rejecting this identity in an effort to gain acceptance, which in the terms of the novel translates into "visibility," among whites.

Almost mid-way through the narrative, just after the Invisible Man succumbs to the lures of the yam vendor, he fantasizes about exposing Dr. Bledsoe as an imposter:

And I saw myself advancing upon Bledsoe, standing bare of his false humility in the crowded lobby of Men's House, and seeing him there and him seeing me and ignoring me and me enraged and suddenly whipping out a foot or two of chitterlings, raw, uncleaned and dripping sticky circles on the floor as I shake them in his face, shouting:

"Bledsoe, you're a shameless chitterling eater! I accuse you of relishing hog bowels! Ha! And not only do you eat them, you sneak and eat them in *private* when you think you're unobserved! You're a sneaking chitterling lover! I accuse you of indulging in a filthy habit, Bledsoe! I accuse you before the eyes of the world!" And he lugs them out, yards of them, with mustard greens, and racks of pigs' ears, and pork chops and black-eyed peas with dull accusing eyes. (258–59)

From a post-*Outweek* vantage point, it is tempting to argue that the "truth" of this famous scene of "outing" is not racial but sexual in nature, that Bledsoe is being exposed (to put it in the crude terms implicit in the Invisible Man's accusation) not as a nigger but as a faggot. Certainly the markers of both a gay sexual encounter and a gay outing are present: One man confronts another, "standing bare," in a public place; the former possesses knowledge of the latter's secret. The accuser "whips" out a "foot or two of chitterlings" in the way he might whip out his penis, and the chitterlings drip "sticky circles on the floor" evocative of semen. The accused is charged with indulging, in private, in a "filthy" habit, which in another context might refer to masturbation but here would surely suggest gay male anal sex as well. The accuser fantasizes, moreover, that after the climactic confrontation the accused "would disintegrate, disinflate!" (259). Contemporary queer theory aside, however, if we recall that by the late 1940s lesbians and gays had already become a main target of anticommunist hysteria, the scene is no less reminiscent of Joe McCarthy than Michelangelo Signorile. Thus one might surmise that the charged double entendre of this decloseting would have been as apparent in 1952, when *Invisible Man* was published, as it is currently.[7]

Recognition that chitterlings can evoke male homosexual or homosocial desire, as well as what LeRoi Jones later called "Negro-ness," may help explain their status as the most fetishized of soul foods by the late 1960s—particularly among aspiring "soul brothers."[8] But it seems to me that we would be mistaken to conclude that this scene from *Invisible Man* is really a scene about sexuality "passing" for one about race.[9] I would focus rather on an ambiguity in the epistemological framework of the Invisible Man's accusations, an ambiguity that discourses of race and sexuality have had in common: "You're a sneaking chitterling lover! I accuse you of indulging in a filthy habit, Bledsoe!" There is a slight discrepancy here. The first charge implies a culinary ontology. Bledsoe does not simply eat chitterlings; he is "a sneaking chitterling lover," and to be a sneaking chitterling lover is to be a particular sort of person, a "filthy" person. The second accusation, that Bledsoe indulges "in a filthy habit," is, by contrast, not necessarily a statement about the sort of being he is. Eating chitterlings does not necessarily a "chitterling lover" make.

Elsewhere in *Invisible Man* the narrator equivocates between the two epistemologies of gastronomy, opting for the former in the renowned yam scene. The choice to eat or not to eat a yam is so fraught because it entails not merely a discrete act of eating but a revelation about the sort of being the Invisible Man is, an admission of the ontological inescapability of, presumably, his blackness.

Historians of sexuality have made an analogous distinction with respect to homosexuality. Following Michel Foucault, they argue that the category of "the homosexual" is not a stable transhistorical identity but instead a creation of the late nineteenth century. Whereas previously a person might have been said to engage in (deviant) sexual acts with members of the same sex, in late Victorian society the homosexual emerged as a deviant, as someone whose sexual desires set him (sic) apart, ontologically, from the heterosexual. Homosexuality began to refer to a category not of deeds but of persons, not to what one did but to what one was.

My point in drawing this analogy is by no means to argue that during the 1950s blackness became ontologized. Rather my point is that in order to understand the complicated evolution of soul food during the civil rights and Black Power eras, one must pay attention not just to the ambiguous, protean relationship between what a black self is or desires, and what a black self eats, not just to how various participants in the debate over soul food attempted to manipulate this ambiguity, but also to the latent potential for the slippage among discourses of race, sexuality, gender, ethnicity, and class. More specifically one must understand how the slippage can operate via food, and thus Ellison is useful in foregrounding connections among blackness, male homosexuality, chitterlings, and filth.

Both blackness and homosexuality have historically been stigmatized as "filthy." According to structural anthropologists, filth is a relational category, one that has no absolute existence, no universal definition. Filth is simply that which remains outside a given system of order, matter (or actions) out of place. This line of thought is most famously explicated by anthropologist Mary Douglas in *Purity and Danger* (1966). Douglas argues:

> Ideas about separating, purifying, demarcating and punishing transgressions have as their main function to impose system on an inherently untidy experience. It is only by exaggerating the difference between within and without, above and below, male and female, with and against, that a semblance of order is created.

One might extrapolate from Douglas that both blackness and gayness have been viewed as "filthy" because they represent social disorder. They are that which is out of place in (yet constitutive of) a system in which heterosexuality and whiteness represented social order.[10] But having said this, we are still left with the discrepancy between filthy "matter" and filthy "actions" and thus with a nebulous perception of where the "disorder" of blackness or homosexuality is supposedly located—whether in the person (who eats chitterlings or engages in sodomy), in the acts (of eating chitterlings or engaging in sodomy), or in the object of action (chitterlings or anus).[11] Furthermore, we are left with the question of why a particular system or order and disorder structures a given society. This is basically the problem that did not but should have plagued Supreme Court Justice Potter Stewart: If we cannot define filth, then how do we know it when we see/eat/fuck it?[12] Another way of posing the question might be to ask what sort of relationship, if any, obtains between subjectivity and social categories. The difficulty in relying on Mary Douglas to answer this question, according to Julia Kristeva, is that subjectivity is precisely what structural anthropology cannot, or at least in Douglas's work does not, confront.

Accordingly, in *Powers of Horror* (1980) Kristeva draws on her own previous work in psychoanalysis to reinterpret Douglas's study of pollution rituals. Her goal is to locate a correspondence between social structures such as the classification pure/impure and the structures of subjectivity. "Why," she asks, "that system of classification and not another? What social, subjective, and socio-subjectively interacting needs does it fulfill?" (92). Or more specifically, "Why does *corporeal waste*, menstrual blood and excrement, or everything that is assimilated to them . . . represent—like a metaphor that would have become incarnate—the objective frailty of the symbolic order?" (70). To help her answer these questions, Kristeva develops her theory of abjection. She derives this theory from, and uses it to explain, the process by which the infant separates itself from the maternal body. Kristeva describes abjection as:

> An extremely strong feeling which is at once somatic and symbolic, and which is above all a revolt of the person against an external menace from which one wants to keep oneself at a distance, but of which one has the impression that it is not only an external menace but that it may menace us from inside. So it is a desire for separation, for becoming autonomous and also the feeling of an impossibility of doing so— whence the element of crisis which the notion of abjection carries with it. (135–36)

Like the dynamic that fuels Stuart Hall's theory of racism, the abject "both attracts and repels. It holds you in spite of your disgust. It fascinates" (Oliver 70). Yet it is not a "lack of cleanliness or health that causes abjection but what disturbs identity, system, order. What does not respect borders, positions, rules. The in-between, the ambiguous, the composite" (Kristeva 4). Not a "quality in itself" or a boundary in itself, the abject is that which has been "jettisoned out of that boundary, its other side, a margin" (ibid. 69). It draws us "toward the place where meaning collapses" (ibid. 2). As Kelly Oliver observes in "Nourishing the Speaking Subject: A Psychoanalytic Approach to Abominable Food and Women" (1992), the abject "is neither good nor evil, subject nor object, ego nor unconscious, nature nor culture, but something that threatens the distinctions themselves . . . The abject is that which points up the arbitrariness of borders" (71).[13]

Kristeva's work has particular resonance for understanding the fascination and disgust with which Ellison's fictional Invisible Man accuses Bledsoe of "relishing hog bowels," as well as with which the historical Elijah Muhammad condemned swine as "the foulest animal" who "lives off nothing but filth." She argues that "food loathing is perhaps the most elementary and most archaic form of abjection" (Muhammad, *How to Eat* 14; Kristeva *PH* 2). Again according to Oliver:

> It is food, what is taken into the body, along with excrement, what is expelled from the body, which calls into question the borders of the body. . . . How can we imagine ourselves as separate bodies when we eat that which is not-us, which in turn becomes us? How can we imagine ourselves as separate bodies when we expel part of us, which in turn becomes not-us? (71)

Kristeva's concern for parturition leads her to privilege breast milk in her analysis because it confounds the separation between mother and infant. But though she never mentions the sausage known in France as *audouille*, it seems to me that her theory might help us account for why chitterlings—rather than, say, "black-eyed peas with dull accusing eyes"—have borne the metonymic burden as the "stone soul" food. Consequently, it can help us account for the twinned responses of attraction and repulsion which a mention of soul food often seems to arouse. As one part of a hog through which food becomes excrement, and accordingly through which hog and not-hog are negotiated, hog bowels point to the fragility of the boundary that divides food from not-food, self from not-self. In Ellison's scenario clearly phallic as well as anal, hog bowels are the "in-between, the ambiguous, the composite," signifying simultaneously both order and disorder, and neither order nor disorder. In effect *doubly disorderly*, they allow us to broaden Kristeva's theory of abjection by formulating connections between food taboos and the prohibitions that found society.

That is, every society is founded on the construction of boundaries. Thus in Kristeva's view every society is founded on the abject, on that which it radically excludes. Because the abject undermines boundaries, it must be prohibited so that society can come into being. Though different cultures may have different abjects, Kristeva argues that in Western culture "the prohibition which founds, and yet undermines, society is the prohibition against the maternal body. It is what is off limits" (Kelly 71). I will defer discussion of the implications of Kristeva's theory for African American maternity until the conclusion of this essay, noting for now only that her work does help explain why maternity provokes fear in a culture that enshrines, literally in law, the myth of the self-made man who has pulled himself up by his own bootstraps. Given that the maternal body that Kristeva theorizes is uninflected, however, by markers of cultural difference such as race, class, and historicity, it would be a tedious undertaking to attempt to derive other taboos (miscegenation, homosexuality) and biases (anti-Semitism, anticommunism) of American culture from an originary maternal prohibition as Kristeva seems to envision it. Yet if more expansively construed, abjection does offer a useful way of thinking about the relationship between the subjective fascination with "filth" (i.e., the abject) and the social stigmatization of certain peoples and practices as "dirty" or "filthy." Since these prohibitions would seem to be related, all underwriting the social structures requisite to the reproduction and maintenance of white patrimony, we might combine the insights of Kristeva and Butler with those of the Combahee River Collective to think of American society as consisting (in historically determined ways) not just of a series of what the Collective called "Interlocking oppressions," but also of a series of interlocking prohibitions and thus interlocking abjections.[14]

What this means for hog bowels is that *in American social order* they are overdetermined to be both fetishized and abjected. They have multiple metonymic possibilities because of the latent potential for slippage between American fascination with male homosexuality and with blackness, a dual obsession displayed after WWII most obviously among the beats.[15] As chitterlings, they are able to signify prohibited actions (coming into contact with shit via mouth or genitals) while simultaneously destabilizing the very boundaries necessary to create and give (filthy) meaning to those actions. As the abject, that which transgresses the boundaries between food and not-food, self and not-self, phallus and anus, origin and decay, purity and danger, they suggest the fragility of the system through which privileged identities such as whiteness, masculinity, and heterosexuality are maintained as what Kristeva calls *corps propre* ("one's own clean and proper body"), blackness, femininity, and homosexuality as unclean and improper (Roudiez viii). Chitterlings remind us that blackness and homosexuality are "filthy" not because they are an "external menace" to social order but because, like our own bowels, anus, and excretions, they "may menace us from inside." Blackness and homosexuality have historically not been what Americans fear in "others"; though certainly the murderous impulses to contain that fear are enacted on "others" who are perceived to embody these dangers. They are what we must abject from ourselves so that American social order can continue coming into being.

Hence the ambiguity of *Sweet Sweetback*'s refrain, which invokes the conflation of blackness and white only to disavow it, suggesting that shit is instead a (prosaic) turd menacing the white man from inside, while blackness is something else entirely, something simultaneously less valued than shit yet potentially even more transgressive, something which draws us "toward the place where meaning collapses" or where. . . .

"The Walls Come Tumbling Down"

You hear a lot of jazz about Soul Food. Take chitterlings: the ghetto blacks eat them from necessity while the black bourgeoisie has turned it into a mocking slogan. Eating chitterlings is like going slumming to them. Now that they have the price of a steak, here they come prattling about Soul Food. The people in the ghetto want steaks. *Beef Steaks.* I wish I had the power to see to it that the bourgeoisie really *did* have to make it on Soul Food.

The emphasis on Soul Food is counter-revolutionary black bourgeois ideology. The main reason Elijah Muhammad outlawed pork for Negroes had nothing to do with dietary laws. The point is that when you get all those blacks cooped up together with beef steaks on their minds—with the weight of religious fervor behind the desire to chuck—then something's got to give. The system has made allowances for the ghettoites to obtain a little pig, *but there are no provisions for the elite to give up any beef!* The walls come tumbling down.

Six years before Melvin Van Peebles released *Sweet Sweetback's Baadasssss Song*, his controversial theatrical contribution to what film historian Donald Bogle has called the "black bourgeois glamourization of the ghetto," Eldridge Cleaver mounted from his jail cell in Folsom Prison this sardonic attack on not white but black *nostalgie de la boue* (Bogle 236). Entitled "Soul Food," the comment is dated 3 November 1965 and was first published in *Soul on Ice* in 1968. Cleaver is referring to the well-known, underanalyzed fact that converts to the Nation of Islam—like Cleaver, predominantly black men of the lower classes—were instructed not to eat pork. While his strictly economistic interpretation of Elijah Muhammad's motivations in proscribing pork requires further scrutiny, Cleaver's attention to the black intraclass dynamics in the Nation of Islam is a needed corrective to analyses that foreground

Muhammad's rhetoric about "white devils." Thus far class has been undertheorized in my discussion of food and abjection. But as was amply illustrated by the efforts of the House Un-American Activities Committee (HUAC) to root out the internal communist menace (often via the feminine/homosexual within which was "soft" on it), belief in the sacred rights of private property must also be maintained for American social and economic order to continue coming into being. When the prerogatives of capital are perceived to be threatened, communists become "dirty" for one of the same reasons the poor have been: both can function as a reminder of the instability of the claim by which the "haves" define themselves against the "have-nots."

Admittedly, this is oversimplified.[16] But my point is that food practices can function within a signifying chain that articulates the conflation of poverty and filth no less than blackness, sexuality, and filth. Thus Cleaver uses the phrase "going slumming" to critique (what he evidently perceives to be) the black bourgeois displacement of filth, via chitterlings, from blackness onto poverty. This is a somewhat futile process, since to the extent that in American social order blackness is already "othered," the "racial exclusion" necessary to create "nonfilthy" blacks would be operative only as an intraracial dynamic. Cleaver implies that this exclusion has entailed efforts by the black bourgeoisie to reconfigure transgression on a somatic level as a function of class rather than race. Rich black bodies become orderly, clean, and pure while poor black bodies are abjected as disorderly, filthy, and polluted. Chitterlings come to signify the difference between the former and the latter, which is to say that their "filthy" meaning is articulated via class rather than sexuality. Certainly Elijah Muhammad's oft-repeated command to his predominantly lower-class black male followers to "go after the black man in the mud" implies that he too viewed mud or filth as separate from "Negroness"—otherwise the phrase would be redundant.

And certainly an analogous slippage is evident in the essay valorizing "Soul Food" by the Rutgers- and Howard-educated LeRoi Jones, who made a point of billing himself as hailing from a "lower middle-class Negro family." (*Black Music* 222). The essay is dated 1962 and was published in his collection *Home* in 1966. Displaying the "*nostalgie de la boue*," which the lower-class Cleaver dismissed as "counterrevolutionary," Jones dwells on soul as the food of poverty and necessity, observing, for example, that "people kill chickens all over the world, but chasing them through the dark on somebody else's property would probably insure, once they went in the big bag, that you'd find some really beautiful way to eat them. I mean, after all the risk involved" ("Soul Food" 102–3). While this image is surely coded in terms of race, the "risk [or transgression] involved" is figured overtly via class: Jones suggests that the slave (her or himself "property") is violating the rights of property by both trespassing and stealing. But this point is problematic for the ideology that supposedly underlies soul, for reasons that will be easier to grasp if we consider a passage from Jones's *Blues People* (1963). Published a year after the "Soul Food" essay was written, *Blues People* offers a fuller explication of Jones's understanding of the meaning of "soul":

> Even the adjective *funky*, which once meant to many Negroes merely a stink (usually associated with sex), was used to qualify the music as meaningful.... The social implication, then, was that even the old stereotype of a distinctive Negro smell that white America subscribed to could be turned against white America. For this smell now, real or not, was made a valuable characteristic of "Negro-ness." And "Negro-ness," by the fifties, for many Negroes (and whites) was the only strength left to American culture. (219–20)

Jones's allusion to Negro "smell" is particularly charged in the context of my topic given the frequent, frequently apologetic references in soul food cookbooks to the smell of chitterlings while they are cooking. "The very idea of chitlings turns up many a nose," Pearl Bailey observes in *Pearl's Kitchen* (1973), just before acknowledging, "I don't care too much for that odor myself" (11). The fact that Bailey also includes the minutiae of her household cleaning practices would suggest that even while taking pride in foods associated with soul, she felt it necessary to distance herself from its "filth." Yet in the interval between Jones's introductory discussion of soul in 1963 and Bailey's publication of her "Extraordinary Cookbook" a decade later, chitterlings had indeed become the "stone soul" food and black, no less tellingly, had become beautiful. Indeed, in an essay from 1971 on "The Lyrics of James Brown," Mel Watkins cites approvingly a comment made by a teenager leaving the Apollo after a concert by the self-styled Godfather of Soul: "The dude is as down as a chitlin'" (22). Chitterlings were no longer a "private" passion to be indulged in shame. Negroness no longer required closeting. "Say it loud," as Brown himself famously commanded, "I'm black and I'm proud."

However, in the passage from *Gender Trouble* that I cited as an epigraph earlier, Judith Butler is drawing on Kristeva to explain the processes of exclusion by which the boundaries of self are constructed. If Butler is correct in arguing that excretory functions are a fundamental model of constructing the boundary between self and other, with the result that "Others become shit," then the problem here is that Jones seems to be suggesting that in the discourses of soul there is no abjection, no process by which others become shit. Rather than attributing "smell" to whites—as does Malcolm X, for example, when he recalls childhood memories of "the different way that white people smelled"—Jones suggests that the "smell" of Negroness becomes valuable in soul (*Autobiography* 17). But the implication of Kristeva's theory is that the construction of hegemonic identities in Western culture requires some form of abjection. It is no more possible for Negroes to embody blackness (or a "Negro smell") than it is for Caucasians, since blackness is always that which is "othered" in the construction of American identity. (Jones, after all, may have changed his name to Amiri Baraka, but he did not begin attributing his work to anonymous "Negroness.") If blackness is embraced, it is embraced not as filth and disorder, but as purity and order. Blackness becomes "one's own clean and proper body"—the Kristevan *corps propre*. In its place, something else will function as the abject. Jones's conflation of "stink" and "sex" in his description of soul suggests one "Other" that something else might have been during the civil rights and Black Power eras.

What I am suggesting, in short, is that while soul is generally either accepted prima facie as an expression of pride in blackness or else analyzed in terms of interracial or black interclass dynamics, the abjection of the black feminine was latent in the discourses of soul from their inception. When in 1971 Julian Mayfield proclaimed "I cannot—will not— define my Black Aesthetic, nor will I allow it to be defined for me," he is one of many who began refusing to define soul (and related discursive practices such as those stemming from the black arts movement) precisely as the women's and gay liberation movements were gaining momentum. Granted, such evasions could be a tactic of resistance to white intrusions. If, however, one takes into account the second half of Mayfield's comment—"but I know that somehow it revolves around this new breed of man and woman who have leaped out of the loins of all those slaves and semi-slaves, who have survived so that we might survive" (27)—my linkage of soul and black maternity should seem less contrived. If one also notes that the slave and semislave mother has no agency in Mayfields depiction, presumably doing nothing while the fully formed "new breed" leapt into the world, then it might also be clearer why I claim that discourses of soul were implicated in Black Power era fears of incarceration in the womb of an enslaved, enslaving mother.

Before offering a few closing remarks about the implications of this issue for the debate over soul food, I will conclude this section with a final reflection on Eldridge Cleaver. If abjection is necessary lest we be drawn "toward the place where meaning collapses" or where, in Cleaver's imagery, the "walls come tumbling down," then we can see that what Cleaver's comment on soul food lacks in historical accuracy, it compensates for in what Kristeva might call "sociosubjective" suggestiveness. His vignette is so compelling precisely because it locates soul food slumming at the nexus where the prohibitions that found the boundaries of the social order are implicated in the exclusions that found the boundaries of the self. By literalizing the decent of self into other (shit) via his association of ghetto dwellers and chitterlings, Cleaver is able to go beyond, as it were, slumming's pleasure principle, to reveal its complicity with our repressed desire for and fear of self-dissolution. For ultimately, Butler observes, it is a fantasy to believe that there are impenetrable boundaries between self and other:

> For inner and outer worlds to remain utterly distinct, the entire surface of the body would have to achieve an impossible impermeability. This sealing of its surfaces would constitute the seamless boundary of the subject; but this enclosure would invariably be exploded by precisely that excremental filth that it fears. (134)

Here I would note that Cleaver not only wrote the soul food comment while he himself was "enclosed" in prison, but he wrote it in the wake of the Watts uprising of August 1965 in Los Angeles. Modulating between individual subjectivity and social structure, his warning that "something's got to give" or else "the walls come tumbling down" gains psychic force from raising the specter not just of class conflict or a race riot but also of a self-annihilating explosion—an explosion, literally from within, of shit.

Coda: *"It Always Starts with Mama"*

Hell, Mary
Bell Jones,
full of groans
the slum lord
is on you
Cursed are you
among women
and cursed is
the fruit of
your womb,
Willie Lee,
as it was
in 1619
is now
and ever
shall be
SHIT
without end
Amen

—Jon Eckels,
"Hell, Mary," 1971

If for Kristeva "abjection" might be loosely defined as the negative attempt to establish the boundaries of self by expelling that which is not-self, then the "primal scene" of abjection would be birth, separation from the mother's body. One implication of her thesis is that fundamental to the construction of the autonomous, independent subject idealized in Western society is the institution of the boundary-constituting taboo by which the feminine becomes abject, by which the womb becomes "cursed," and the "birthmark" is denied. And though I realize this will seem a distant leap from the argument I have outlines thus far, what has most interested me from the start about soul food is this curious historical coincidence: widespread celebration of a primarily black female practice, soul cooking, started escalating around 1968 in the wake of a virulent outbreak of hostility toward and scapegoating of the practitioners, particularly in their role as mother of sons. I refer here, of course, to the popular hegemony during the late 1960s and early 1970s (not to mention the present) of the myths of black matriarchy and black male emasculation. Catalyzed in large part by the writings of E. Franklin Frazier and Daniel Patrick Moynihan, these twinned obsessions generally surfaced in expressions of racist gyno- and homophobia.

Given this historical context, it is surely noteworthy that "authoritative" discourses of soul food (such as cookbooks) were by 1970 not only emanating primarily from diverse African American women, but that often they merged with or functioned as discourses of black grandmotherhood, motherhood, and daughter- hood.[18] (To cite one example of the sort of convergence I have in mind, the first chapter in Pearl Bailey's *Pearl's Kitchen* is called "Mama Looking over My Shoulder.") Given, moreover, the era's increasingly public preoccupation with the reproductive rights and practices of American women in general, a preoccupation that was animated not just by high profile campaigns to legalize abortion and halt sterilization abuse, it is surely noteworthy as well that two of the most prominent of soul food's critics, Elijah Muhammad and Dick Gregory, focused their critique of African American dietary practices especially on pregnant and nursing women. In fact, they used their concern for what Gregory called "purifying the system" as a springboard to attack the birth control pill as being, like soul food, a method of racial genocide (*Political Primer*, Dedication).[19]

In an extended version of this essay, I bring these ostensibly separate strands of argument together by exploring the anxieties that led these two originally lower-class black men to associate "filth" and "danger," *via food*, primarily with gender and sexuality rather than race or class. In other words, they created their own poor black male *corps propre* by displacing the filth of selfhood onto black women. Yet Muhammad and Gregory are interesting in this context less because of their mutual opposition to soul food than because of what are otherwise marked divergences in their sociopolitical agendas. To understand the widespread cultural fears of black female pollution and control the procapitalist, antifemi- nist Muhammad and the anticapitalist, profeminist Gregory openly express is, I think, to understand more clearly some of what was being *contained* by those equally divergent proponents of soul who during the late 1960s began claiming, along with *Soul Food Cook Book* (1970) author Jimmy Lee, that "It's not soulful to try and spell out exactly what soul is" (7). It is better to appreciate not just the fervor but also the ambivalence with which many African American women have participated in the debate over soul food.

For one "danger" that appears to have motivated much of the era's fascination with blackness in general, and slave cuisine in particular, is that it can raise the specter of incarceration, contamination, and ultimately self-dissolution in the womb of an enslaved, enslaving mother. As one last example of this Black diet- and weight-conscious George Jackson. He begins the prison letters collected in *Soledad Brother* (1970) as follows:

> It always starts with Mama, mine loved me. As testimony of her love, and her fear for the fate of the manchild all slave mothers hold, she attempted to press, hide, push, capture me in the womb. The conflicts and contradictions that will follow me to the tomb started right there in the womb. The feeling of being captured . . . this slave can never adjust to it, it's a thing that I just don't favor, then, now, never. (9–10)

Jackson's comment perfectly epitomizes the double-bind of Black Power: how to valorize black manhood when manhood, of necessity, "always starts with" womanhood.[20] Hortense Spillers has argued eloquently that the stigmatization (or, in Kristevan terms, abjection) of African American women is thrice overdetermined because the child historically followed the condition of the enslaved, black mother.[21] As a result, she says, "the female . . . breaks in upon the imagination with a forcefulness that marks both a denial and an 'illegitimacy.' Because of this peculiar American denial, the black American male embodies the only American community of males which has had the specific occasion to learn who the female is within itself" (80)

If we can unravel what Freud might have termed the convoluted "cloacal" connection between the Black Power era's dual fetishization of chitterlings and black wombs, we may even find new modes of fathoming the recent spate of medical and legal efforts to construe the womb of color as the gravest of all possible dangers to the zygote, embryo, or fetus, which it is eternally presumed to harbor within. These modes would view the criminalization of black uteruses as a model for, not a derivation from, the criminalization of white ones.[22] Yet the even more unspeakable danger, which, one might further speculate, actually underwrites the resilience of this obsession with black maternity in American culture is that African-American women might have an existence apart from their wombs; they might be not "mother" but in fact truly "other." Soul food, in this sense, is where the chitterling hits—yet misses—the (primal) pan.

Notes

I grateful to the staff and fellows of the Commonwealth Center for Literary and Cultural Change and the Carter G. Woodson Institute for Afro-American and African Studies, both affiliated with the University of Virginia. My debt to Deborah McDowell is far greater than a mere acknowledgment could ever express. David Lupton aided my research immeasurably by generously sharing his bibliography of cookbooks by African Americans. I would also like to thank Eric Lott, Susan Fraiman, and Bluford Adams for their commentary and encouragement.

⋯⋯⋯⋯

1. To the extent I have been able to draw on the work of Hall and others at the Birmingham Centre, I am indebted to the example of Eric Lott. In his own study of early blackface minstrelsy ("The Seeming Counterfeit"), Lott uses Hall's model to argue that "audiences involved in early minstrelsy were not universally derisive of African-Americans or their culture" (224). Lott, not Hall, refers to this interracial dynamic as a complex play of repulsion and attraction" (227).

2. In a footnote to his chapter on white patronage of black culture ("Hip and the Long Front of Color") in *No Respect* (1989), for example, Andrew Ross presumes that the popularity of black music and soul food during the sixties are analogous:

> A similar set of conditions inspired the black middle-class craze for "soul food" in the sixties . . . which, while it served as a gesture toward the historically binding ties of ethnic community, was largely confined to those who could afford expensive foods, and who could therefore afford to abstain from them. (See endnote 43 on page 243.)

Though my own reading of soul is indebted to Ross's compelling analysis of how the black music scene inflected American cultural dynamics in the 1950s and 1960s, I am writing against not only this scholarly bias toward privileging music as the vehicle for discussing soul, but also against the penchant for construing soul only in terms of class and race. Even in his recent and impressively researched history *New Day in Babylon* (1992), William L. Van Deburg subdivides his lengthy chapter on "Black Power in Afro-American Culture" into soul style, soul music, soulful talk, soulful tales and soul theology. Not even granted its own section, soul food is subsumed under "soul style" and given a cursory treatment in less than three pages. Gender is neither a category of soul food analysis nor (until page 296 of a 312 page book) of Black Power analysis.

3. Some of the more obvious examples of the groups I have in mind here would include the Urban League, Southern Christian Leadership

Conference (SCLC), Student Nonviolent Coordinating Committee (SNCC), Congress of Racial Equality (CORE), National Council of Negro Women (NCNW), National Welfare Rights Organization (NWRO), Republic of New Africa (RNA), US Organization, Nation of Islam, Black Panthers, and Black Arts Movement. These organizations and movements were divergent in membership, structure, and purpose—some separatist, others assimilationist, some oriented primarily toward conventional political issues, others toward artistic and cultural expression. What they nevertheless shared was a fundamental concern with how to be black, with how to counter the continued denial of political rights and cultural recognition to blacks, in white America—I have relied on the works cited in the bibliography by Evans, Giddings, Gitlin, Marable, and Van Deburg as general guides to the civil rights and Black Power eras. One could cite any number of sources to discuss poststructuralist criticism of the Western humanistic subject, beginning most obviously with psychoanalytic theories of the unconscious stemming from Freud, Lacan, Kristeva, and others. But as my reference to the "juridical" subject would suggest, my own thinking has been particularly influenced by scholarship in feminist legal theory. See especially the works cited in the bibliography by Eisenstein, MacKinnon, Rhode, and Williams, as well Patricia Hill Collins's *Black Feminist Thought* (1990), which sets forth an Afrocentric feminist epistemology.

4. I borrow quite loosely here from Eve Sedgwick, who has popularized among academics the clinical and juridical diagnosis "homosexual panic." Her discussion of the term in *Epistemology of the Closet* (1990) would suggest, however, that Sedgwick would not be entirely comfortable with my appropriation of the phrase to describe hatred of African American women. See p. 19 of *Epistemology* in particular.

5. In the spring of 1993 President Clinton nominated black female law professor Lani Guinier to be assistant attorney general for civil rights in his administration. Guinier was branded a "quota queen" by conservatives and purported moderates, and her nomination was withdrawn by Clinton in early June.

6. My use of the term "practices" stems in part from Michel de Certeau's *The Practice of Everyday Life* (1984). De Certeau argues that everyday practices—speaking, writing, walking, cooking, etc.—should bot be dismissed "as merely the obscure background of social activity," but should instead by analyzed as "tactics" through which seemingly passive consumers act upon, resist, and function as producers of late capitalist society (xi ff.)

7. Signorile was the feature's editor of *Outweek*, a short-lived gay and lesbian weekly in New York City. The contemporary practice of "outing" is intricately associated not with anticommunism but with the AIDS epidemic. For a useful discussion of outing, see Douglas Crimp's "Right

On, Girlfriend!" (1992), especially pp. 6–7. For an informative history of the emergence and development of the lesbian and gay community during the three decades preceding Stonewall, see John D'Emilio's *Sexual Politics, Sexual Communities* (1983).

8. Lest my meaning be misconstrued, however, I should note that I intend "fetish" to be understood here in its Marxian as well as its Freudian sense. Thus by "fetishized" I refer to a dual process of self-delusion whereby 1) "the definite social relation between men [sic]" assumes "the fantastic form of a relation between things" (Marx 165); and 2) "a substitute phallus [is] created in the unconscious of a little boy who does not want to surrender the belief that his mother has a penis" (Williams 103). As to the former, the arduous labor that turned hog bowels into chitterlings had traditionally be that of black women. In their function as restaurant "commodities," therefore, the chitterlings that enabled men to "eat like soul brothers" may very well have been the products of the unacknowledged and poorly or unpaid labor of "soul sisters." To bend Marx sideways, the "fantastic form" of a relation "between men" might have obscured the "definite social relation" of dominance and subordination toward Linda Williams's comment in *Hard Core* (1989) that "a Marxian, political analysis of the prior *social* fact of the devaluation of women must always be factored into a discussion of the Freudian fetish" (106)

9. If anything, I think Ellison is drawing on the charged metaphor of the "closet" to articulate the damage inflicted on the psyches of those targeted by racism. By contrast, in her introduction to the American Women Writers series edition of Nella Larsen's *Quicksand and Passing* (1987), Deborah McDowell argues convincingly that the reader is encouraged "to place race at the center of any critical interpretation" of *Passing* when, in fact, a more subversive reading might focus on sexual passing, on the closeting of lesbian desire (xxiii). McDowell's argument has stimulated my own thinking about the potential for slippage between discourses of race and sexuality. See especially pp. xxiii–xxxi of her introduction.

10. Whereas Douglas appears to assume that the terms in a given binary are not just equally *necessary* but also equally *valued*, poststructuralist theory (most notably that of Jacques Derrida) would insist that, at least in Western culture, a binary is also, constitutively, hierarchical: thus, for example, "above" is valued over "below," "male" is valued over "female," "pure" would be valued over "impure," and "cleanliness" over "dirt" or "filth."

11. I conflate gay male sexuality with anal sexuality advisedly. As D. A. Miller has pointed out in his essay "Anal Rope" (1990), in American social order the anus is the "popularly privileged site of gay male sex, the orifice whose sexual use general opinion considers (whatever happens to be the state of sexual practices among gay men and however it may vary

according to time and place) the least dispensable element in defining the true homosexual" (134).

12. See *Jacobellis v. Ohio* (1964).

13. Oliver's article has been very helpful in my efforts to understand Kristeva's theory of abjection. My summary of Kristeva here basically paraphrases Oliver's own summary on pp. 75–76 of "Nourishing the Speaking Subject."

14. As exemplified by the Combahee River Collective's "A Black Feminist Statement" (1977), many women of color have consistently addressed "racial, sexual, heterosexual, and class oppression" and have been in the vanguard of those arguing for "the development of integrated analysis and practice based upon the fact that the major systems of oppression are interlocking" (13).

15. In this context Jack Kerouac's fond recollection in *On the Road* (1955, 1957) of his night at the Imperial Bar in Boston becomes rather interesting:

> I drank sixty glasses of beer and retired to the toilet, where I wrapped myself around the toilet bowl and went to sleep. During the night at least a hundred seamen and assorted civilians came in and cast their sentient debouchments on me till I was unrecognizably caked. What difference does it make after all?— Anonymity in the world of men is better then fame in heaven, for what's heaven? What's earth? All in the mind. (202)

Barbara Ehrenreich argues in *The Hearts of Men* (1983) that the beat ideal was indeed a "world of men," in which here Kerouac would appear to equate with being "unrecognizably caked" by "sentient debouchments."

16. The cold war specter of a communist takeover was also deceptively used, for example, to justify enormous ongoing government appropriations for the military and "defense" industries. But as Slavoj Zizek has argued in *The Sublime Object of Ideology* (1989), it matters little whether we believe in the legitimacy of a hegemonic ideology such as capitalism, for "even if we do not take things seriously, even if we keep an ironical distance, *we are still doing them*" (sic) (33). We can, for example, recognize that our legal system by and large serves the interests of capital, yet still act in keeping with the belief that everyone is equal under the law. Likewise, even if we recognize *consciously* that *unconscious* processes of abjection are functioning as a method of "social regulation and control," it does not matter as long as our actions are in keeping with the belief that nonwhites, women, lesbians, gays, communists, jews, the poor, or other "Others," are, in reality, filthy or dangerous (Butler 133). With such complexities factored in, my argument for interlocking abjections becomes

even more useful in explaining the fluidity (or cynical flaccidity, as Zizek might say) of psychic mechanisms that have enabled "dirt" or "filth" to permute as danger through a variety of discursive formations, with the result that eventually everyone is implicated. Indeed, the process of identity formation in American social order has been so effective in maintaining the status quo because it allows for individual variations in what is abjected: everyone can locate "filth" elsewhere, in actions if not fetishistic belief, and thus everyone can come to have a stake in the maintenance of the boundaries and prohibitions that found American society.

17. In his well-known study *Black Nationalism* (1962), E. U. Essien-Udom paraphrases Muhammad as having informed him that the "official policy of the Nation of Islam . . . is to recruit the 'Negro in the mud' into the movement and to 'alienate him from giving support to middle-class Negro leadership' " (201). "Negro in the mud" is Muhammad's phrase, a phrase also attributed to him by Malcolm: "Always Mr. Muhammad instructed us, 'Go after the black man in the mud' " (262). In the context of my previous discussion of the implications of black bourgeois *"nostalgie de la boue* (literally, as Wolfe explained, "nostalgia for the mud") it should not be difficult to understand the relevance of Muhammad's comment to the construction of lower-class black selfhood (Wolfe 32). In their public rhetoric, Muhammad and his ministers commonly targeted the "white devil" as the enemy of the "black man." But as his remarks to Essien-Udom and Malcolm reveal, Muhammad also viewed middle-class blacks—especially middle-class black Christians—with tremendous anger and distrust. Likewise Malcolm displayed a strong class-based resentment of the black bourgeoisie. For instance, in discussing his own efforts to recruit among black Christians, he recollects: "We by-passed the larger churches with their higher ratio of so-called 'middle class' Negroes who were so full of pretense and 'status' that they wouldn't be caught in our little storefront"

18. To mention just a few of the cookbooks by African American women that have "soul" in the title: Ethel Brown Hearon's *Cooking with Soul* (1968), Inez Yeargen Kaiser's *The Original Soul Food Cookery* (1968), Hattie Rhinehart Griffin's *Soul-Food Cookbook* (1969), Princess Pamela's *Soul Food Cookbook* (1969), Pearl Bowser's *A Pinch of Soul* (1970), Mahalia Jackson's *Mahalia Jackson Cooks Soul* (1970), Charleszetta Waddles's *Mother Waddles Soul Food Cookbook* (1970), Mary Jackson and Lelia Wishart's *The Integrated Cookbook, or The Soul of Good Cooking* (1971), Mary Keyes Burgess's *Soul to Soul: A Soul Food Vegetarian Cookbook* (1976), Ruth Jackson's *Ruth Jackson's Soulfood Cookbook* (91978), Marva Joy Curry's *Everything You Always Wanted to Know about Soul Food Cooling . . . And Were Afraid to Ask* (1983), Sheila Ferguson's *Soul Food: Classic Cuisine from the Deep South* (1989), and Kathy Starr's *The Soul of Southern Cooking* (1989).

19. Muhammad attacked the pill in both of his dietary manuals, *How to Eat to Live* (1967) and *How to Eat to Live, Book Two* (1972), as well as in his *Message to the Blackman in America* (1965). Gregory's most notorious attack on the pill is his essay "My Answer to Genocide," which appeared in Ebony in 1971. Angela Davis's "Racism, Birth Control and Reproductive Rights" (1981) offers a good overview of the sometimes "blatantly racist premises" of the campaign for "voluntary motherhood" as epitomized by many white middle- and upper-class feminists (202). The best overall history of abortion in America is Rosaling Petchesky's *Abortion and Woman's Choice* (1984, 1990). Linda Gordon's *Woman's Body, Woman's Right* (1976) offers a somewhat dated but still comprehensive history of birth control in the United States.

20. Even more to the point here is Elijah Muhammad's notorious dictum that "Woman is man's field to plant his nation." In addition to reducing woman to womb, he also literalizes the conflation of womb and filth. Black women are both constitutive of Muhammad's nation of "original" black men yet also the dirt that must be abjected for those men to be pure. Similarly, Dick Gregory opines in his *Political Primer* (1972) that "more boy babies die at birth or shortly thereafter than girl babies, because they are unable to survive the mucus in the mother's system" (260). Mucus is equivalent to "filth" in Gregory's schema.

21. In "Mama's Baby, Papa's Maybe," Hortense Spiller dissects this myth of black matriarchy by formulating a careful genealogy of its historical roots in slavery. Spillers argues that "legal enslavement removed from the African American male not so much from sight as from *mimetic* view as a partner in the prevailing social fiction of the Father's name, the Father's law" (80).

22. I refer here to the purported epidemic of crack babies and fetal alcohol syndrome, as well as increasing use of forced caesareans. Rather than viewing these efforts as a backlash against white feminism, which is simply played out on the bodies of lower-class women of color, we might instead suggest that women of color have been the primary target of these efforts because of fear of the black womb has in fact provided an important model from which the contemporary fear of white wombs has been derived. See the works by Corea (1985), Pollitt (1990), and Rowland (1992) for feminist perspectives on reproductive technologies and the emergence of fetal rights. In "The Abortion Question and the Death of Man" (1992), Mary Poovey formulates a brilliant analysis of how the contemporary debate over abortion contains, even within its most reactionary elements, the potential for a radical questioning of the "embodiment" of the Western juridical subject. Poovey's argument has been very influential in guiding my thinking about the relationship among soul food, black motherhood, and the juridical subject of American culture.

Works Cited

Bailey, Pearl. *Pearl's Kitchen: An Extraordinary Cookbook*. New York: Harcourt, 1973.

Baraka, Amiri. See Jones, LeRoi.

Baro, Gene. "Soul Food." *Vogue*, Mar. 1970: 80+.

Baruch, Elaine Hoffman, and Lucienne J. Serrano, eds. *Women Analyze Women: In France, England, and the United States*. New York University Press, 1988.

Bersani, Leo. "Is the Rectum a Grave?" *AIDS: Cultural Analysis/Cultural Activism*. Ed. Douglas Crimp. Cambridge: MIT Press, 1988: 197–222.

Bogle, Donald. *Toms, Coons, Mulattoes, Mammies, and Bucks: An Interpretive History of Blacks in American Films*. 1973. New expanded edition. New York: Continuum, 1991.

Bowser, Pearl. *A Pinch of Soul*. New York: Avon, 1970.

Burgess, Mary Keyes. *Soul to Soul: A Soul Food Vegetarian Cookbook*. Santa Barbara, Calif.: Woodbridge Press, 1976.

Butler, Judith. *Gender Trouble*. New York: Routledge, 1990.

Cleaver, Eldridge. *Soul on Ice*. New York: Ramparts-Dell, 1968.

Collins, Patricia Hill. *Black Feminist Thought: Knowledge, Consciousness, and the Politics of Empowerment*. New York: Routledge, 1990.

Combahee River Collective. "A Black Feminist Statement." *All the Women are White, All the Blacks are Men, But Some of Use are Brave: Black Women's Studies*. Ed. Gloria T. Hull, Patricia Bell Scott, and Barnara Smith. New York: Feminist, 1982: 13–22.

Corea, Gena. *The Mother Machine: Reproductive Technologies from Artificial Insemination to Artificial Wombs*. New York: Harper, 1985.

Crimp, Douglas. "Right On, Girlfriend!" *Social Text* 33 (1992): 2–18.

Curry, Marva Joy, *Everything You Always Wanted to Know About Soul Food Cooking . . . And Were Afraid to Ask*. Author, 1983.

Davis, Angela. "Racism, Birth Control and Reproductive Rights." *Women, Race and Class*. New York: Vintage-Random, 1981: 202–21.

De Certeau, Michel. *The Practice of Everyday Life*. Trans. Steven Rendall. Berkeley: University of California Press, 1984.

D'Emilio, John, *Sexual Politics, Sexual Communities: The Making of a Homosexual Minority in the United States, 1940–1970.* Chicago: University of Chicago Press, 1983.

Douglas, Mary. *Purity and Danger: An Analysis of the Concepts of Pollution and Taboo.* London: Ark-Routledge & Kegan Paul, 1966.

"Eating Like Soul Brothers." *Time,* 24 Jan. 1969: 57.

Eckels, Jon. "Hell, Mary." *A Broadside Treasury.* Ed. Gwendolyn Brooks. Detroit: Broadside, 1971: 43.

Ehrenreich, Barbara. *The Hearts of Men: American Dreams and the Flight from Commitment.* Garden City, N.Y.: Anchor-Doubleday, 1983.

Eisenstein, Zillah. *The Female Body and the Law.* Berkeley: University of California Press, 1988.

Ellison, Ralph. *Invisible Man.* New York: Vintage-Random, 1952.

Essien-Udom, E. U. *Black Nationalism: A Search for an Identity in America.* New York: Dell, 1962.

Evans, Sara. *Personal Politics: The Roots of Women's Liberation in the Civil Rights Movement and the New Left.* New York: Vintage-Random, 1980.

Ferguson, Sheila. *Soul Food: Classic Cuisine from the Deep South.* New York: Weidenfeld & Nicolson, 1989.

Foucault, Michel. *The History of Sexuality: An Introduction.* Trans. Robert Hurley. Vol. 1. New York: Vintage-Random, 1978.

Frazier, E. Franklin. *The Negro Family in the United States.* University of Chicago Sociological Series. Chicago: University of Chicago Press, 1939.

Freud, Sigmund. *Three Essays on the Theory of Sexuality.* Rpt. of Standard Edition. Trans. and rev. James Strachey. New York: Basic, 1962.

Giddings, Paula. *When and Where I Enter: The Impact of Black Women on Race and Sex in America.* New York: Bantam, 1984.

Gitlin, Todd. *The Sixties: Years of Hope, Days of Rage.* New York: Bantam, 1987.

Gordon, Linda. *Woman's Body, Woman's Right: Birth Control in America.* New York: Penguin, 1976.

Gregory, Dick. *Dick Gregory's Natural Diet for Folks Who Eat: Cooking with Mother Nature.* New York: Harper, 1973.

———. *Dick Gregory's Political Primer.* Ed. Jams R. McGraw. New York: Perennial-Harper, 1972.

———. "My Answer to Genocide." *Ebony,* Oct. 1971: 66–72.

Griffin, Hattie Rhinehart. *Soul-Food Cookbook.* New York: Carlton, 1969.

Hall, Stuart. "New Ethnicities." *Black Film/British Cinema.* London: 1988: 27–31.

Hearon, Ethel Brown. *Cooking with Soul.* Milwaukee: Rufus King High School, 1968. Rpt. 1971.

Jackson, George. *Soledad Brother: The Prison Letters of George Jackson.* New York: Bantam, 1970.

Jackson, Mahalia. *Mahalia Jackson Cooks Soul.* Nashville: Aurora Pub., 1970.

Jackson, Mary, and Lelia Wishart. *The Integrated Cookbook, or The Soul of Good Cooking.* Chicago: Johnson Pub., 1971.

Jackson, Ruth. *Ruth Jackson's Soulfood Cookbook.* Memphis: Wimmer, 1978.

Jones, LeRoi [Amiri Baraka]. *Black Music.* New York: William Morrow, 1967.

———. *Blues People.* New York: William Morrow, 1966: 101–104.

———. "Soul Food." *Home.* New York: William Morrow, 1966: 101–4.

Kaiser, Inez Yeargen. *The Original Soul Food Cookery.* New York: Pitman, 1968.

Kcrouac, Jack. *On the Road.* Ncw York: Signct-Viking, 1955, 1957.

Kristeva, Julia. *Powers of Horror: An Essay on Abjection.* trans. Leon S. Roudiez. New York: Columbia University Press, 1982.

Lee, Jimmy. *Soul Food Cookbook.* New York: Award Books, 1970.

Lott, Eric. " 'The Seeming Counterfeit': Racial Politics and Early Blackface Minstrelsy." *American Quarterly* 43:2 (1991): 223–54.

MacKinnon, Catherine. *Feminism Unmodified: Discourses on Life and Law.* Cambridge: Harvard University Press, 1987.

———. *Toward a Feminist Theory of the State.* Cambridge: Harvard University Press, 1989.

Marable, Manning. *Race, Reform and Rebellion: The Second Reconstruction in Black America, 1945–1982.* Jackson: University Press of Mississippi, 1984.

Marx, Karl. *Capital: A Critique of Political Economy.* 3 vols. 1867–1894. Trans. Ben Fowkes. New York: Vintage-Random, 1977. Vol. 1.

Mayfield, Julian. "You Touch My Black Aesthetic and I'll Touch Yours." *Black Aesthetic.* Ed. Addison Gayle Jr. New York: Anchor-Doubleday, 1972. 23–30.

McDowell, Deborah. Introduction. *Quicksand and Passing.* By Nella Larsen. Ed. Deborah McDowell. American Women Writers Series. New Brunswick, N.J.: Rutgers University Press, 1987. ix–xxxvii.

Miller, D. A. "Anal *Rope.*" *Representations* 32 (Fall 1990): 114–33. Rpt. in *Inside/Out.* Ed. Diana Fuss. New York: Routledge, 1991: 119–41.

Moynihan, Daniel P. *The Negro Family: The Case for National Action* ["The Moynihan Report"]. Washington, D.C.: U.S. Department of Labor, 1965.

Muhammad, Elijah. *How to Eat to Live.* Chicago: Muhammad Mosque of Islam No. 2, 1967.

———. *How to Eat To Live.* Book No. 2. Chicago: Muhammad Mosque of Islam No. 2, 1972.

———. *Message to the Blackman in America.* Chicago: Muhammad Mosque of Islam No. 2, 1965.

Oliver, Kelly. "Nourishing the Speaking Subject: A Psychoanalytic Approach to Abominable Food and Women." *Cooking, Eating, Thinking: Transformative Philosophies of Food.* Ed. Deane W. Curtin and Lisa M. Heldke. Bloomington: Indiana University Press, 1992: 68–84.

Pamela, Princess. *Princess Pamela's Soul Food Cookbook.* New York: Signet-NAL, 1969.

Petchesky, Rosalind Pollack. *Abortion and Woman's Choice: The State, Sexuality, and Reproductive Freedom.* 1984. Rev. ed. Boston: Northeastern University Press, 1990.

Pollitt, Katha. " 'Fetal Rights': A New Assault on Feminism." *Nation,* 26 March 1990: 409–18.

Poovey, Mary. "The Abortion Question and the Death of Man." *Feminists Theorize the Political.* New York: Routledge, 1992: 239–56.

Rhode, Deborah L. *Justice and Gender: Sex Discrimination and the Law.* Cambridge: Harvard University Press, 1989.

Ross, Andrew. *No Respect: Intellectuals and Popular Culture.* New York: Routledge, 1989.

Roudiez, Leon S. Translator's Note. *Powers of Horror: An Essay on Abjection.* By Julia Kristeva. New York: Columbia University Press, 1982. vii–x.

Rowland, Robyn. *Living Laboratories: Women and Reproductive Technologies.* Bloomington: Indiana University Press, 1992.

Sedgwich, Eve. *Epistemology of the Closet.* Berkeley: University of California Press, 1990.

Spillers, Hortense J. "Mama's Baby, Papa's Maybe: An American Grammar Book." *Diacritics* 17: 2 (1987): 65–81.

Starr, Kathy. *The Soul of Southern Cooking.* Jackson: University Press of Mississippi, 1989.

Stewart, J., concurring. *Jacobellis v. Ohio,* 378 U. S. 184, 197 (1964).

Torgovnick, Marianna. *Gone Primitive: Savage Intellects, Modern Lives.* Chicago: University of Chicago Press, 1990.

Van DeBurg, William L. *New Day in Babylon: The Black Power Movement and American Culture, 1965–1975.* Chicago: University of Chicago Press, 1992.

Van Peebles. Melvin, dir., writer, prod., and actor. *Sweet Sweetback's Baadasssss Song.* 1971.

Waddles, Charleszetta. *Mother Waddles Soulfood Cookbook.* Detroit: Mother Waddles Perpetual Mission, 1970. 3rd ed., 1976.

Watkins, Mel. "The Lyrics of James Brown: Ain't It Funky Now, or Money Won't Change Your Licking Stick." In *Amistad 2.* Ed. John A. Williams and Charles F. Harris. New York: Random, 1971: 21–42.

Williams, Linda. *Hard Core: Power, Pleasure, and the "Frenzy of the Visible."* Berkeley: University of California Press, 1989.

Williams, Patricia. *The Alchemy of Race and Rights: Diary of a Law Professor.* Cambridge: Harvard University Press, 1991.

Wolfe, Tom. *Radical Chic and Mau-Mauing the Flak Catchers.* New York: Farrar, 1970.

X, Malcolm. *The Autobiography of Malcolm X.* 1964. With Alex Haley. New York: Ballantine, 1973.

Zizek, Slavoj. *The Sublime Object of Ideology.* London: Verso-New Left, 1989.

Chapter 18

"Fable Number One":
Some Myths about Consumption

Ed Schiffer

Although most theories of cultural production consider it axiomatic that advertising is the means by which capitalism perpetuates itself, it is possible to approach advertising, and television commercials in particular, in other ways. Indeed, to ask what it really means to "consume" these innumerable invitations to consume, it may be necessary to suspend any systemic view of advertising in favor of an almost "aesthetic" approach to commercials. Far from being instances of crude and bullying rhetoric, commercials frequently adopt a self-conscious and self-reflexive stance toward both their putative function and the act of consumption itself.

No commercial displays this tendency better than a spot for "Nature's Favorite Apple Chips" that ran in the early 90s. Introduced by a placard proclaiming "Nature's Favorite presents Fable #1," the commercial that follows features live actors against crudely drawn backdrops meant to evoke the Garden of Eden. Acting as narrator, the announcer explains: "Strolling through the garden, Eve was in a quandary. Being new in the neighborhood, she had no *earthly* idea what to eat." Out of nowhere, a bag of apple chips appears on a tree. "Suddenly she was tempted by a bright shiny . . . bag of Nature's Favorite Apple Chips—an all-natural snack made with pure orchard-fresh apples. They were *sinfully* delicious— crisp and wonderfully satisfying." Discreet script appears at the bottom of the screen informing us that these chips have "No Added Salt. No Cholesterol. No Preservatives," and the announcer continues: "Nature's Favorite Apple Chips—four delicious flavors in your supermarket's produce section. A temptation few can resist," he concludes, as "Adam's" naked arm thrusts into the frame from the left, grabbing for the bag, which "Eve" moves out of his reach, as she continues munching happily.

For even a mildly suspicious viewer, this commercial might seem one of those uncanny, if not infrequent, moments when advertising almost compulsively reveals its own workings. Doesn't it, after all, dare us to succumb as surely as Eve did? Indeed, the repetition of "natural" seems to be belied by the highly stylized graphics, and the revisions in the biblical story of the fall put us on our guard even as they seek to "program" us as consumers. Unlike the biblical Eve, this one has unproblematic appetites. Her refusal to share her chips with "Adam" makes it self-evident that the individual's satisfaction of her desires is a first priority.

Even more telling is what we might call the "secularization" of the story. There are no divine injunctions setting limits to human consumption in this landscape, and most important, the omission of the serpent in this version of the fall points to a mystification of advertising's own role in *creating* the supposedly "natural" desires it caters to. Insofar as this is on some level the mission of all commercials, it is indeed advertising's "fable number one."

The revisionist force of the commercial, however, may be read in other ways. In returning to the original act of meaningful consumption, the Apple Chips spot rewrites it as a moment of empowerment, rather than deception and error. In that respect, it is a direct, if somewhat illegitimate, descendent of someone like Milton, who saw the story of the fall as the foundational myth of human identity. For the seventeenth-century Puritan poet, the moment in the garden radicalized the category of choice with its imperative to negotiate between reason and appetite. The decision to eat, to consume, to act on one's desires, thus became what made us, for better *and* worse, human. Is it ridiculous to suggest the Apple Chips commercial holds out the possibility of similarly exalting our innumerable "choices" as consumers?[1]

If this notion seems patently absurd, we do well to consider the degree to which "personhood" in capitalist culture (and it is frankly pointless to conjure an alternative) is tied to, if not located in, one's ability to be a consumer. From Adam Smith to Thorstein Veblen, theorists have suggested that a major motive for consumption is a basic human desire for a kind of communication. It is no accident that aspirations of emergent classes are so often figured as a desire for "a place at the table."[2] When the North American Free Trade Agreement was debated, nativist opponents of the pact offered an unwitting but subtle demonstration of the ways in which conceptions of "humanity" are tied to one's status as consumers. The promise that loss of jobs to Mexico would be offset by the prospect of eighty million new "consumers" could not make sense to those who could not see Mexicans as sufficiently human to be consumers. And, indeed, the best hope for an end to racism toward Mexicans lies in their ability to emerge, like the Japanese before them, as consumers able to put their money where their mouths are.

Critics might concede that consumption itself is indeed a primary human activity, but the problem with advertising lies in the mystified *images* of consumption it forcefeeds the consumer. There is no need to rehearse at length the profoundly mistrustful version of advertising that is to be found in many of the most perceptive books on the subject. For Stewart Ewen, advertising was invented as "an aggressive device of corporate survival." He quotes numerous captains of industry as they fantasize about controlling the consciousness of the consumer, whose anger at his grim place in industrial society is bought off by the promise of the supposed fruits of the same system that is exploiting him. For Ewen, unlike, say, Vance Packard, it is not a matter of the "abuse" or "corruption" of advertising discourse; the discourse itself is founded on the abuse of the consumer.[3] Though far less inclined to see advertising as a grand capitalist conspiracy, Michael Schudson is no less sweeping in his account of how it functions as a kind of "capitalist realism," which seeks to construct a coercive view of the good life.[4]

As comprehensive and compelling as such versions of advertising may be, they suffer precisely to the degree that they are "systemic." Though far from vulgar Marxism in their appreciation for advertising's semiotics, they have insufficient respect for the lived experience of the individual consumer whose autonomy they claim to defend.[5] The degree to which the consumer is a force to be reckoned with is suggested by the degree to which so many commercials must acknowledge and assuage skepticism (e.g., "Velveeta *is* real cheese!"). If advertising were completely successful at inscribing the consumer, it would not insist on depicting him/her as an at least potentially oppositional force. Any defense of advertising (and that, it should be clear by now, is what this is) must therefore focus on the viewer who, like Eve in the garden, must decide if she is being tempted with the fruit of the tree of knowledge of good and evil—or some meretricious new snack food. Debates about advertising, therefore, take their place as a modern instance of venerable disputes about the status of fiction. Such defenses always amount to defenses of the reader because the reader (or viewer or consumer) is the specific site of the offending discourse's supposedly pernicious effects.

In the case of advertising, two seemingly contradictory ways of defending its effects on the consumer come to mind. With a backhanded salute to Marcuse, one might venture that, given its unabashed appeal to the full range of human desire, advertising is always at least potentially liberatory. This fact about advertising is usually sidestepped by switching attention from the consumer to the producer of the image, as if it were somehow easier to intuit the sinister motivations of the producer rather than the complex response of the viewer. And indeed it *is* easier to discuss the aesthetics of commercials in terms of "quick cuts" and other "editing techniques" than to grapple with the frank gratification offered by certain forms of sensual stimulation. Unfortunately, when critics on the cultural left decry the tendency toward "wish-fulfillment" in popular culture, they evince a curiously puritanical suspicion of human wishes, as if the fact that desires can be manipulated somehow discredits them.[6]

On the other hand, one might equally argue that the real power of advertising lies not in its power to gratify our desires, but to make us conscious of them. With their insistent, if frequently romanticized, thematization of what it means to consume, commercials may actually serve to make us conscious of our consumerist practices, and consumption may actually become perspicuous, rather than merely conspicuous. Indeed, the entire rise of the "consumerism" movement is predicated on the belief that consumers need not be passive in their consumption of advertising.

These two ways of defending advertising are, of course, part of one dialectic, and a true characterization of the discourse would have to acknowledge its ability to balance the two views of the consumer we have just encountered—one that grants the consumer intelligence and one that figures him as some sort of unpleasant hybrid of stomach and ego that has no choice but to consume and thereby be consumed. The genius of the most successful commercials lies in their ability to negotiate between these two views of its audience, either by appealing to one in the name of the other, or by using an appeal to one to legitimate the other. In a very practical way, commercials are a modern version of the mind/body problem, although it might be more correct now to call it a mind/stomach problem.

We are now in a position to appreciate why the most paradigmatic commercials are so often for food products. "It's the oldest question in the world," one famous spot says before offering its answer to the query, "What's for dinner?" Eating *is* primal, and it offers the prime example of the human need to adjudicate between pleasure and utility. We may not experience any residual conflicts about eating in our daily lives, but commercials memorialize the problem in the most matter-of-fact ways. Consider the vast range of ads that feature various edibles that have been anthropomorphized so as to dramatize their eagerness to be eaten. Preeminent here would be the long-running "Charlie the Tuna" commercials for Star-Kist. In spot after spot, Charlie took pains to demonstrate his superior understanding of art, music, and literature, only to find out "Star-Kist doesn't want tuna with good taste, they want tuna that tastes good." We may join the announcer in saying "Sorry, Charlie," but his misunderstanding actually names the equivocation that is so central to most commercials. The play on the word "taste" reminds us that our acts of consumption may be simultaneously a matter of refined judgment and crude desire.[7] Consumption in general, and eating in particular, is an activity that highlights much that is equivocal in the human condition, and commercials have their peculiar power because they "manage"—and, yes, frequently mystify—our unease.[8]

It is important to emphasize this phenomenological approach to consuming commercials because there is something hopelessly naive and beside the point about analyses of advertising that somehow find it scandalous that commercials lie or misrepresent. As the frankly mendacious "Joe Isuzu" commercials of the late 80s indicate, advertising often *expects* to be taken with more than a grain of salt. The claims of commercials are rarely probative and always rhetorical. Indeed, in many ways, attacks on advertising are reminiscent of nothing so much as Plato's quarrel with the Sophists. And as with Plato, there is something futile about attempts to thwart the thoroughgoing "rhetoricizing" of public discourse that may be the true triumph of advertising language. There are no doubt many good reasons why modern man is so susceptible to a discourse that reaches out, touches, and molds him with its insinuating mode of address, but there is no return to Eden.

And yet we continue to act as if there were. What better modern redaction of the story of the fall could there be than the recent attempt of Chris Whittle to bring commercials into public schools. Here was the well-spoken but satanic businessman offering schools millions of dollars of video equipment if only they wouldn't choke on the requirement that they feed students several minutes of commercials each day in homeroom. Few schools signed up for Whittle's "Channel One," even though sponsored sporting events and franchised food operations are now commonplace features of public education. Rather than gag at the idea of commercial language "polluting" the classroom, teachers might have felt challenged to seize the opportunity to teach students how to "read" the kind of appeals they encounter in this already all-too-fallen world. It is the very worst form of "wishful thinking" to see Whittle or advertising itself as the serpent in the garden. To attribute such demonic agency to those who would tempt us is to minimize the choices the Eve in all of must make.

Notes

1. James R. Lewis has attempted a structuralist analysis of how certain print advertisements have manipulated the symbolism of the fall in "Adam and Eve on Madison Avenue: Symbolic Inversion in Popular Culture," *Studies in Popular Culture* X:1 (1987) 74–82.

2. For a useful and concise overview of theories of consumption—and the cultural myths supporting them—see Niels Thorsen, "Two Versions of Human Need: The Traditional and the Modern Understanding of Consumption," *Consumption and American Culture*, ed. David E. Nye and Carl Pedersen (Amsterdam: VU University Press, 1991), pp. 5–17.

3. *Captains of Consciousness: Advertising and the Social Roots of the Consumer Culture* (New York: McGraw-Hill, 1976), pp. 54, 187ff.

4. *Advertising, The Uneasy Persuasion: Its Dubious Impact on American Society* (New York: Basic Books, 1984).

5. For an analogous debate, see Jennifer Wicke's quarrel with Fredric Jameson and Franco Moretti, over the impact of print advertising, in her important work, *Advertising Fictions: Literature, Advertisement, and Social Reading* (New York: Columbia University Press, 1988).

6. For an interesting demonstration of this logic, see Mark Crispin Miller's attempt to trace the degradation of American movies to the influence of commercials in "Hollywood: The Ad," *The Atlantic* 265:4 (April 1990) 41–68.

7. For the historical importance of the concept of "taste" in mediating less decorous forms of desire, see Maggie Kilgour, *From Communion to Cannibalism: An Anatomy of Metaphors of Incorporation* (Princeton: Princeton University Press, 1990).

8. This may explain, for instance, why commercials anthropomorphize not only food itself (cf. the California Raisins, the Pillsbury Dough Boy ad nauseum), but other nonhuman "consumers." Commercials for pet food ascribe "finickiness" and other marks of sensibility to dogs and cats as half of an implied syllogism: if animals eat like humans, then surely humans are not merely animals in how they eat.

Chapter 19

Bubbie's Challah

Stephen Steinberg

After my grandfather passed away in 1955, my grandmother would come to our house for Friday-night dinner. She always arrived on the doorstep with two challahs, one for the Sabbath meal, the other to sustain us until the next Sabbath meal. We would eat it for breakfast schmeared with cream cheese. Add another schmear of jelly, and it was an instant lunch. Dipped in soup, it was the perfect supper complement. After a few days, when the bread began to stale, we would saturate it in eggs and fry it on the griddle to produce the best French toast west of Kiev. By the time both challahs had been consumed, we knew that our supply would soon be replenished.

This was a challah like none other. It was large and puffy, with bulbous protrusions on the top, brown from the oven and sprinkled with poppy seeds. The interior was light and fluffy, with air pockets that were delectable. This was my Jewish grandmother's pièce de résistance. She nourished the entire extended family with her challahs, fusing us, like the genes we shared, with her culinary magic. We paid her back with extravagant praise, ostensibly for her gift to our palates, but also for her spiritual nourishment. In all cultures "bread" signifies the stuff of life itself. It is because of its potent symbolism that bread is so often incorporated into religious ceremonies. Challah was our connection with our grandmother, and through her, to our ancestors. It may have been our palates that defined the moment, but each time we consumed my grandmother's challah, it was a ritual affirmation of our sense of peoplehood and our place in history. Perhaps challah was my grandmother's cultural artifice for tantalizing us into the world of our fathers.

In any event, I feasted on her challah for thirty-two years, until my grandmother passed away, taking the recipe to her grave. Only then did it dawn on me that nobody in the entire family—not one of her eighteen progeny—had acquired her skill. None of us, or our children, would ever savor her challah again.

What does this rupture of a family tradition signify about our family, or about ethnic continuity in general? Why was there no one with the foresight to safeguard this family secret, not to speak of our symbolic link to our past? How is it that we are bereft of the food that sustained our family for over half a century? Surely, this loss cannot be assuaged by purchasing a challah from a local store, not even one that advertises "challah just like your grandmother made."

Perhaps the answer is obvious: that we all conspired in the comfortable illusion that my grandmother and her challah would be here forever. Perhaps we wished to remain children, which was possible so long as we were fed by this family matriarch. Perhaps we realized, on some level of consciousness, that my grandmother's challah would not be the same if the dough were not kneaded by *her* hands, if it were not baked in *her* oven, and if it were not purveyed by *her* outstretched arms, accompanied by her loving embrace. Perhaps it was right that the secret should remain hers, not to be simulated by some pretender.

But then again, how was culture ever purveyed from one generation to the next? How, after all, did my grandmother acquire her culinary magic? It required an elder not just willing but determined to share her powers with a neophyte. And it required an upstart who craved to follow the path treaded by forbears. Is it possible that, as much as my grandmother's eighteen progeny revered her, that none of them wanted to *be* her? That her daughters and granddaughters—no less than her sons and grandsons—did not want to be *defined* by a challah, with all of the ingratiation that it evoked from their children? Is it possible, also, that my grandmother had another design for her daughters, as well as her sons? In *World of Our Fathers* Irving Howe wrote, "In behalf of its sons the East Side was prepared to commit suicide; perhaps it did." Is it possible that my grandmother's act of omission was her sacrifice on behalf of her daughters?

Perhaps my grandmother and her eighteen progeny were guided by the same vision—of a new generation that would forge its own identity, even if this meant foregoing some of the rich culture and flavors of their childhood. Perhaps everybody was resigned to the fact that challah would be a fond memory of a passing tradition.

Contributors

Carol J. Adams is the author of *The Sexual Politics of Meat* and *Neither Man Nor Beast*. She is the editor of several anthologies, including *Ecofeminism and the Sacred* and, with Josephine Donovan, *Animals and Women*. She is currently working on a vegan cookbook, and her current fascination is sourdough cultures.

Marianna Beck, Ph.D., lives in Chicago where she has been co-publishing *Libido: The Journal of Sex and Sensibility* for the last decade.

Susan Bordo is Professor of Philosophy and holds the Otis A. Singletary Chair in the Humanities at The University of Kentucky. She is the author of *The Flight to Objectivity: Essays on Cartesianism and Culture* (SUNY Press, 1987) and *Unbearable Weight: Feminism, Western Culture, and the Body* (University of California, 1993), which was named one of the New York Times' notable books for 1993. Her most recent book is *Twilight Zones: The Hidden Life of Cultural Images from Plato to OJ* (University of California, 1997). She is working on a book on the male body, to be published by Farrar Straus & Giroux.

Priscilla Parkhurst Ferguson is Professor of Sociology at Columbia University, where she teaches courses in cultural sociology. Her publications include books on literary and urban culture in France; she is currently completing a study of culinary culture tentatively entitled *Eating Disorders and Culinary Transformations*.

Joanne Finkelstein is Associate Professor of Sociology and Cultural Studies at Monash University, Victoria, Australia. She has recently published *Slaves of Chic* (1996) and *Fashion: An Introduction* (1998).

Diana Fuss is Associate Professor of English at Princeton University. She is the author of *Essentially Speaking* (Routledge, 1989) and *Identification Papers* (Routledge, 1995). She is also the editor of two volumes, *Inside/Out* (Routledge, 1991) and *Human All Too Human* (Routledge, 1995).

Deborah R. Geis is Associate Professor of English at Queens College of the City University of New York, where she specializes in modern/contemporary drama and women's studies, and is also a member of the Ph.D. faculty in Theater at the CUNY Graduate Center. She is the author of *Postmodern Theatric(k)s* (University of Michigan Press, 1993) and coeditor, with Steven F. Kruger, of *Approaching the Millenium: Essays on Angels in America* (University of Michigan Press, 1997). Her other publications include articles on David Mamet, David Rabe, Adrienne Kennedy, Maria Irene Fornes, Ntozake Shange, and Edward Albee; she is currently writing a book on American feminist drama and performance art.

bell hooks, writer, cultural critic, feminist theorist, the author of sixteen books, most recently two memoirs, *Bone Black: Memories of Girlhood* and *Wounds of Passion: A Writing Life* (Holt), and a collection of essays, *Remembered Rapture: The Writer at Work*.

David Farrell Krell is Professor of Philosophy at DePaul University in Chicago. Krell is author of *Contagion: Sexuality, Disease, and Death in German Idealism and Romanticism* (Indiana University Press, 1998). He has coauthored, with Donald L. Bates, *The Good European: Nietzsche's Work Sites in Word and Image* (University of Chicago Press, 1997). Other books include *Architecture: Ecstacies of Space, Time, and the Human Body* (SUNY Press, 1997), *Infectious Nietzsche* (Indiana University Press, 1996), and *Lunar Voices: Of Tragedy, Poetry, Fiction, and Thought* (University of Chicago Press, 1995). He has published two works of fiction with SUNY Press; *Nietzsche: A Novel* (1996) and *Son of Spirit: A Novel* (1997).

Steven F. Kruger has taught medieval and queer studies at Queens College (CUNY), the Graduate School and University Center (CUNY), and the University of Alberta. He is author of *Dreaming in the Middle Ages* (Cambridge University Press, 1992) and *AIDS Narratives: Gender and Sexuality, Fiction and Science* (Garland,

1996), and coeditor, with Deborah R. Geis, of *Approaching the Millenium: Essays on Angels in America*. His current work includes coediting, with Glenn Burger, a collection of essays on medieval culture and postmodern theory, *Queering the Middle Ages/Historicizing Postmodernity*. His next book will investigate the connections among medieval categories of religion, race, gender, and sexuality.

Alphonso Lingis is a professor of philosophy at the Pennsylvania State University. He is the author of *Excesses: Eros and Culture* (1984), *Libido: The French Existential Theories* (1985), *Phenomenological Explanations* (1986), *Deathbound Subjectivity* (1989), *The Community of Those Who Have Nothing in Common* (1994), and *Sensation: Intelligibility in Sensibility* (1995).

Mary Lukanuski. After completing her MS in Library Science at Columbia University, Lukanuski catalogued rare books and "non standard" formats at Columbia, Disney, RAND, and The Getty. Seeing the wonders of NCSA mosaic in late 1993, she moved into Web development and onto production positions at Universal-MCA and Hotwired. She is now a producer with Studio Verso in San Francisco. Thinking about food and eating continue to provide Mary with solace in the swirl of an ever changing technology.

Gary Paul Nabhan is the Director of Science Outreach at the Arizona-Sonora Desert Museum and author of twelve books, including *Cultures of Habitat* (Centerpoint Press).

Ron Scapp is director of the Graduate Program in Urban and Multicultural Education at the College of Mount St. Vincent, The Bronx, where he teaches education and philosophy. He is currently completing *A Question of Voice: The Search for Legitimacy*. He is also working on a book entitled, *Teaching Values: Education, Politics, and Culture*, and continues to collaborate with Brian Seitz, coediting *Etiquette* and *Fashion Statements*.

Ed Schiffer has taught in the English Departments of Yale, Reed College and UCLA. His television criticism has appeared in *The Wall Street Journal* and other publications. He currently practices law in San Francisco.

Brian Seitz teaches philosophy at Babson College. He is the author of *The Trace of Political Representation* (SUNY Press, 1995), and is currently writing, *A Material Phenomenology of Political*

Representation. In addition to other projects, he is also currently coauthoring *Politology: A Tale of Two Cities,* with Thomas Thorp, and continues to collaborate with Ron Scapp, coediting *Etiquette* and *Fashion Statements.*

Stephen Steinberg teaches in the Department of Urban Studies at Queens College and the Ph.D. Program in Sociology at the CUNY Graduate Center. His books include *Turning Back: The Retreat from Racial Justice in American Thought and Policy,* which received the Oliver Cromwell Cox Award for Distinguished Anti-Racist Scholarship, and *The Ethnic Myth: Race, Ethnicity, and Class in America.* In addition to his scholarly publications, he has published articles in *The Nation, New Politics, Reconstruction,* and *The UNESCO Courier.*

Laura Trippi is a curator, writer and new media project manager working at the intersection of art, science and popular culture. From 1988–95 she was a curator at The New Museum, New York. From 1996–98 her web site Drawing On Air (dn/a) was housed at adaweb <www.adaweb.com/~dn/a>. Her writing appears in *Acme Journal, The Guggenheim Magazine, 21C* and *World Art.* She is currently the Web/New Media Services Manager at Carnegie Hall <www.carnegiehall.org>.

Allen S. Weiss has most recently published *Perverse Desire and the Ambiguous Icon* (SUNY Press, 1994); *Flamme et festin: Une poétique de la cuisine* (Paris, Éditions Java, 1994); *The Mirrors of Infinity: The French Formal Garden and 17th Century Metaphysics* (Princeton Architectural Press, 1995); *Phantasmic Radio* (Duke, 1995); *Unnatural Horizons: Paradox and Contradiction in Landscape Architecture* (Princeton Architectural Press, 1998); and has edited *mental Sound & Radio* (The Drama Review 151, 1996) and *Taste, Nostalgia* (New York, Lusitania Press, 1997). He teaches in the Departments of Performance Studies and Cinema Studies at New York University.

Jeff Weinstein, restaurant critic and food essayist for New York's *Village Voice* for more than 17 years, is author of *Life in San Diego* (novella) and *Learning to Eat,* both published by Sun & Moon Press. He has written for *The New Yorker, Artforum, Art in America,* and many other publications; his short story, *A Jean-Marie Cookbook,* reprinted in *Contemporary American Fiction,* was awarded a Pushcart Prize. Weinstein is Fine Arts Editor of *The Philadelphia Inquirer.*

Doris Witt is an Assistant Professor of English at The University of Iowa, where she teaches twentieth-century U.S. literary and cultural studies. She is the author of *Black Hunger* (Oxford University Press).

Sharon Zukin is Brooklundian Professor at Brooklyn College and professor of sociology at the City University Graduate School. Author of *The Cultures of Cities, Loft Living,* and *Beyond Marx and Tito,* she is also the winner of the C. Wright Mills Award for *Landscapes of Power: From Detroit to Disney World.*